PASS PMP IN 21 DAYS I -STUDY GUIDE

Step 1: Understand Concepts

KAVITA SHARMA

SIGNIFICANT CONTRIBUTOR – PMBOK 6TH EDITION

BASED ON NEW PMP 2021 CONTENT

VERSION: 7.1, RELEASED ON: 3 June 2022

I want to thank all my students for making this book possible and continue updating it. This is the 7th version of the book in your hands.

Your feedback emails/WhatsApp keep me motivated.

Thanks to all of you.

कर्मण्येवाधिकारस्ते मा फलेषु कदाचन ।
मा कर्मफलहेतुर्भुर्मा ते संगोऽस्त्वकर्मणि ॥

It is the work that you control and not the outcome.

TABLE OF CONTENTS

1 PREFACE

1.1 HI FROM KAVITA SHARMA

Most people, when they start preparing for the PMP, They search. So many resources. Some are good, and some are confusing. Worse, some try and put fear.

I started this book to make PMP concepts simpler and easy to grasp. PMP is easy. You will pass if you know and understand concepts.

The PMP Exam tests your skills and understanding of the concepts. If you know them, You will pass.

The first version of the study guide came out in 2014. A lot of mistakes ☺, But you loved it. Your feedback and encouragement made this book a success.

This new version is to continue with the effort and help you succeed.

The design principles of the book are:

1. Use Keywords for easier and faster learning.
2. Repeat important concepts
3. Explain things using small examples
4. Build around a manager's life
5. Make you confident in concepts

With this, I present the book to you. Do one chapter one day, and you will attain a pace. It is easy, and you will achieve your goal of being a PMP in 21 Days. Follow the plan ☺

1.2 ABOUT THE BOOK

The book uses scientific learning techniques to help you understand the key concepts and remember them. There are the following tools for your pursual:

KEYWORDS

If you see a definition – try and find the keyword for that. By default, the keywords are marked as BOLD for you. Try and pay attention when you see them.

LET'S PLAY

A chapter is divided into a logical set of study capsules. Once you learn a concept, a quiz is placed towards the end of the concept. This will help with two things – 1. Help you evaluate your knowledge. 2. Boost confidence when you get going with a concept. The studies feel easy.

MODULE END QUESTIONS

Module End questions are PMP-style questions. These will help you understand the PMP style of questions to get in the exam and prepare you for it. These are complex questions. Please complete them as part of your completion of the chapter. A chapter reading is not complete until and unless you do the questions and check and verify the answers.

MIND MAPS:

You will see mind maps to help you see the concepts in a picture. It helps (visual readers) set the context and get consolidated information in one place.

VIDEOS AT YOUTUBE

Video Available ▶ You Tube

SEARCH THIS TOPIC AT THE CHANNEL

If you have difficulty understanding the concept, you can search for the video with the keywords on my YouTube channel. **You will find the video.** I'm working towards creating more videos as this book is published. You can also request a video through email or comment on my channel.

DAY WISE PLAN:

Your prep for PMP starts with this study guide. Read **one chapter a day** and finish all the chapters in 15 days (A total of 13 chapters). **Do ensure that you complete the module end quizzes.** A chapter is not complete until and unless you complete all questions and review them.

1.3 THE 21 DAYS TEST PREP PLAN

Phase	Day	Book Chapters	Commitment (Hours)
Phase: Understand and Evaluate			
	Day 1	2. The Basics	2 - 4 Hours
	Day 2	3. Agile – Let's Get Started	2 - 4 Hours
	Day 3	Buffer	NA
	Day 4	4. Project Integration Management	2 - 4 Hours
	Day 5	5. Project Scope Management	2 - 4 Hours
	Day 6	6. Project Schedule Management	2 - 4 Hours
	Day 7	7. Project Cost Management	2 - 4 Hours
	Day 8	8. Project Quality Management	2 - 4 Hours
	Day 9	9. Project Risk Management	2 - 4 Hours
	Day 10	10. Project Procurement Management	2 - 4 Hours
	Day 11	11. Project Stakeholder Management	2 - 4 Hours
	Day 12	12. Project Resource Management	2 - 4 Hours
	Day 13	13. Project Communications Management	2 - 4 Hours
	Day 14	Buffer	NA
Phase: Simulate			
	Day 15	Full-Length PMP Test	4-5 Hours
	Day 16	Full-Length PMP Test	4-5 Hours
	Day 17	Full-Length PMP Test	4-5 Hours
	Day 18	Full-Length PMP Test	4-5 Hours
	Day 19	Buffer - If you missed any day	NA
	Day 20	Buffer - If you missed any day	NA
	Day 21	**Pass the PMP EXAM**	

You can refer following documents for optional studies.

1. Agile Practice Guide available ta PMI.org
2. PMBOK 6th Edition available ta PMI.org
3. Student Handbook is available at https://pmi.lochoice.com (Part of the updated course of 2021) available for students who have availed of the 35 PDU training from any Authorized Training Provider(ATP).

1.4 BASELINE ASSESSMENT TEST

Surprized to see the questions before we start our studies? Let us do them to understand PMP questions. Don't worry if you get them wrong. We will get them right by the end of this book ☺.

1. You are managing a hybrid project. Your team is busy developing the design of the prototype at this stage. One of the designers, Rachel, is working with you on this. She is creative and loves to hear feedback on the design. She is outgoing and a good communicator. People like her. However, if you ask her about the progress, she is noncommittal. Today when you asked her about an upcoming deadline, she responded that she would get you something. You are unsure if she has any plan in place. Who is Rachel? Select 2 personality traits:

    ☐. A.   Extrovert

    ☐. B.   Introvert

    ☐. C.   Sensing

    ☐. D.   Intuitive

    ☐. E.   Thinking

    ☐. F.   Feeling

    ☐. G.   Judging

    ☐. H.   Perceiving

2. In a hybrid project, the Project Manager discovers a defect in a deliverable that is due to be submitted to the customer in the coming week. The Project Manager knows the customer does not have the technical understanding necessary to notice the defect. The deliverable fulfills the contract requirements. What is the BEST thing to do?

    A.   Start the process to get formal acceptance from the customer

    B.   Log the issue in the lessons learned

    C.   Discuss the issue with the customer and ask for his inputs

    D.   Assess the situation and make changes to the plan if required.

3. The Project Manager's responsibilities consist of the four basic functions:

    A.   Thinking, planning, controlling, and monitoring

    B.   Planning, doing, briefing, and reviewing

    C.   Planning, controlling, tracking, and acting

    D.   Planning, organizing, monitoring, and controlling

4. To build and deliver the defect-free increment for the next iteration, the development team should focus on

    A.   Takeaways from Sprint Retrospective meetings
    B.   Constantly reminding people of the core values of agile
    C.   Burndown charts for updates on the Sprint completion
    D.   Carefully planning the Sprint planning meetings

5. Due to the project end phase, 5 team members were released. You had 8 team members before the release. There are 3 sponsors of the project. Calculate the total communication channels of the project as of now.

    A.   21
    B.   15
    C.   132
    D.   20

6. For effective communication, the listening ability plays an important role. The following could be the ways of improving the listening ability except:

    A.   Listening and giving feedback
    B.   Working on another activity while listening
    C.   Allowing the speaker to complete his message
    D.   Focusing on concepts and ideas

7. In a hybrid project, formal acceptance by the sponsor of the project indicates that they have accepted the product, and a formal transition can start. The formal acceptance for handover should be signed off during which stage of the project?

    A.   Administrative closure
    B.   As the last milestone in the project plan
    C.   After the project is closed out
    D.   When requested by the program manager

8. Ground rules are established in a project team to set clear expectations regarding acceptable behavior by any member. Whose responsibility is it to establish and enforce ground rules?

    A.   The Project Manager
    B.   All Project Team Members
    C.   The Human Resource team
    D.   The Functional Manager

9. In a one-on-one communication process, the sender is the one who transmits the signals, while the receiver _____ the signals (fill in the blank).

    A. Decode

    B. Encode

    C. Intercept

    D. Receives

10. The incremental project life cycle is one of the agile project life cycles

    A. True

    B. False

11. Part of the project closure process is receiving the formal acceptance. From whom should you obtain the official acceptance of your agile deliverable?

    A. The Quality Director

    B. The Head Of The Project Management Office

    C. The Product Owner

    D. The Customer

12. Your team is using planning poker, and you are given some cards. What are the most likely values in the cards?

    A. T-shirt sizes S, XM, L, XL, XXXL, etc

    B. Fibonacci series like 1, 2, 3, 5, 8, 13, 21, 34, etc

    C. Odd number 1, 3, 5, 7, 9, 11, etc.

    D. Random numbers as per your team's suggestions

13. In the case of agile development methodology, who should know the most about the progress toward a business objective or a release and be able to explain the alternatives?

    A. Project Manager

    B. Customer

    C. Scrum Master

    D. Product Owner

14. Punishment power is also known as:

    A. Coercive power

    B. Bad Power

    C. Formal Power

    D. Good Power

15. You are managing a product called OPLAY. The product is a collaboration platform where people can find their friends or communities and play games with them. You have a few games in mind to launch. Some of the games are:
   - Tetris (2 player game)
   - UNO (2 and 4 Player game)
   - Checkers (2 Player game)

   You want to ensure that each game variant works perfectly on all mobile platforms. No errors can be tolerated, as this will be bad for your brand and application. Which methodology would work best for such a scenario?

   A. Waterfall
   B. Springfall
   C. Agile
   D. Iterative

16. The following are examples of deliverables, except:

   A. The planning team submitted the project Management plan
   B. The software Development Team developed the application software
   C. Task A started a day late
   D. The project charter was created

17. The key to promoting optimum team performance in project teams that are not collocated is to:

   A. Exercise power and authority
   B. Establish a reward and recognition system
   C. Obtain the support of Functional Managers
   D. Build trust through effective communication

18. While selecting the team members for my agile team, I should focus more on:

   A. Team members who have competency in core skills (I shaped)
   B. Team members who have generic skills
   C. Skills do not matter - attitude matters
   D. Team members who have a broad level of skill plus specialty in-depth (T shaped)

19. The purpose of the phase-end review is to:

   A. Determine ETC (expected time to complete)
   B. Determine ETC (estimate to complete)
   C. Get customer sign off

    D.   Make a Go/No-go call for the next phase

20. You are working in the healthcare industry to work on producing an oral vaccine. Recently the govt introduced a new legal regulation on the vaccine testing process. This would greatly impact the outcome of the project. How would you handle this?

    A.   Ignore and continue working as per the plan

    B.   Log it as a change of low priority

    C.   Log it as an issue and make necessary arrangement

    D.   Log it as a Risk and plan for it

21. The weather forecast was a cloudy day with a 90% probability of rain. Carrying an umbrella would be classified as a _____ risk strategy. Fill in the blank.

    A.   Avoid

    B.   Mitigate

    C.   Transfer

    D.   Accept

22. The _____ lists the observations that reflect if the process is in control or not by listing the observations within the context of upper control limit and lower control limit. Fill in the blank.

    A.   Interrelationship diagrams

    B.   Control charts

    C.   Ishikawa diagrams

    D.   Tree diagrams

23. Your team has gotten into a lot of arguments recently. Tom and Harry have been constantly at war with each other. You are now at a point where you need to intervene. Else the project environment is affected and impacting the morale of other team members. Which of the following is not a valid conflict management technique?

    A.   Force

    B.   Withdraw

    C.   Focus Groups

    D.   Avoid

24. Which of the following statement is valid about the crashing technique?

    A.   It adds to cost and/or risk

    B.   It leads to rework

    C.   It is implemented when the project is on schedule

    D.   Crashing is another name for fast-tracking

25. The team has produced detailed requirements but is yet to develop the work breakdown structure. The senior manager Bob asked you to provide a definitive estimate of the project costs. What would be your next step?

    A.   Say no to Bob as you do not have this estimate worked out yet

    B.   Tell Bob that you are new to the project and can't provide the estimate

    C.   Tell Bob that you would be able to provide the estimate after the team develops a bottom-up estimate

    D.   Tell Bob that you would be able to provide the estimate after the team develops the top-down estimate

1.5 ALL ANSWERS

ANSWERS: 1.4: BASELINE ASSESSMENT TEST

No	Answer	Domain	Remarks
1.	A, H	People (MBTI)	Rachel is an Extrovert and Perceiving. Expect one question in the PMP Exam on this.
2.	D	People	This is a question of the ethical working of the Project Manager. The most ethical choice is D
3.	D	Process	A PM should know what's expected from him.
4.	D	Process: Agile	Sprint retrospectives can help to identify the problem areas and can help improve the quality by acting on the suggested improvement by the team.
5.	A	Process	Total Stakeholders: 8 - 5 + 3 + 1. **(Total 7)** You need to count yourself as one of the stakeholders and then calculate the communication channels. PM is a stakeholder in the project - right?
6.	B	People	This is an EXCEPT question. Use the TRUE/FALSE method to arrive at the correct answer.
7.	A	Process	The formal acceptance refers to the administrative closure of the project.
8.	B	People	Everyone contributes to team formation and establishing ground rules.
9.	A	People	A receiver DECODES the signals.
10.	B	Process: Agile	The incremental project life cycle does not use a timebox and cannot be classified as agile.
11.	C	Process: Agile	The product owner is the owner of all requirements and signoff with the agile team.
12.	B	Process: Agile	Planning poker may use Fibonacci series cards to establish the efforts of PBIs The cards may have values: 1, 2, 3, 5, 8, 13, 21, 34, etc
13.	D	Process: Agile	The Product Owner is accountable for maximizing the value of the product resulting from the work of the Development Team.

No	Answer	Domain	Remarks
14.	A	People	Punishment power is also known as coercive power.
15.	D	Process	Project life cycles is one of the key topics.
16.	C	Process	Task A started late is more of a status update.
17.	D	People	Getting the team to trust you and other team members is the first step toward building a high-performing team.
18.	D	Process: Agile	Know what is I and T-shaped skillsets.
19.	D	Business Environment	Learn governance in the business environment.
20.	C	Business Environment	Learn compliance in the business environment.
21.	B	Process: Risk	Mitigate is to reduce the probability or/and impact. The umbrella will reduce the impact of the rain.
22.	B	Process: Quality	A control chart contains the mean, UCL, LCL, and observations. This is help understand and monitor the product quality.
23.	C	People	A Focus group is a tool and technique to gather data.
24.	A	Process: Schedule	Crashing adds to the cost and/or risk.
25.	C	Process	The detailed and most accurate estimates can be developed using bottom-up estimates.

BUSINESS ENVIRONMENT

2. THE BASICS

TOPICS WE COVER IN THIS CHAPTER

→ Project vs. Operations

→ Program And Portfolios

→ Development Life Cycle

→ Project Value

→ Project Phases

→ Project Selection Methods

→ Phase Gate/Kill Points

→ EEF and OPA

→ Organization Structures

→ PMO Types

→ Project Life Cycles

→ PDCA

→ Process Groups

→ PMO

The chapter is divided into sections as displayed:

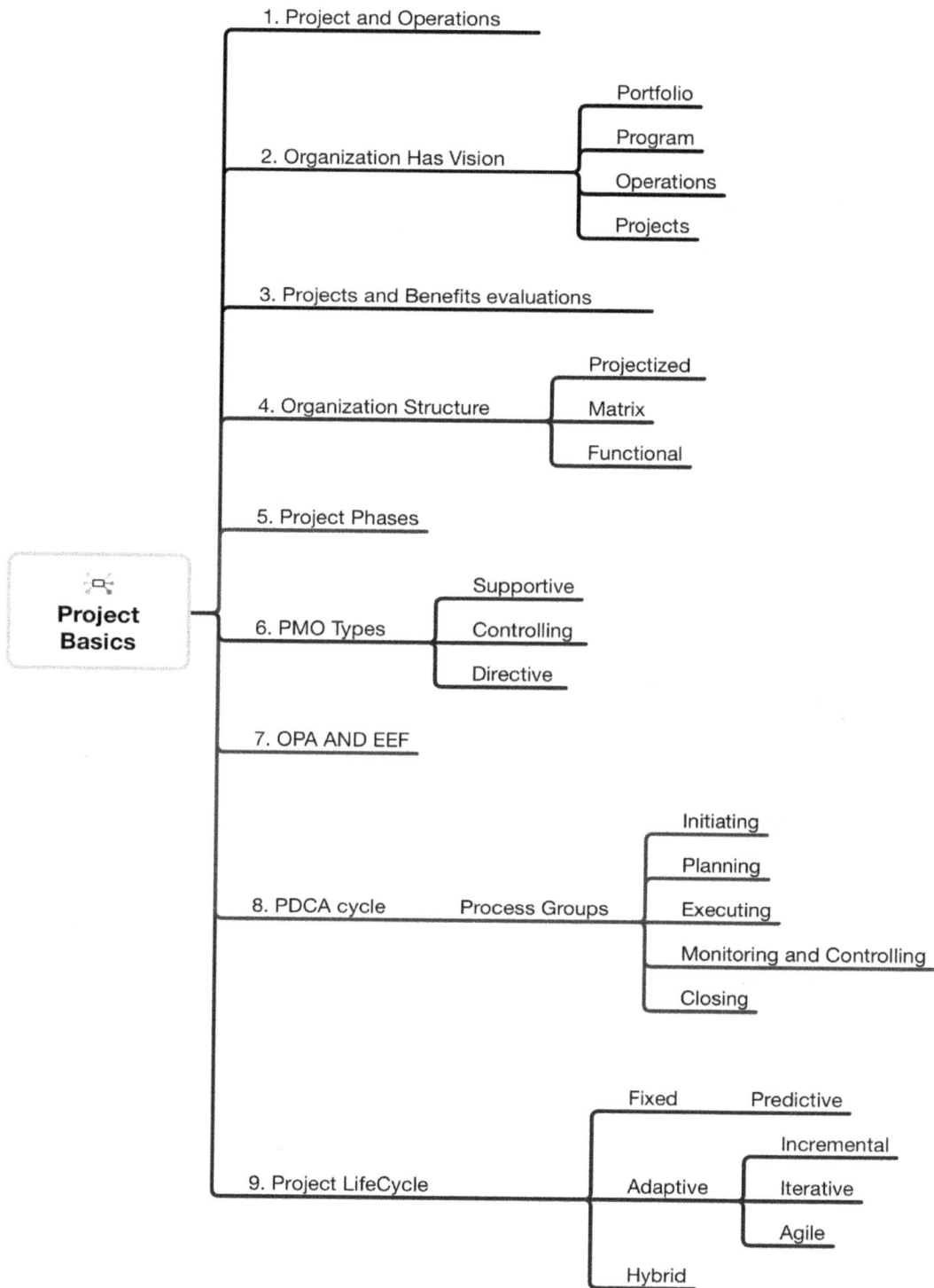

- **Project Basics**
  - 1. Project and Operations
  - 2. Organization Has Vision
    - Portfolio
    - Program
    - Operations
    - Projects
  - 3. Projects and Benefits evaluations
  - 4. Organization Structure
    - Projectized
    - Matrix
    - Functional
  - 5. Project Phases
  - 6. PMO Types
    - Supportive
    - Controlling
    - Directive
  - 7. OPA AND EEF
  - 8. PDCA cycle — Process Groups
    - Initiating
    - Planning
    - Executing
    - Monitoring and Controlling
    - Closing
  - 9. Project LifeCycle
    - Fixed — Predictive
    - Adaptive
      - Incremental
      - Iterative
      - Agile
    - Hybrid

2.1 PROJECT AND OPERATIONS

PROJECT:

What are the keywords in the project definition? Let's see.

OK, if you said "Temporary endeavor" and "Unique," then you are absolutely on target and found the right keywords. If not, we need to practice more.

Let's understand what a project is.

→ A project is temporary.

→ It has a start date and an end date.

→ It should create a unique offering.

→ The offering could be a product or a service result.

A project brings a change in an organization and should align with the organization's vision.

How is a project different than operations?

OPERATIONS

An operation is repetitive in nature and is ongoing. Look for keywords like daily, monthly, yearly - That is, operations.

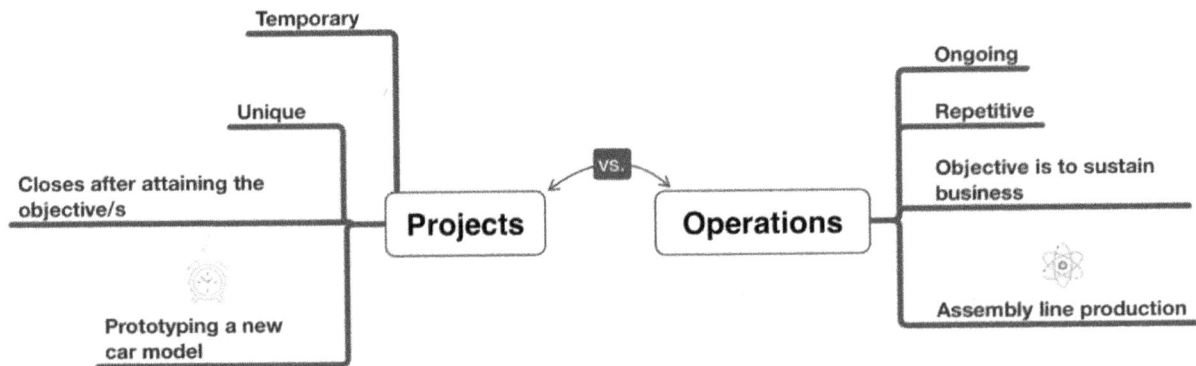

2.1.1 LET'S PLAY: PROJECT VS. OPERATIONS

Select if the scenario given represents a project or an operation

SCENARIO	ANSWER
1. Construction of a new building at a new location.	A. Project B. Operations
2. Baking a grand cake at home for a 50th Birthday celebration.	A. Project B. Operations
3. Crossing the road every day while coming back home.	A. Project B. Operations
4. A college student selecting the theme and venue for an upcoming fresher party. They are planning the party for the first time.	A. Project B. Operations
5. Watching TV after work, every day.	A. Project B. Operations
6. The teacher prepares the quarterly tests for the class.	A. Project B. Operations
7. A seasoned writer, writing a new article for an old publication.	A. Project B. Operations
8. Conducting disaster recovery drills every quarter by the operations head.	A. Project B. Operations
9. Getting a dental checkup every year.	A. Project B. Operations
10. Setting up a game station with the TV for the first time.	A. Project B. Operations

11. The disaster recovery drills procedure to be implemented for the first time in a new building.

    A. Project
    B. Operations

12. The student needs to prepare for upcoming exams for the boards. It's a difficult task, as the student is taking it for the first time and wants to pass the exam with flying colors.

    A. Project
    B. Operations

13. The tuition center, ABC, is conducting coaching for all the students. This year there has been a 20% increase in the number of students.

    A. Project
    B. Operations

14. A bakery chef is known for his wedding and birthday cakes. He gets an order to bake a cake for a 50th Birthday celebration.

    A. Project
    B. Operations

15. A new writer plans to write and publish a book on a technical subject. He is the SME (Subject Matter Expert) on the subject. This book will be his first.

    A. Project
    B. Operations

2.2 Project Is Part of A Program or A Portfolio

PROGRAM

A program is a collection of **related projects**.

Why do we combine related projects? So that we can get cumulative benefits by managing them under one umbrella.

A program manager may not have the authority to kill or initiate a new project. The main goal of Program Managers is to align/**optimize resources.** So from a pool of resources, i.e., under the program, they can shift resources from one project to another based on resource urgency.

PORTFOLIO

A portfolio is aligned with the organization's **vision and strategy**.

A portfolio is directly responsible for carrying out the projects, programs, and/or operations. A portfolio manager **can kill projects** (also called components) and can initiate new components for portfolio alignment and optimization.

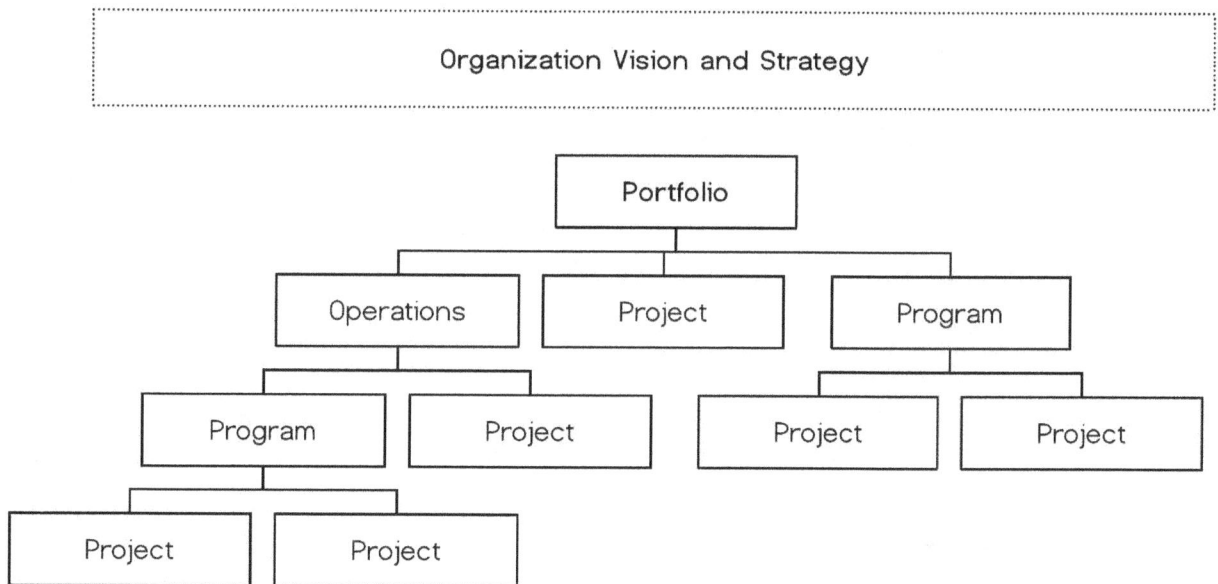

```
┌─────────────────────────────────────────────────────────┐
│            Organization Vision and Strategy              │
└─────────────────────────────────────────────────────────┘

                    ┌──────────────┐
                    │  Portfolio   │
                    └──────────────┘
      ┌──────────────────┼──────────────────┐
┌────────────┐    ┌────────────┐      ┌────────────┐
│ Operations │    │  Project   │      │  Program   │
└────────────┘    └────────────┘      └────────────┘
   ┌──────┴──────┐                      ┌──────┴──────┐
┌─────────┐ ┌─────────┐          ┌─────────┐  ┌─────────┐
│ Program │ │ Project │          │ Project │  │ Project │
└─────────┘ └─────────┘          └─────────┘  └─────────┘
 ┌────┴────┐
┌─────────┐ ┌─────────┐
│ Project │ │ Project │
└─────────┘ └─────────┘
```

Figure 1: Project, program, and portfolio

2.2.1 LET'S PLAY: PROJECT, OPERATION, PROGRAM, PORTFOLIO
Find if you are managing a project, operation, program, or portfolio:

1. You work with an airline help desk. Your job is to ensure that each passenger is given help when needed. You also issue tickets after verifying passenger details. The processes are described, and you follow them to ensure smooth work.

    A. Project

    B. Operation

    C. Program

    D. Portfolio

2. You are planning the initiative SMART as per your organization's vision of being lean and green. This initiative needs to be taken across the entire organization and will affect all divisions. The success or failure of SMART will impact the profits and employee salaries for next year.

    A. Project

    B. Operation

    C. Program

    D. Portfolio

3. You have a few team managers reporting to you. Each manager complains of having difficulties in getting the right workforce. Team ALPHA forecasts the need for 1 technical resource, team BETA wants 3 technical resources, and team GAMMA is forecasting a need for 5 resources by next month. When you analyzed this closely, you found that the Team GAMMA has 2 underutilized resources from the last few weeks. They only need them in the coming month. You get the resources reallocated to team ALPHA and BETA.

    A. Project

    B. Operation

    C. Program

    D. Portfolio

4. You are managing the project CLASSIC HOMES. This is the name given to the project to construct a residential township. As per the blueprint, it is comprised of 7 high-rise buildings and 30 low-rise studio apartments.

    A. Project

    B. Operation

    C. Program

    D. Portfolio

2.3 PROJECTS ARE INITIATED TO ACHIEVE RESULTS

PORTFOLIO MANAGEMENT AND PROJECTS:

Portfolio managers keep evaluating the market, risks, and other factors and decide to introduce a new component in the portfolio. The new component may introduce a few new initiatives, the re-bundling of old elements, and a few changes/upgrades to current components. Any of the changes lead to a project within the portfolio.

A project typically can be initiated by:

→ New technology
→ Competition
→ Material issues
→ Political changes
→ Market demand
→ Economic changes
→ Customer request/Stakeholder demand
→ Legal requirement
→ Business process improvement
→ Strategic opportunity
→ Social need
→ Environmental considerations

PROJECT SELECTION METHODS

How do portfolio managers select a project?

NEED AND DEMAND:

How much of a market demand does the project/product have?

Feasibility Study:

Is the project realistic and feasible for the team?

CASH FLOW ANALYSIS TECHNIQUES

These methods use comparative approaches to compare the benefits obtained from the candidate projects so that the project with the maximum benefit will be selected. Various benefit measurement methods are:

SCORING MODELS

A score is given to every project idea by different parameters such as cost, the risk involved, resource availability, in-house expertise, similar projects done in the past, etc.
The one with the maximum score gets selected and initiated.

PAYBACK PERIOD

The intent of the project payback period is to estimate the amount of time that will be necessary to recover the investment in a project. That is, how long it will take for the project to pay back its original budget and begin to generate positive cash flow for the company.

Lower payback time is better for the project.

NET PRESENT VALUE (NPV)

The present value of the project in dollars/today's currency rate. Present Value compares the value of the future cash flows from the project to current dollars.

$PV = FV / (1+r)n$

> PV=Present Value
>
> FV=Future Value
>
> r is the rate of interest (as a decimal, so 0.10, not 10%)
>
> n is the number of years

More the net present value, the better the project.

INTERNAL RATE OF RETURN (IRR)

The discount rate at which the present value of cash inflows is equal to the original investment. IRR asks the simple question: What percentage of return will this project earn? Under this model, the project must meet some required minimum rate applied to all projects under consideration.

The higher the internal rate of return, the better the project.

RETURN ON INVESTMENT (ROI)

Profit earned as compared to the capital invested.

Return on investment (%) = (Net Profit / Investment) × 100

The higher the ROI, the better the project.

QUICK RECAP ON THE PROJECT SELECTION METHODS

Project Selection Method	Selection Criteria
Payback Period	Lowest
Benefit Cost Ratio	Highest
Net Present Value (NPV)	Highest
IRR	Highest
ROI	Highest

2.3.1 LET'S PLAY: PROJECT SELECTION MECHANISM

A local construction firm is evaluating retail projects to be undertaken to build. They researched the following information:

Projects	Payback Period (Years)	Benefits/Cost Ratio	NPV (Million)	IRR (%)	ROI
Project A	3	2.5	3	12	250
Project B	2	1.5	4	11.5	200
Project C	2.5	1.6	3.2	23.2	160
Project D	6	2	5.3	12.1	210

1. Which project would you select if the selection criteria are the payback period?

    A.   Project A

    B.   Project B

    C.   Project C

    D.   Project D

2. Which project would you select if the selection criteria are IRR?

    A.   Project A

    B.   Project B

    C.   Project C

    D.   Project D

3. Which project would you select if the selection criteria are Return on investment?

    A.   Project A

    B.   Project B

    C.   Project C

    D.   Project D

4. Which project would you select if the selection criteria are Present Net Value?

    A.   Project A

    B.   Project B

    C.   Project C

    D.   Project D

2.4 ORGANIZATION STRUCTURES

Does the structure of the Organization influence the way projects are carried out?

Yes, for sure.

Organizations are structured to optimize the work which they perform. The work can either be unique or repetitive in nature.

A car manufacturing company's majority of works in the assembly line production of cars. They want the people to be experts in their work. Functional structure is the best fit for this type of organization.

Some organization does the projects for their clients, like advertising. The work is a burst of work to be finished within a timeline and is unique. A projectized structure is the best structure for them.

A virtual organization is required in covid like pandemic situations and can perform optimally even when the team is spread around the world.

Senior management decides on the org structure. A Project Manager has no authority to define the structure. However, it is a good idea to know the org structure you work with so that you can perform the work better.

TYPES OF ORGANIZATIONS

Org. Type	Subtype	Work in	Allocations	Headed By	Keywords
Simple/ Organic		Flexible	Part-Time	Owner	No Formal Division Of Work
Functional	Centralized	Departments	Part-Time	Functional Head	Departments, One Boss
Functional	Decentralized	Departments	Part-Time	Functional Head	Departments, One Boss
Matrix	Weak	Departments	Part-Time	Functional Head, Project Manager	Departments, Two Or More Bosses
Matrix	Balanced	Departments	Part-Time	Many	Departments, Many Supervisors
Matrix	Strong	Departments	Part-Time - Full Time	Project Manager	Departments, Two Or More Bosses
Virtual	Matrix	Network, Assignment Based	Part-Time	Functional Head, Project Manager	Departments, Two Or More Bosses
Project-Based	By PM	Projects	Full Time	Project Manager	Project - One Boss
Project-Based	By PMO	Projects	Full Time	Project Manager	Project - One Boss
Hybrid		Mixed	Mixed	Mixed	Mixed

PROJECTIZED ORGANIZATION:

Senior management forms this type of organization when they expect the **majority of work as projects.** In this structure, the team members report to the Project Manager. The teams are formed at the time of project initiation and adjourn when the project/phase terminates.

This structure gives **a lot of authority to the Project Manager** since the Project Manager controls all resources once they are allocated to the project, including the people reporting to the PM. So, what happens when a project is closed?

You are aware that a project is temporary in nature, which means that the project has a start date and an end date. Now, if the project ends, what would happen to people under the Project Manager hierarchy? What happens to the Project Manager himself?

Typically, in this type of organization, a support function, which might be called RMG (Resource Management Group) or PMO (Project Management Office), is responsible for people who are not allocated to a project. If you have heard of a **bench** period in an organization, then you would know for sure that the organization type is Projectized.

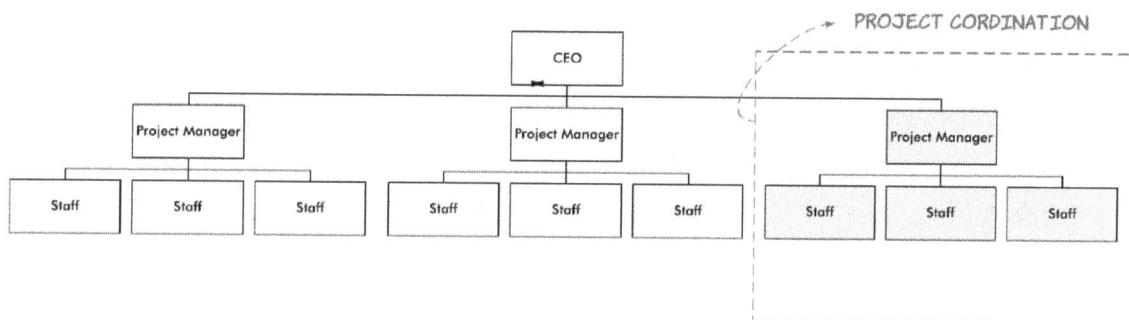

FUNCTIONAL ORGANIZATION:

These types of organizations are formed where the **work expected is repetitive in nature.** In other words, this type of organization is formed around functions that are repetitive and form the overall operations. Now, we know from the definition of operations that these are ongoing; **work is ongoing.**

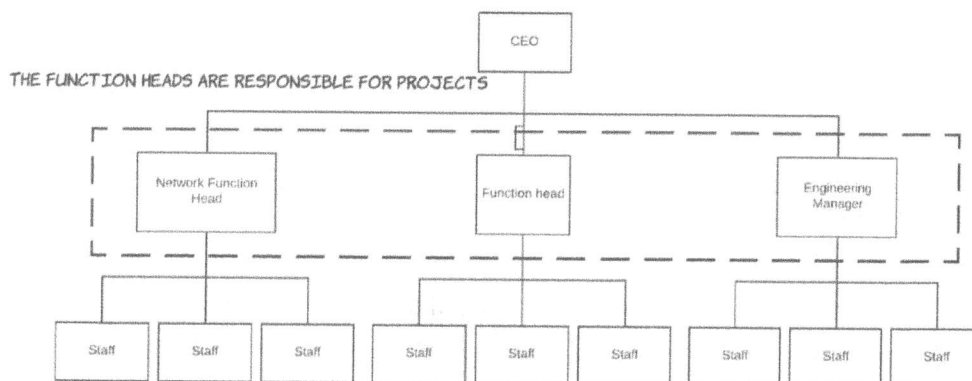

The teams are **structured around operations/functions**. Since this is repetitive work and is always going on, the hierarchy of the function is **permanent**. This means there is no bench period in a team member's life. Why? Because operations/functions are ongoing and typically never cease to exist, unlike projects.

Now, if this type of organization gets a project to work on, who would be carrying out the project? **Typically, the responsibility of completing projects will fall to the Functional Manager.** They might choose a person from their team to help take notes, but the Functional Manager would be responsible for the project.

What will happen if any issue comes up in operations? What would be the priority for the Functional Manager? Would it be a new project or operation work?

If you thought about operations, then you are absolutely correct! **A Functional Manager's core task is to keep the operations continuous. In such a scenario, the projects take a back seat.**

…But there are organizations that want to prioritize both the projects and operations, and they typically form a matrix structure.

MATRIX ORGANIZATIONS

These are the type of organizations that expect both project and operation work to happen. Typical features of matrix organization:

→ The team members report to more than one boss.
→ The team reports to both the Function Manager and the Project Manager (more than 1 supervisor)
→ Project coordination happens across departments.

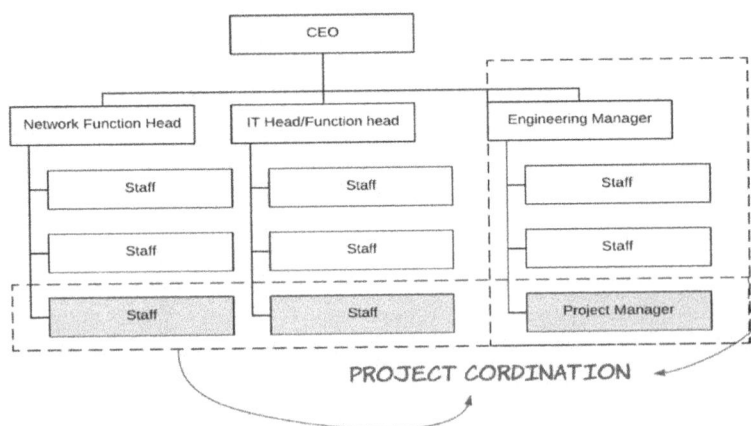

The detailing of weak matrix and strong matrix organization is omitted because, in the new PMP exam, you won't see such questions. Just remember the key features of the matrix organizations:

→ Two supervisors

→ The presence of a home, i.e., a functional head

→ The temporary allocation to a project and a PM

PROJECT MANAGER AUTHORITY GRAPH

The below diagram shows that the more you move towards a functional organization, PM's authority is low. The more we move towards a Projectized organization, The more the PM gains authority.

In the real world, most of us may work in a matrix organization where the authority is shared among the functional head and the PM.

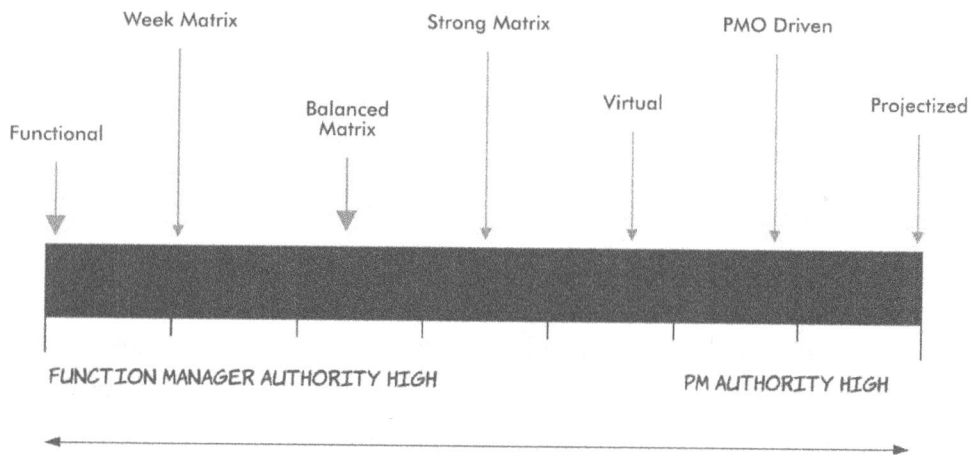

2.4.1 LET'S PLAY: ORGANIZATION TYPES

Can you find out the organization type, as represented by the interviewer?

1. We are looking for an end-to-end program lead. You'd be responsible for working with the finance, sales, and marketing department. You also need to work with some specialists to ensure a better architecture. Remember these people will be working in their respective teams and should be busy with their respective work. The trick is to get your work done on time. Are you up to it?

A.	Functional	B.	Matrix
C.	Projectized	D.	Simple

2. We have a very difficult client that can behave in abrupt ways. We need a Project Manager who can understand the business context and client requirements and can deliver as per the organization framework. We need people who can think and deliver. The team will report to you, and you will be responsible for the project outcome. It's a big responsibility, are you up to it?

A.	Functional	B.	Matrix
C.	Projectized	D.	Simple

3. There has been some pressure from our stakeholders to look at alternate energy sources. Everyone in the department is fully occupied with work, and hence we need someone who could help us to accelerate work on this new initiative. I need you to take notes in the meetings. All the decisions will be taken by the functional head, so in case of doubt – talk to him.

A.	Functional	B.	Matrix
C.	Projectized	D.	Simple

4. I need someone dynamic who can multi-task. We have some great success in one home automation product, named MAALEE. Currently, half of the team is busy with fulfillment and customer care. We are also developing low-cost variants of MAALEE, and that may require your expertise. I need you to be part of as many initiatives as possible. Can you do it?

A.	Functional	B.	Matrix
C.	Projectized	D.	Simple

2.5 PROJECTS ARE DIVIDED INTO PHASES

PROJECT PHASE

A project phase is a collection of related project activities that results in the completion of one or more deliverables. The phases in a life cycle can be described by a variety of attributes. Attributes may be measurable and unique for a specific phase.

A phase is a logical division between project work.

Some Project Managers may want to divide the project work into types of work. For example:

→ Construction

→ Coding

→ Integration testing

→ Testing etc.

Phases in Sequence

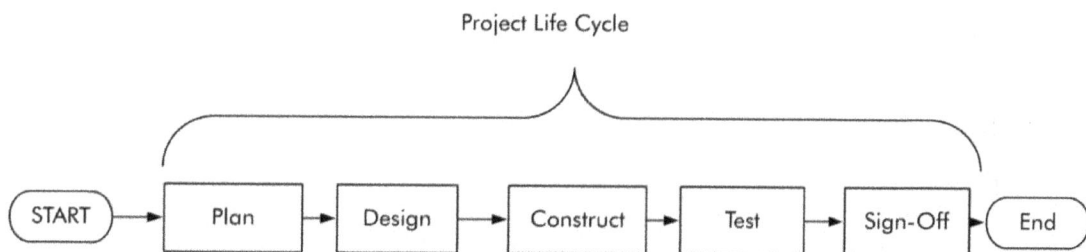

Project Life Cycle

START → Plan → Design → Construct → Test → Sign-Off → End

Phases in Parallel

Project Life Cycle

START → Plan → Pilot → Sign-Off
Plan → USA → Sign-Off → End
Plan → UK → Sign-Off

Some project managers may want to divide the work using deliverables/location or any other parameter which works. For example:

→ Phase 1 – Roll out in the USA

→ Phase 2 – Europe

→ Phase 3 – The rest of the world

A few managers divide the work according to features. For example:

Phase 1 – Site's basic features up and running

Phase 2 – Extra features up and running

Combining all the phases together is called a project life cycle.

PHASE END REVIEWS:

A phase-end review by senior management is a point where the portfolio manager can evaluate the project's effectiveness and the environment. The decision to give the nod to continue the project or not is one of the key decisions which is taken by the portfolio managers at these review meetings. Thus these meetings are also referred to as **kill points.**

2.6 PROJECT MANAGEMENT OFFICE

Have you heard of the following groups?

→ PMO

→ RMG (Resource Management Group)

→ Quality

→ Excellence

Combine all of them for your reference and call them PMO.

The PMO is responsible for helping projects so that project management practices can be standardized, measured, and improved.

In some organizations, the PMO supplies the templates, while in others, it is referred to as the quality department and audits the projects. Different level of authority is exerted by different PMOs.

SUPPORTIVE PMO

Supportive PMOs provide a consultative role to projects by providing templates, best practices, training, and access to information and lessons learned from other projects. This type of PMO serves as a project repository.

THE DEGREE OF CONTROL PROVIDED BY THE PMO IS LOW.

Controlling PMO

Controlling PMOs provide support and require compliance through various means. Compliance may involve adopting project management frameworks or methodologies, using specific templates, forms, and tools, or conformance to governance.

The degree of control provided by the PMO is moderate.

Directive PMO

Directive PMOs take control of the projects by directly managing them.

The degree of control provided by the PMO is high.

2.7 OPA AND EEF

ORGANIZATIONAL PROCESS ASSETS (OPA)

When an organization claims that they have specialized in telecom software integrators, what does that mean?

Does it mean that each and every employee in the organization understand telecom? Not necessarily.

Then what does it signify?

It means that the organization is learning and is compiling the best practices for telecom software integration (SI) over a period of time so it can help them to be more efficient in executing telecom-related projects. These assets may include:

→ Lessons learned
→ Plans
→ Templates
→ Best practices
→ Estimation guidelines
→ Execution guidelines
→ Risk information

Organizational Process Assets **help the organization and Project** Managers to be **more effective** in their work.

PMO is the custodian of Organizational Process Assets

OPAs are enablers.

ENTERPRISE ENVIRONMENTAL FACTORS (EEF)

Let's consider an example to understand EEF:

EXAMPLE 1:

You need to staff your team and have to align the work hours with another country. To have maximum overlap hours, you decided to work from 12 noon till 9 pm. However, as per your state's policy, you need to ensure that any female staff is dropped back home safely. Your organization is a start-up and does not have any drop-off arrangements yet.

Would you think twice before selecting female staff for the project, considering the drop-off costs?

EXAMPLE 2:

You have a team member who is always late. His attitude towards work is not good, and on top of that, he does not even attend the daily team meetings. You gave him feedback twice in the last month. This is getting out of control, and you are not happy with the situation. You feel that you can do better without this person on your team. What would you do?

→ Can you just terminate the person's employment?

→ Would you go to HR and ask HR to put him on a PIP (Personal Improvement Plan)?

→ Would you ask the Functional Manager to replace him with another team member? Your action depends on the company policy – doesn't it?

In the given examples, there were certain factors that can influence you to behave/work in specific ways. These factors could be external (Example1) or internal (Example2).

Typically, an Enterprise Environmental Factor would constrain you. Enterprise Environmental Factors refer to conditions not under the control of the project team that influence, constrain, or direct the project.

Enterprise Environmental Factors are CONSTRAINTS.

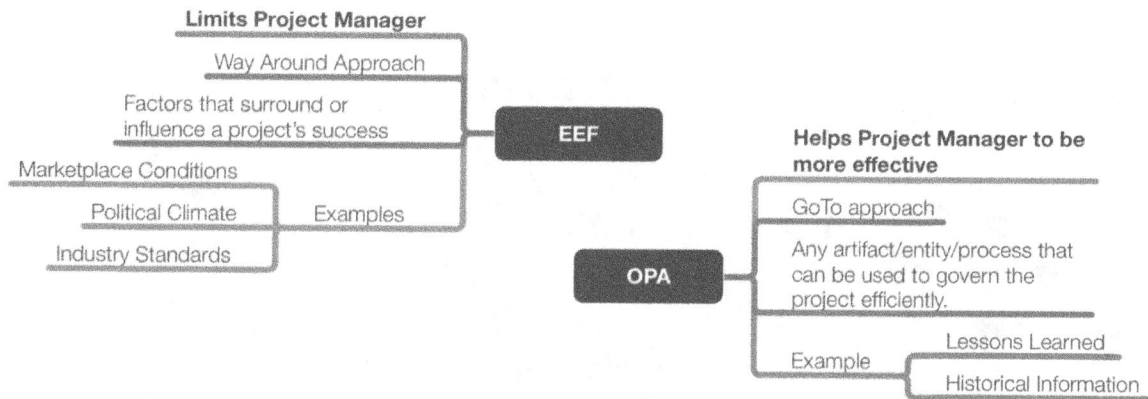

2.7.1 LET'S PLAY: OPA VS. EEF

Select the right option:

1. A team member complains of a sexually oriented remark made by a colleague. You refer to the human resource policy on harassment to initiate appropriate action.

    A. Organizational Process Assets

    B. Enterprise Environmental Factors

2. To develop the Project Management Plan, you look for a predefined template.

    A. Organizational Process Assets

    B. Enterprise Environmental Factors

3. Since the office is in a remote place, you must arrange for pickup and drop-offs so that people can commute to the office safely.

    A. Organizational Process Assets

    B. Enterprise Environmental Factors

4. You change the project team timings from 11 am till 7 pm because no one seems to be in the office at 11 am at the customer's office. This will help you overlap with customer times and give better project efficiency.

    A. Organizational Process Assets

    B. Enterprise Environmental Factors

2.8 THE PDCA

INTRODUCTION: INDIAN WEDDING

Think of a Big Fat Indian Wedding. How do people plan it? Is there any planning in that? When I was a kid, we used to have a meeting with all the Chachas and Taus (Uncles), and responsibilities were assigned to people. I remember that keeping track of the money was one responsibility, and there were others, like:

→ Food menu

→ Beds

→ Getting the rooms cleaned

→ Flowers

→ The puja pandal

And you name it.

Was it a project? Yes, you bet!

Our elders have some re-defined ways of carrying out the project work.

Therefore, PMBOK has divided the project into SIMILAR types of work, called the KNOWLEDGE AREA. The examples of the knowledge areas are:

→ Cost

→ Quality

→ Scope

→ Etc.

Understand that a project goes through certain stages (initiation, planning, and execution). These are referred to by PMBOK as PROCESS GROUPS.

Process groups are not project phases.

In fact, every project phase goes through all the process groups. What does it mean? Each phase will be initiated, planned, executed, and closed, along with monitoring and closing processes.

PROCESS GROUP INTERACTION

The process interaction shows that:

→ Initiating processes happen first.

→ Planning and execution are conducted simultaneously

→ Monitoring and controlling processes are umbrella processes and are performed all the time, starting from project initiation until the closing of the project.

→ There is a trigger in monitoring and controlling, which would trigger the close of the project.

→ Closing processes are performed together.

PROCESS GROUPS

INITIATING

Each project is initiated. This means that the organization has committed to putting resources into the project and has allocated a Project Manager.

PLANNING

Once the project is initiated, the Project Manager plans the scope, time, and other success factors, including the quality necessary to meet the project objectives.

EXECUTING

The actual work happens here. Your team does the work and produces deliverables.

MONITORING AND CONTROLLING

The Project Manager creates dashboards every month/week to determine the project status. In an Agile project, the monitoring and controlling happen DAILY. The team updates the burndown charts and takes control of the work.

CLOSING

These processes are performed to finalize all activities across all Process Groups and to formally close the project or phase.

KNOWLEDGE AREAS

A Knowledge Area is a complete set of concepts/activities performed in an area of specialization.

The Knowledge Areas as per PMBOK 6th are:

1. Project Integration Management
2. Project Scope Management
3. Project Schedule Management
4. Project Cost Management
5. Project Quality Management
6. Project Resource Management
7. Project Communications Management
8. Project Risk Management
9. Project Procurement Management
10. Project Stakeholder Management

Let's go back to the wedding:

Imagine that you are managing the cash/payments, etc. You estimated the wedding. At the end of every day, you may have to look at how much money you are left with and ask yourself — Is it enough? All of these activities or areas of specialization can be combined under the Cost Management Knowledge Area.

Managing activities and ensuring that you complete them on time is a schedule management knowledge area. Similarly, the rest of the knowledge area follows.

Let's see what happens in each process group:

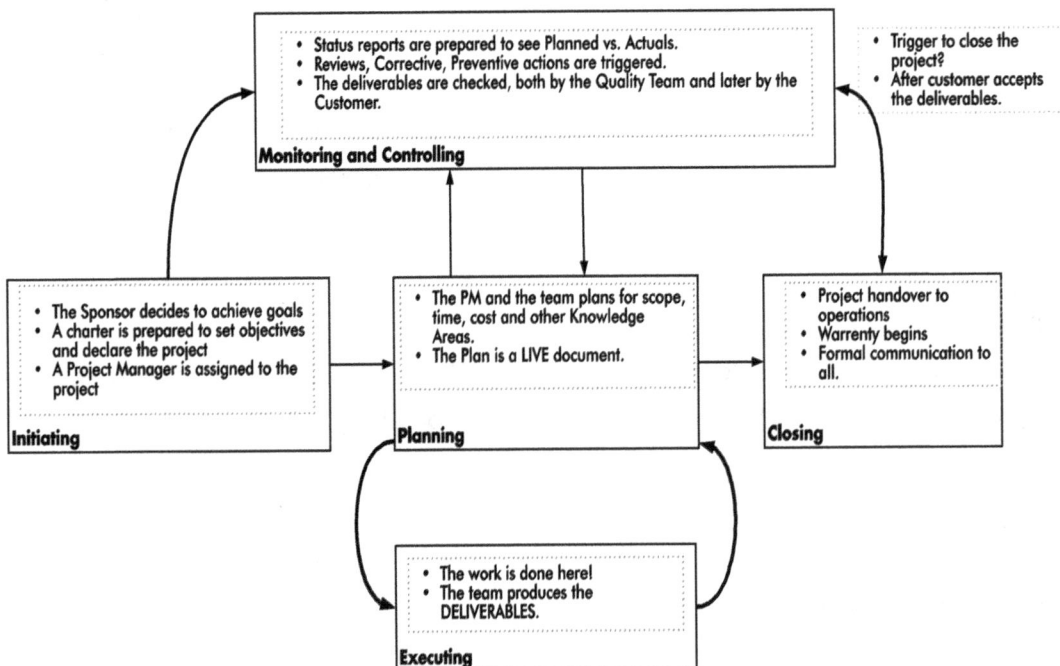

Monitoring and Controlling
- Status reports are prepared to see Planned vs. Actuals.
- Reviews, Corrective, Preventive actions are triggered.
- The deliverables are checked, both by the Quality Team and later by the Customer.

- Trigger to close the project?
- After customer accepts the deliverables.

Initiating
- The Sponsor decides to achieve goals
- A charter is prepared to set objectives and declare the project
- A Project Manager is assigned to the project

Planning
- The PM and the team plans for scope, time, cost and other Knowledge Areas.
- The Plan is a LIVE document.

Closing
- Project handover to operations
- Warrenty begins
- Formal communication to all.

Executing
- The work is done here!
- The team produces the DELIVERABLES.

2.8.1 LET'S PLAY: PMBOK PROCESS GROUPS

Refer to the PMBOK process chart and map the activities with the relevant process group:

Activity Description	Process Group
1. The team plans for the overall work and delivery approach	Planning
2. The team does the work as per the allocated task and updates the task information	
3. Forecasts are created in the group	
4. A status is compiled to check if the project is within schedule or not	
5. Audit happens here	
6. Testing happens here	
7. A schedule is created in this process group	
8. The work is divided into smaller, manageable units	
9. Handover is performed	
10. Plans are created in this process group	
11. The project goals are defined, and resources are committed to achieving goals	
12. Daily stand-up meetings to understand progress and update the task progress	

2.9 PROJECT LIFE CYCLE

Video Available YouTube

SEARCH THIS TOPIC AT THE CHANNEL

How would you define the project life cycle? What methodologies are available, and which methodology could be best for your project? That's a complicated question so let's try to solve it.

EXAMPLE 1:

There are a few industries where the cost of change is too high. You want to **do it right the first time**. For example, the construction of a building of 25 floors. Would you finish the 25th floor first and then think that the design needs to be optimized, let's rebuild the entire building? That's just not feasible.

So, in this case, you would want to ensure that you get the specifications right, do due diligence on the type of surface, soil, air, and water, as well as get adequate regulatory nods, then start the actual development/construction of the building. Here:

→ The cost of change is huge

→ Specifications are clear

→ The construction industry has mature regulations and processes

EXAMPLE 2:

Another example. A new technology (IT – software) has evolved, and a lot of things can be achieved. You, as a customer, want some work to be done using new technology. However, you are not aware of the capabilities of the new technology. The relevant new feature can bring immense value to the business. You want to explore those features and build based on market feedback and the features available. Here in this scenario:

→ The cost of change is low

→ Specifications are changing

→ Industry is new

How would you go about developing the project for each scenario?

Before we this question, let us understand various ways to develop and deliver the product (Project Life Cycle - PLC).

PREDICTIVE LIFE CYCLES

This is also known as **fully plan-driven**. A predictive life cycle is an excellent methodology when customer requirements are **precise**, the industry is **mature**, and the cost of change **is high**. Think construction.

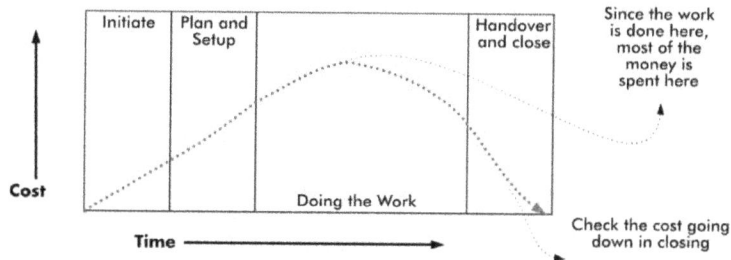

When we speak about predictive life cycles, things to keep in mind are:

→ Cost and staffing levels are low at the start, at their peak as the work is carried out, and drop as the project moves towards closing.

→ Risks in any project are greatest at the start and decrease during the later stages.

→ The ability to implement the changes in the product is lowest at the start.

→ Changes cost a lot as the project progresses towards completion.

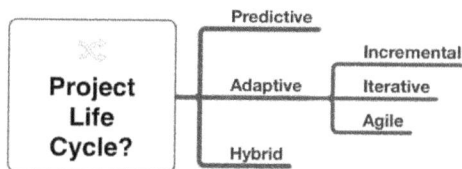

ADAPTIVE LIFE CYCLES

If the requirements are evolving, do you wait to get all of them uncovered before you start the project? That's not even possible in some scenarios where the next set of requirements will evolve only when the customer sees the response from the market of the product/project. In such cases, we can opt for an adaptive life cycle. We deliver some part of the requirements and then build on it. The approaches to work on adaptive life cycles are:

INCREMENTAL LIFE CYCLES

Deliver in phases. We do it all the time. The requirements are mature. We finalize them and develop them, and deliver them in the first phase. We then work with the customer for the next set of requirements and deliver them in the next phase. We deliver in phases.

ITERATIVE LIFE CYCLES

Think products! Windows and Mac operating systems are the best examples that may come to mind. If you are a gamer, think of the different versions of Wii or Play station.

A product team can think of releasing a major version as and when the industry demands or as per the team release cycle. Each version may focus on new additional features for the customer.

AGILE LIFE CYCLES

Agile projects follow the Agile Manifesto. The delivery approach combines the iterative and incremental lifestyle to deliver value to customers. Many agile techniques exist but just remember that agile follows the agile manifesto. **Iterations are released in small burst cycles of a week or a month.** These small iterations are focused on new features or additional functionality. The iterations are repeated until the whole product is released.

Small cycle iterations help the project team to seek input from the customer in a shorter time frame. Any changes can then be incorporated into later iterations. This allows both the customer and the project team to work through details on the fly and can be very useful when the requirements are hazy or unclear.

Agile Manifesto

Individuals And Interactions	over	Processes And Tools
Working Software	over	Comprehensive Documentation
Customer Collaboration	over	Contract Negotiation
Responding To Change	over	Following a Plan

That is, while there is value in the items on the right, we value the items on the left more.

* Taken from: http://agilemanifesto.org/

PLC SUMMARY

	Requirements	Activities	Delivery	Goal
Predictive	Fixed	Performed once	Single delivery	Manage cost
Iterative	Dynamic	Repeated until correct	Single delivery	Correctness of solution
Incremental	Dynamic	Performed once for a given increment	Frequent small deliveries	Speed
Agile	Dynamic	Repeated until correct	Frequent small deliveries	Customer value via frequent deliveries and feedback

2.9.1 LET'S PLAY: PROJECT LIFE CYCLE
Suggest the life cycle suitable for the scenarios:

1. The customer is new to mobile application development. Their requirements keep changing as the team learns new possibilities of features in mobile development/applications every day. They are very excited to start rolling out new features to their users. The key focus is to roll out valuable features, see the market feedback, and build on the feedback.?

2. The customer wants to build a website for their upcoming new segment of clothing lines. The clothing lines are supposed to be rolled out in a specific sequence. There are few designers that the fashion brand employs, and they are expected to launch their collection soon (The dates keep changing). Each designer's work, once finished, can be showcased on the new platform. However, the current emphasis is to roll out a campaign to showcase the upcoming new fashion lines and build excitement. The next set of rollouts would depend on the designers and their completion of the designs. The designers are yet to commit to the timelines.

3. You are managing a product called OPLAY. The product is a collaboration platform where people can find their friends or communities and play games with them. You have a few games in mind to launch. Some of the games are Tetris (2-player game), UNO (2 and 4 player game), and Checkers (2-player game). You want to ensure that each game variant works perfectly on all mobile platforms. No errors can be tolerated, as this will be bad for your brand and application.

4. You are tasked to make a bridge between two villages over a river. The bridge should be constructed to allow a seamless journey for vehicles and people from both villages. The government body issued a contract to your organization with the required specifications. The emphasis is that the bridge should be rolled out soon and at a fixed cost.

5. You work as a manager with an automobile manufacturing unit. The company is facing a challenge now that the government has come out with new emission and safety laws. This would require a redesign of the engine and interior, including safety gears, to pass the new tests mandated by the law. The engine design is complex and goes through lots of trials and errors. For the rest of the other phases of the vehicle production, once the engine and safety norms are satisfied, they are easier to follow. They follow the standard approach of development like assembly, painting, and testing jobs.

2.10 MODULE END QUESTIONS

1. You are asked to coordinate a new initiative named CODE-B. This is a new and complex initiative and requires the involvement of other departments. You are published as the coordinator for CODE-B. You are given the authority to call meetings. The team member, at any point in time, is working on multiple initiatives. Your core responsibility as the project coordinator is to track progress and flag any issues so that an action can be initiated at the management level. Which type of organization do you work with?

    A. Projectized

    B. Functional

    C. Matrix

    D. Organic

2. The research division head asks you to develop a prototype for facial recognition. He further tells you that you have the authority to get the resource allocation as needed, but the product needs to be ready within the next 6 months. The product needing to be ready within the next 6 months is an example of:

    A. A requirement

    B. Stakeholder expectation

    C. An assumption

    D. A constraint

3. Your organization is structured to do projects. Once a project is completed, the team member searches for another appropriate project matching his skill set and growth path. The PMO helps the team member with the next allocation as per his skill match. Once the project is completed, whom would the team member report to?

    A. Functional Head

    B. Project Manager

    C. Manager of Project Manager

    D. Project Management Office

4. The research division head asks you to develop a prototype for facial recognition. The software should be accurate. However, a few features like searching in the federal database for prints and health records can be added as features later. Which methodology can work for your project?

    A. Agile so that customer gains confidence in the team

    B. Incremental to keep on adding required functionality

    C. Iterative so that features are accurate and function work well

    D. Predictive as its straight forward project

5.   You are managing the project GHANA. The project is to develop services for telecom network operators. You are also part of the PMO (Project Management Office). Which type of organization do you work with?

    A.   Projectized

    B.   PMO

    C.   Matrix

    D.   Organic

6.   You are working with a robotics firm. A new robot for a manufacturing client is expected to be delivered in the next ten months. You seek advice and historical data from the PMO. They have all the information. The PMO is rather helpful and in no way questions your authority as the Project Manager. Which type of PMO is discussed in this scenario?

    A.   Supportive

    B.   Controlling

    C.   Directive

    D.   Servant-leader

7.   Select the incorrect statement:

    A.   A stakeholder can be a project resource

    B.   A stakeholder can be a group

    C.   A stakeholder can be an organization

    D.   A stakeholder can be a vendor human resource

8.   You joined an organization as a team member. You have one supervisor. Your role and growth path are clearly defined. Which type of organization did you join?

    A.   Projectized

    B.   Weak Matrix

    C.   Strong Matrix

    D.   Functional

9.   The following scenario depicts a project EXCEPT:

    A.   Temporary endeavor by one person

    B.   Temporary endeavor by team & manager

    C.   Implementing the changed standard operating procedures (SOPs)

    D.   Adhering to the standard operating procedures (SOPs)

10. To get started on the project, you spoke to the PMO and obtained the old project estimates and historical data. This will help you to plan and control the project. This is an example of:

    A.   Controlling PMO

    B.   Organizational Process Assets

    C.   Enterprise Environmental Factors

    D.   Directive PMO

11. You work with the design and technical team as a manager for new product development. The customer wants an innovative cutting edge designed product. The customer can explain the functionality, and your technical team has developed the specifications. Design, on the other hand, has yet to be evolved. The challenge is that no one (including the customer) knows what they want. What time of project/phase life cycle would you choose for design and why?

    A.   Design should be developed iteratively by redesigning till the team achieves what the customer likes

    B.   Design should be developed incrementally by developing features in phases

    C.   Design should be developed as a predictive life cycle using a prototype approach

    D.   Design should be developed as an agile life cycle with active customer inputs

12. Your firm makes bestseller vehicles for the rural market. The last product, which was launched two years back, was a major hit with the consumers and your team won several awards. Now you are in the process of developing a new model, YANNA, which should comply with newly announced government regulations. The extent of the work is mostly known, but one of the components is tricky and needs lots of iterations to be perfect. This is the most crucial component of the entire project, which can make or break the product. What and how would you select the project life cycle for the new-age truck, YANNA?

    A.   Combination of predictive for known components plus agile development for unknown component

    B.   Combination of predictive for known components plus iterative development for unknown component

    C.   Use an iterative life cycle for the entire project

    D.   Use agile life cycle for the entire project

13. You have joined as a service lead with one of the leading organizations. You work on several leads at any point in time and form different teams from across departments to fulfill the services. The team members report to you part-time. What makes it difficult to coordinate is that the team is not even collocated. This is also good in a way and works well because you save on project costs, and you can get resources from across all the departments and geographies. This helps get a better global output. Which type of organization do you work with?

    A.   Projectized

    B.   Virtual

    C.   Matrix

    D.   Organic

14. Which project stage takes huge efforts and expenditures?

    A.   Controlling stage

    B.   Closing stage

    C.   Planning stage

    D.   Executing stage

15. Select the TRUE statement:

    A.   The cost of implementing a change is huge at the start and diminishes later

    B.   It's OK to make changes at later stages

    C.   The cost of change at the start is less

    D.   A change management process can be created when the need arises

2.11 ALL ANSWERS

ANSWERS: 2.1.1 LET'S PLAY: PROJECT VS. OPERATIONS

Question No	Select the answer	Why?
1.	Project	Unique
2.	Project	Unique
3.	Operations	Daily
4.	Project	Unique
5.	Operations	Daily
6.	Operations	Quarterly
7.	Project	New article
8.	Operations	Quarterly
9.	Operations	Yearly
10.	Project	First time
11.	Project	First time
12.	Project	First time/Unique
13.	Operations	Every year
14.	Operations	Daily work
15.	Project	New, the First book

ANSWERS: 2.2.1 LET'S PLAY: PROJECT, OPERATION, PROGRAM, PORTFOLIO

Question No	Answer	Why
1.	Operation	Processes are followed.
2.	Portfolio	Across organization.
3.	Program	Resource optimization.
4.	Project	Clear goals, unique start, and end date.

ANSWERS: 2.3.1 LET'S PLAY: PROJECT SELECTION MECHANISM

Question No.	Answer
1.	Project B has the lowest payback period.
2.	Project C has the highest IRR.
3.	Project A has the highest ROI.
4.	Project D has the highest NPV.

ANSWERS: 2.4.1 LET'S PLAY: ORGANIZATION TYPES

1. MATRIX - Check the allocation
2. PROJECTIZED - One Boss
3. FUNCTIONAL - Check that the person has no authority
4. MATRIX - Check the allocation

ANSWERS: 2.7.1 LET'S PLAY: OPA VS EEF

Question.	Answer	Why
1.	Enterprise Environmental Factors	You need to follow the policy even if your first choice of decision is something else.
2.	Organizational Process Assets	It aids you in creating a plan in a shorter time frame.
3.	Enterprise Environmental Factors	Limiting factor.
4.	Enterprise Environmental Factors	You need to find a way to deal with a limitation.

ANSWERS: 2.8.1 LET'S PLAY: PMBOK PROCESS GROUPS

ACTIVITY DESCRIPTION	PROCESS GROUP
1. The team plans for the overall work and delivery approach	Planning
2. The team does the work as per the allocated task and updates the task information	Executing
3. Forecasts are created in the group	Monitoring and Controlling
4. A status is compiled to check if the project is within schedule or not	Monitoring and Controlling
5. Audit happens here	Executing
6. Testing happens here	Monitoring and Controlling
7. A schedule is created in this process group	Planning
8. The work is divided into smaller, manageable units	Planning

9. Handover is performed	Closing
10. Plans are created in this process group	Planning
11. The project goals are defined, and resources are committed to achieving goals	Initiating
12. Daily stand-up meetings to understand progress and update the task progress	Executing

ANSWERS: 2.91 LET'S PLAY: PROJECT LIFE CYCLE

Scenario	Life Cycle
1. The customer is new to mobile application development. Their **requirements keep changing** as the team learns new possibilities of features in mobile development/applications every day. They are very **excited to start rolling out new features** to their users. The key focus is to **roll out valuable features, see the market feedback, and build on the feedback.?**	**Agile** Value, Market feedback – all points toward Agile PLC
2. The customer wants to build a website for their upcoming new segment of clothing lines. The clothing lines are supposed to be rolled out in a **specific sequence**. There are few designers that the fashion brand employs, and they are expected to launch their collection soon (The dates keep changing**). Each designer's work, once finished, can be showcased on the new platform.** However, the current emphasis is to roll out a campaign to showcase the upcoming new fashion lines and build excitement. The next set of rollouts would depend on the designers and their completion of the designs. **The designers are yet to commit to the timelines.**	**Incremental** Changing dates and specifications, Few Requirements, at least the first phase is clear.
3. You are managing a product called OPLAY. The product is a collaboration platform where people can find their friends or communities and **play games with them.** You have a few games in mind to launch. Some of the games are Tetris (2-player game), UNO (2 and 4 Player game), and Checkers (2 Player Game). You want to ensure that each **game variant works perfectly on all mobile platforms.** No errors can be tolerated, as this will be bad for your brand and application.	**Iterative** Complete game, No errors.

Scenario	Life Cycle
4. You are tasked to make a bridge between two villages over a river. The bridge should be constructed to allow a seamless journey for vehicles and people from both villages. The government body issued a contract to your organization with the required specifications. The emphasis is that the bridge should be rolled out soon and at a fixed cost.	**Predictive** Clear requirements Fixed cost Physical outcome – rework is a lot of waste
5. You work as a manager with an automobile manufacturing unit. The company is facing a challenge now that the government has come out with new emission and safety laws. This would require a redesign of the engine and interior, including safety gears, to pass the new tests mandated by the law. **The engine design is complex and goes through lots of trials and errors.** For the rest of the other phases of the vehicle production, once the engine and safety norms are satisfied, they are easier to follow. They follow **the standard approach of development like assembly, painting, and testing jobs**.	**Hybrid** One phase – new engine design can follow agile The rest of the phases can be Predictive

ANSWERS: 2.10 MODULE END QUESTIONS

Answer	Why of the Answer
1. C	You have the authority to call meetings, and people are reporting to more than one boss—a typical matrix organization. Most of the decisions are made by the departmental head. This shows that it is a MATRIX organization.
2. D	Six months is a constraint to be accounted for while you plan for the project.
3. D	This is a great question. First of all, you need to find the type of organization in the given scenario. Then, you need to find the reporting authority. The scenario showcases a Projectized organization. We know that in a Projectized organization, the team does not have a HOME/ Department. Once the project is over, the team, including the Project Manager, goes to the BENCH or waiting area. These bench/ unallocated resources are managed by PMOs in Projectized organizations.

Answer	Why of the Answer
4. C	The emphasis is on the accuracy of the features. An iterative approach will work the best.
5. B	The controlling PMO gets involved in managing the project directly. The Project Manager is thus part of the PMO itself.
6. A	A supportive PMO manages the Organizational Process Assets and does not have authority to control the project aspects
7. A	Using the TRUE/FALSE method: A. A stakeholder can be a project resource: This looks like an OK statement but let's see if the rests of them are more TRUE or False B. A stakeholder can be group: TRUE C. A stakeholder can be an organization: TRUE D. A stakeholder can be a project human resource: TRUE Now by looking at all the options, you know that options B, C, and D are definitely TRUE, whereas option A contains the word resource. This could be a printer or an office meeting room. So, choice A is most correct.
8. D	One supervisor means that it is either Projectized or Functional. In this case, it is a functional organization. Notice the keywords, role, and growth paths are defined.
9. D	Using the TRUE/FALSE technique to select the right option: A. Temporary endeavor by one person – TRUE B. Temporary endeavor by the team & manager - TRUE C. Implementing the changed Standard operating process (SOPs) – TRUE. D. Adhering to SOPs (Temporary and unique) – FALSE – This is ongoing, and operations

Answer	Why of the Answer
10. B	This is an example of how well you read the intent of the question. The question asks you about the historical data that can help you in your project. This is a clear example of the usage of Organizational Process Assets. In case you get side-tracked into finding the PMO, then you may not be able to select the PMO type because not much information on the role of PMO is described in the question.
11. D	In case of new technology and where the specifications are evolving, the agile approach can be used to work and firm up the specifications.
12. A	See that some of the phases are known, and the customer is performing them in earlier products. However, only one component is evolving. This can be the best example of a mixed lifecycle. Predictive for the phases which are known and agile for the one which needs to be evolved.
13. B	The team is virtual (Not collocated) and reports to many bosses. Gets formed only for the project—all the keywords for Virtual teams.
14. D	Most of the efforts and costs are incurred when your team starts putting in efforts to develop the deliverables (i.e., carrying out the work/executing stage).
15. C	Do not necessarily go with the most verbose answer! Those could be wrong as well. The picture shows that cost of change is low in the starting phases of the project and expends a huge amount of money and efforts to incorporate the change towards the later stages of the project. Thus, a Project Manager's emphasis should be on getting the correct requirement from the customer so that changes due to incorrect requirements are eliminated.

AGILE

3. AGILE – LET'S GET STARTED

TOPICS WE COVER IN THIS CHAPTER

→ What Is Agile	→ User story
→ Agile Manifesto	→ Persona
→ MoSCoW	→ Product Backlog
→ Scrum Roles	→ DOR and DOD
→ Scrum Events	→ Relative Estimation
→ Scrum Artifacts	→ Team Velocity
→ Kanban Charts	→ Spikes

3.1 CONTEXT

There was a point in time when software projects started, software developers were doing the development, testers were doing testing, and the Project Manager was doing project management. The developers and testers (typically of the same orientation, started thinking of the work. They do all the work, and the kudos go to the PM. If the Project Manager does not know or contribute much to the development process, then why should the PM be the one in the limelight? Why do they take all the credit, whereas the developers are the ones who created the product? Why such emphasis on plans when at the same time – some work can be done? Why does someone else dictate them? Does someone else estimate for their work? So a few developers developed a new way of software working. They developed a manifesto and principles. This is called agile manifesto and agile principles. Let us see the agile manifesto available at https://agilemanifesto.org

Agile Manifesto

Individuals And Interactions	over	Processes And Tools
Working Software	over	Comprehensive Documentation
Customer Collaboration	over	Contract Negotiation
Responding To Change	over	Following a Plan

*That is, while there is value in the items on
the right, we value the items on the left more.*

So, they changed the typical roles in the software projects and said that there should not be any Project Managers. Instead, there should be someone who would coach us and help us achieve the results – This role is known as a Scrum Master or, in some approaches still – Project Manager. They emphasized that the Development Team should be able to have all the skillsets (multi-skilled or T-shaped) so that they can deliver the working software.

One of the key things which were agreed upon was that the agile teams should show something working in a required time frame, e.g., some teams agreed that a good time to show progress by showcasing the completed features in 2 weeks, and some said 4 weeks. It was later established as the best practice to have a roll-out period of 1 -4 weeks (No/little documentation -right) to show that the team is progressing in the right direction.

The concept of TIMEBOX emerges – It means that the agile teams would produce something of value within the selected period (1-4 weeks).

It changed everything. How?

In the standard (predictive) way of project management – the Project Manager and the team used to agree on the scope with the customer and then used it to estimate time and cost and prepare the plan and milestones to get started. These plans were agreed upon by the customer and sign-off (baselined), and the team would start working to deliver the products – a building, a ship, or a road – you get the idea.

Since the agile team said that we would be producing something of value within some predefined time limit – it would mean that – The TIME IS FIXED. The team would now select the features to be developed within that period. So the estimation techniques are evolved to estimate scope. Since the time was FIXED, and the Agile team members are fixed – The cost more or less is typically fixed (remains the same), so an emphasis on the cost tracking is gone. We will revise the above concepts in each chapter and see how the agile way of working impacts when we think of cost or schedule.

But for now – Let's start with a new project – Using AGILE.

3.2 PROJECT WOOFED

You are a dog lover. You are faced with a problem. You had two dogs, and they gave birth to 6 puppies. You want the puppies to be adopted by good families. You are a software engineer, and you think it's a problem on a bigger scale. So you envision a solution (website/app) for the collaboration of people. Users can list their dogs for adoption. Interested people (Dog lovers) can browse the available dogs and adopt.

Can you think of other features for this offering?

Let me give you another one: Dogs lovers should have some way to reach out to animal shelters or NGOs to report any problems.

3.2.1 LET'S PLAY: PRODUCT THINKING

Think to list the features of the proposed solution. List at least 5 features

1.

2.

3.

4.

Based on the kind of vision you have, you may have added features like:

1. Payment for the dogs (Dog Listing - prices)
2. Pictures or short clips of dogs
3. Details and care of various dogs (Breeds)
4. Healthcare/Animal shelters contacts (location-aware)
5. Most important – Registration for different users. (Dog owners, Lovers, Hospitals, NGOs, etc.)

A structured way to develop the product specifications is using Persona.

3.3 AGILE PERSONAS

A persona is a specific type of user who would interact with the system. It can be based on real users.

Let's try persona with an example:

Persona - Jerry

Jerry owns a dog, works in a multinational firm, and lives alone. He has a girlfriend, but she lives in another town. Jerry travels very often and needs someone to take care of the Dog in his absence.

Persona - Katie

Katie loves dogs. She is an old lady and stays home – most of the time. She walks regularly, and whenever she spots a pet in need – she calls up the helpline to get the required help. Due to her age, she cannot wait for long on the streets.

Now you got the idea. Let us think and write a few more personas:

3.3.1 LET'S PLAY – PERSONA

Describe a few types of people who can interact with your WOOFED:

1.

2.

3

Each persona would have some specific needs from the solution/product. Let's give this product a name - how about WOOFED? Or you can name it as you want.

3.4 USER STORY USING PERSONA

A user story describes the type of user (persona) that they want and why. A user story can help understand the specific requirement of typical users. A user story also will help you find the value it holds for the user and thus business.

A user story has a format:

As a user, I would like to _____(feature), So that _____(Value)

WRITING THE USER STORY FOR JERRY:

- As Jerry, since I travel a lot, I would like WOOFED to provide pet care services so that I can travel without any guilt knowing my dog is taken care of.

Let's write another one:

- As Katie, I would like to know the helpline numbers of nearby hospitals or NGOs so that I can inform them of any dog that needs care.
- As Katie, I would like to rate the hospitals/NGOs – based on the response and care so that other people are aware of the NGO/Hospital attitude and interactions.

Now you get the idea...

3.4.1 LET'S PLAY – USER STORIES

Let's write 2 user story for each persona which you created:

Persona 1: _____

1.

2.

Persona 2: _____

1.

2.

Persona 3: _____

1.

2.

Great work so far. Let's dig deeper.

3.5 AGILE TEAM AND ROLES

Since we are talking about a timeboxed release and the requirements that keep evolving, a role who knows and owns the product vision and who can work with the team to clarify and feature or collaborate to build a vision for the product becomes very important. A customer can play that role. However, if you look around yourself, you will see that you are dealing with products everywhere. Think of the Zoom Product team, Think of your team for WOOFED, and so on. This person who owns the vision of the product and works with the Development Team would be called the Product Owner.

PRODUCT OWNER

The Product Owner owns the Product Backlog. They own the entire product portfolio and decide on the feature's priority or value. A Product Owner is responsible for grooming the Product Backlog (prioritizing it) and providing a sense of direction and vision of the product to the Development Team. Who can be this person? Normally a role within the performing organization (the organization where the project is getting developed).

TEAM

The agile team consists of T shaped skillset - enthusiastic individuals. Agile teams should be cross-functional. What does it mean? The Team members have a specialization in one skill plus a breadth of multiple skills. These are also called **T Skill people**. Think of it as a DBA (database administrator having testing and coding skills as well).

How are I shaped, skill people? The people who have a single specialization.

Since Agile teams are small, the rule is plus or minus 7, i.e., 5 - 9 people in the agile development. Less than five is too few, and more than 9 is too big (Scrum rule may not be applicable to all agile methodology. But there is a general consensus that agile teams should be small.

The agile team member should be:

FULLY COMMITTED

100% Allocated on the project (When a person multitasks between two projects, that person is not 50% on each project. Instead, due to the cost of task switching, the person is somewhere between 20% and 40% on each project * Agile Practice Standard)

PAIRED PROGRAMMING

One person does the actual work, and the other observes. This improves the code quality and adds another set of eyes to ensure quality. This practice also creates a backup resource just in case of any issue. It can be used in virtual teams by using the remote pairing concept where the paring is observed using a video conferencing link to have the overlap between the team pairs.

AGILE TEAM SPACE

Collaborative work environments, where the agile teams can share progress and update the progress for everyone to see.

COLLOCATED

Better coordination and trust lead to better productivity.

What about geographically distributed teams? Can't they be agile? Yes, but then the recommendation is to create a **FISHBOWL WINDOW** (People can see each other while working) by using a pre-configured daily window of video conferencing.

SCRUM MASTER/ PROJECT MANAGER

The project manager role is not recommended in the Agile teams. Why? Because Agile teams are supposed to be self-organizing, No manager is required to plan and control.
Scrum Master is the new role that replaces the Project Manager in SCRUM methodology (One of the most adopted agile methodologies). However, Project Manager is still a term used in many agile teams like Disciplined Agile and XP. It is expected that a manager should serve as a coach rather than control and manage the development. They should show the traits of servant leadership, coach the team, and help and coordinate with the stakeholders. They are also responsible for ensuring that the Development Team performs focused on the key deliverables, and in case there is any issue/impediment they face, the PM/Coach pitch into work with the issues. So that the team does the work which they are good at, ie. Programming. **What are the traits of a servant leader?**

- Educate stakeholders about why and how to be agile
- Support the team through mentoring and encouragement. Advocate for team members' training and career development. The quote "We lead teams by standing behind them."
- Help the team with technical project management activities like quantitative risk analysis
- Celebrate team successes
- Support and bridge-building activities with external groups

3.5.1 LET'S PLAY – AGILE ROLES

Identify the roles played in each scenario:

1. Harry is responsible for working within a timeline. He attends daily team meetings to work with his peers. He is expected to call for help in case of issues beyond his control

    A. Product Owner

    B. Team Member

    C. Scrum Master

    D. Stakeholder

2. Ria is coaching the team on how to adopt agile. She attends the daily meetings but does not lead them. She ensures that if the team is facing some blockers, she works with management to handle them.

    A. Product Owner

    B. Team Member

    C. Scrum Master

    D. Stakeholder

3. Blu is working with the business to understand the requirements. He also works with the testing team to get the defects on the current product. The team comes to him for any clarity on the work under development. He does not attend the daily meetings.

    A. Product Owner

    B. Team Member

    C. Scrum Master

    D. Stakeholder

4. Ray is emotional to the core and is very devoted to product success. He checks out the competitor products and works on the feature list to outrun the competition. He maintains the features list and works with the Development Team to see the outcome.

    A. Product Owner

    B. Team Member

    C. Scrum Master

    D. Stakeholder

3.6 TIMEBOX:

Timebox is an **agreed-upon time** to finish development and release the working software. The Development Team decides the duration of the timebox using considerations like customer preference /software complexity and organization guidelines. The iteration duration is one of the few things to establish when the team chooses to go agile. Also, note that **The team cannot continue the work beyond the timebox.**

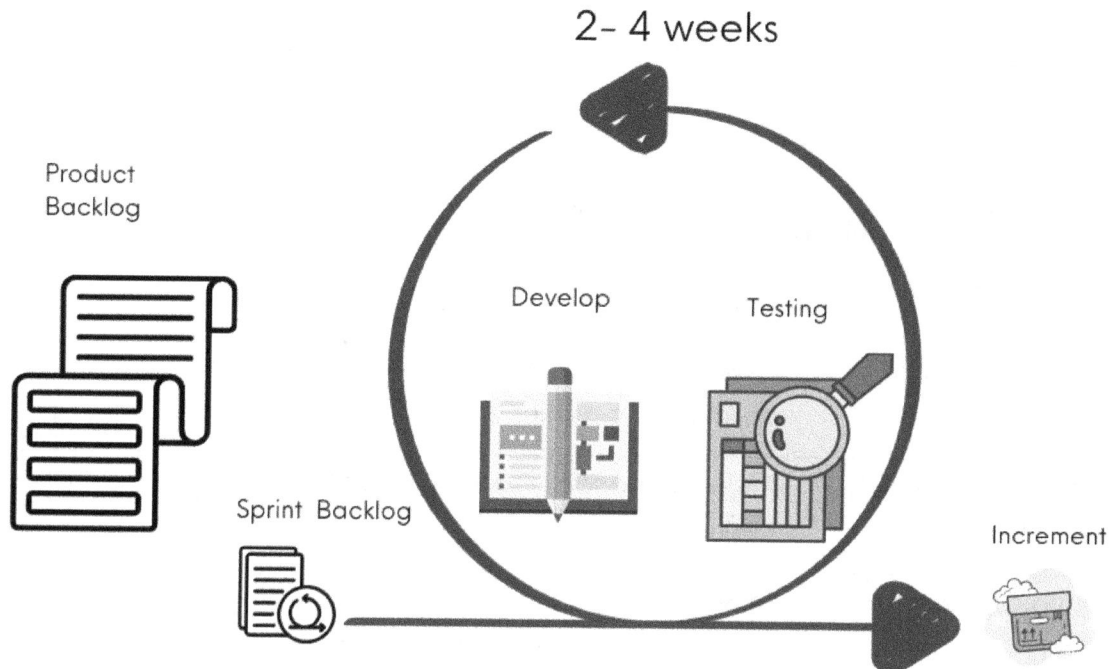

So what happens in the timebox?

The development team selects the features which are of high value as per the Product Owner (he has an ultimate say). The stories are estimated, and the team agrees to deliver them in the upcoming planned iteration of 2/4 week. There are different prioritization techniques that can be applied while selecting the Items for the upcoming sprint/iteration. The selected items for the sprint are called SPRINT BACKLOG. A Sprint Backlog is a SUBSET of Product Backlog.

The team works and shares status every day using daily stand-up meetings. And delivers the working product, also referred to as INCREMENT, at the end of the sprint/iteration.

So if you are from predictive life cycle background, just think that all the planning, execution, testing, and acceptance testing is done within the timebox. The duration of the phase is FIXED, i.e., Timeboxed.

In the case of traditional (Predictive models) the scope is fixed, and the team plans for schedule and cost.

However, in the case of Agile, the TIME of the phase/iteration is fixed, and the team estimates which PBI Items can be developed in the iteration. Ie. The Time is fixed, and the scope is estimated.

3.7 REQUIREMENT PRIORITIZATION METHODS

You can use them with customers or in the sprint planning meetings to decide on the correct (high-value) features to be taken for development for the iteration or for a phase(in the case of the predictive approach).

KANO MODEL

Must-be Quality	One-dimensional Quality	Attractive Quality	Indifferent Quality	Reverse Quality
Must be included Think MVP	Satisfaction when fulfilled Dissatisfaction when not fulfilled.	Exciters Not expected attributes	No one cares Does not help the product	Can lead to dissatisfaction Not to be included

Must-be Quality	These are the requirements that must be included and are the price of entry into a market. (Think MVP)
One-dimensional Quality	These result in satisfaction when fulfilled and dissatisfaction when not fulfilled.
Attractive Quality	These product features result in higher satisfaction when provided but do not cause dissatisfaction if not achieved. These are generally not expected attributes, such as a thermometer on a milk package showing the temperature of the milk.
Indifferent Quality	These attributes refer to neither good nor bad aspects, and they do not result in either customer satisfaction or customer dissatisfaction.
Reverse Quality	These features may result in dissatisfaction since not all customers are alike—for example, loud music in a restaurant.

MOSCOW

This method uses four priority groups: MUST have, SHOULD have, COULD have, and WON'T have. With this technique, stakeholders can collaboratively prioritize requirements. The acronym represents the following:

- MUST (Mandatory)
- SHOULD (Of high priority)
- COULD (Preferred but not necessary)
- WON'T (Can be postponed and suggested for future execution)

PAIRED COMPARISONS

A User Story is picked up and compared with the other User Stories of the Product Backlog items to arrive at the relative value. This will ensure that the most valued user stories are shortlisted.

$$P\,B\,I-1$$
$$P\,B\,I-2$$
$$P\,B\,I-3$$
$$P\,B\,I-4$$

$$= \begin{array}{c} PBI\,2 \\ PBI\,1 \\ PBI\,3 \\ PBI\,4 \end{array}$$

$$= \begin{array}{c} PBI\,2 \\ PBI\,3 \\ PBI\,1 \\ PBI\,4 \end{array}$$

100 POINT METHOD

Each stakeholder is given 100 points. The person can then give any point to their preferred feature.

Value and thus prioritization is determined by calculating the total points allocated to each feature/ User Story.

This is also an example of a decision analysis matrix.

Functionality	Marketing Representative	IT Manager	Business Head
Customer sign-up	30	25	35
Social Media Sharing	20	15	25
Customer Profile	25	25	20
Track Order	25	35	20
Total	100	100	100

DOT VOTING

Individuals use sticky dots to prioritize items/PBIs for development. Typically a team member/decision-maker is given less no of dots than the decisions. The person selects the choices and puts the dot as per their priority.

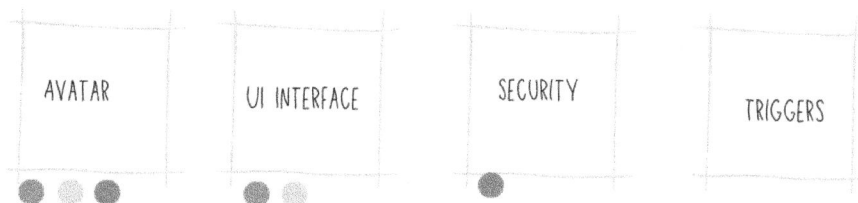

AVATAR	UI INTERFACE	SECURITY	TRIGGERS

3.7.1 LET'S PLAY: PRIORITIZATION.

1. You are working with your team to select the product features essential for the product. Your team has categorized the user stories in "Must be" and "Attractive" qualities to begin with. What other qualities do you think the team should be aware of to get the maximum benefits of this prioritization method? (Select all that apply)

    ☐ A.   One-dimensional Quality

    ☐ B.   Indifferent Quality

    ☐ C.   Reverse Quality

    ☐ D.   Nice to have Quality

2. The Moscow prioritization scheme follows the following categorization techniques: (Select all that apply) Select one or more:

    ☐. A.   Must have

    ☐. B.   Should have

    ☐. C.   Could have

    ☐. D.   Won't have

    ☐. E.   Exciters

    ☐. F.   Delighters

    ☐. G.   Satisfiers

    ☐. H.   Dissatisfiers

3. Each Story is paired against all other stories for further prioritization. The Story, which comes first, is the only Story selected for execution in the Paired Comparisons technique. That way, the team is sure to have selected the winner feature.

    A.   True

    B.   False

4. You asked your team to select the top features of the product for the next iteration. To achieve the same, you asked your team to put their vote on the user story. The team member has only five votes. It is possible to give more than one vote to a feature/user story if they feel that the feature is essential. Which technique did you use?

    A.   Dot voting

    B.   100 point method

    C.   Paired Comparison Analysis

    D.   Requirement Prioritization Meeting

3.8 PRODUCT BACKLOG

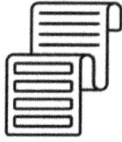

A Product Backlog is a list of the new features, changes to existing features, bug fixes, infrastructure changes, or other activities that a team may deliver in order to achieve a specific outcome. The Product Backlog is the single authoritative source for things that a team works on. (Definition from agile alliance). Who owns the Product Backlog? The Product Owner.

The Product Owner keeps the list of features or user stories in prioritized order. The variable which derives the prioritization is business value. The Product Owner gets feedback from the market, user polls, defect lists, also competitor analysis. With all that help, the Product Owner creates and adds items to the Product Backlog and puts the business value to each item in the Product Backlog.

PRODUCT BACKLOG ITEMS (PBIs)

The features which are yet to be developed. The bugs which are yet to be closed and other required items like regulations that need to be adhered to. The Product Owner does many things like competitor analysis, regulations applicability, and defect reports and adds the required changes to the Product Backlog. Understand the PBIS are features to be developed but also defects and regulations requirements. But which should be developed first?

PRODUCT BACKLOG GROOMING

The Product Owner works with the Development Team to bring clarity to the features. The meeting when all of the Development Team and Product Owner meet and discuss Product Backlog Items (PBI) which may result in the change of PBIs priority is called the Product Grooming Session, and the activity is called Product Backlog Grooming. This is an ongoing exercise in general.

3.9 DEFINITION OF READY (DOR)

Each PBI should follow the DOR so that Development Team can clearly estimate the PBI's development for the upcoming iteration. If the PBIs are unclear and broad, then the Development Team would not be able to complete the feature in the iteration. So to ensure that requirements are good and ready to be developed, the team may establish a certain checklist for the Product Owner. This checklist could be like this:

- Is the PBI small enough to be developed in 2 weeks?
- Is the PBI clear?
- Can the PBI be developed by one team member?
- Is the PBI testable?

Having a DOR would make the Sprint planning meetings more productive. What is the Sprint planning meeting? We will discuss them next. The DOR may follow INVEST criteria, i.e., Individual, Negotiable, Valuable, Estimable, Small, Testable for the Product Backlog Items.

I	(Independent).
	The PBI should be self-contained and it should be possible to bring it into progress without a dependency upon another PBI or an external resource.
N	(Negotiable).
	A good PBI should leave room for discussion regarding its optimal implementation.
V	(Valuable).
	The value a PBI delivers to stakeholders should be clear.
E	(Estimable).
	A PBI must have a size relative to other PBIs.
S	(Small).
	PBIs should be small enough to estimate with reasonable accuracy and to plan into a time-box such as a Sprint.
T	(Testable).
	Each PBI should have clear acceptance criteria which allow its satisfaction to be tested.

SPRINT PLANNING MEETINGS

At the start of the iteration, the Development Team and the Product Owner choose the PBIs, resulting in a valuable product for the business. This requires discussion on the PBIs to understand the feature in detail and estimates to select the total PBIs for the iteration development.

SPRINT BACKLOG

The selected list of user stories is called Sprint Backlog. The sprint backlog is a subset of the Product Backlog.

The team may use several methods to select the features/PBIs/user stories for development. For example, for the WOOFED product, I may have several features on the Product Backlog, and I may want all of them to be developed:

- Registration for the dog owner
- Registration for dog lovers
- Dog listings

- Breed caring videos
- Nearby pet care
- Discussion boards
- Meetups for dog owners
- Food services

The team has only 7 members and 2 weeks to develop the iteration. They need clarity on all the features so that they can estimate and develop them. It is essential that the PBI items follow the INVEST criteria or DOR. What is DOR? Go back and read pl.

3.10 SIZING THE STORY/FUNCTIONALITY

Video Available YouTube

SEARCH THIS TOPIC AT THE CHANNEL

How do we estimate the work for the iteration? Which features should be selected in the upcoming sprint/iteration?

Thoughts?

This brings us to how we estimate if the stories can fit in the iteration.

The Development Team can estimate using the following methods:

To stay away from absolute hours or days sizing, the Agile team works on some abstraction, and that makes the sizing very interesting.

STORY POINT

Story point is an estimation technique where each user story is rated by the team to arrive at a general consensus on the effort to develop the feature/story.

A story point can be 5 hours of work for one team and 10 hours of work for another team. So the team estimates each PBI item using RELATIVE sizing, i.e., using story points.

A few of the ways to size the PBIs are:

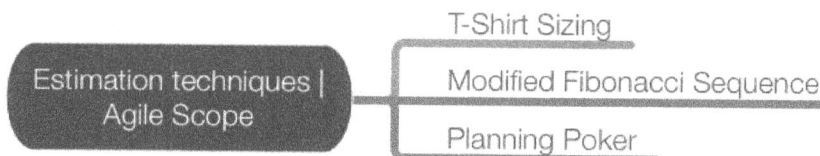

Estimation techniques | Agile Scope	T-Shirt Sizing
	Modified Fibonacci Sequence
	Planning Poker

T-Shirt Sizing

One of the simplest methods is to size a story or feature. The features are categorized as T-shirts starting from Extra small, medium, large, and extra-large. This will help the team establish a consensus on the feature under discussion. The team, in turn, may associate the sizes to story point or working hours. For example, the XS size of the PBI may mean that it can be finished in 1 day. Small may take 2 days. Medium - 4 days, Large may take 6 days, and XL may take 10 days to be ready.

Modified Fibonacci Sequence:

Do you know Fibonacci Sequence?

What is it?

We start from numbers 0 and 1, add them with the last number, and get the sequence.
The formula gives us the series: 1, 1, 2, 3, 5, 8, 13, 21,...

The modified series is to calculate the size of the story is: 1, 2, 3, 5, 8, 13,20,40,100

The numbers are referred to as story points. A story point can be 5 hours of work in one team and 10 hours of work in another team. The team can then use the above numbers to establish the complexity and effort of the feature. 100 may mean that the story is too big to be built and needs to be divided into further sub-features.

Planning Poker

In the Sprint Planning meeting, each team member is given a card to represent the effort on the user story/feature. Each feature is discussed, and all members pick their cards to show the efforts needed to develop the feature in the discussion. If there is slight variation - that's good - discussion would bring clarity, and finally, the consensus on the effort of the story.

If the team picks up cards that vary in the estimate, e.g., one developer feels that the story is small and another feels that the story is XL, then a discussion may be required to clarify the estimate. The team gets into discussion and arrives at the final size.

Planning poker can use any estimation technique (T-shirt size or Fibonacci series) to arrive at the estimates for each PBI.

3.10.1 LET'S PLAY | ESTIMATION AGILE
Select the correct estimation method

1. This estimation technique uses a format: 0, 0.5, 1, 2, 3, 5, 8, 13, 20, 40, 100. It may sound counter-intuitive, but that abstraction is helpful because it pushes the team to make tougher decisions around the difficulty of work.

    A. T-shirt sizing

    B. Story point

    C. Fibonacci series

    D. Planning poker

2. The team will take an item from the backlog, discuss it briefly, and each member will mentally formulate an estimate. Then everyone holds up a card with the number that reflects their estimate. If everyone agrees, great! If not, take some time (but not too much time–just a couple of minutes) to understand the rationale behind various estimates.

    A. T-shirt sizing

    B. Story point

    C. Fibonacci series

    D. Planning poker

3. This is one of the Story points sizing techniques to estimate user stories usually used in agile projects. It's a relative Estimation Technique. Rather than using several planning pokers, items are classified into XS, S, M, L, and XL.

    A. T-shirt sizing

    B. Story point

    C. Fibonacci series

    D. Planning poker

4. The team takes an item from the backlog, discusses it briefly, and each member will mentally formulate an estimate. Then everyone holds up a card that shows XL, L, M, and S that reflect their estimate. If everyone agrees, great! If not, take some time to understand the rationale behind various estimates. (Select two)

    ☐ A. T-shirt sizing

    ☐ B. Story point

    ☐ C. Fibonacci series

    ☐ D. Planning poker

3.11 SCRUM EVENTS

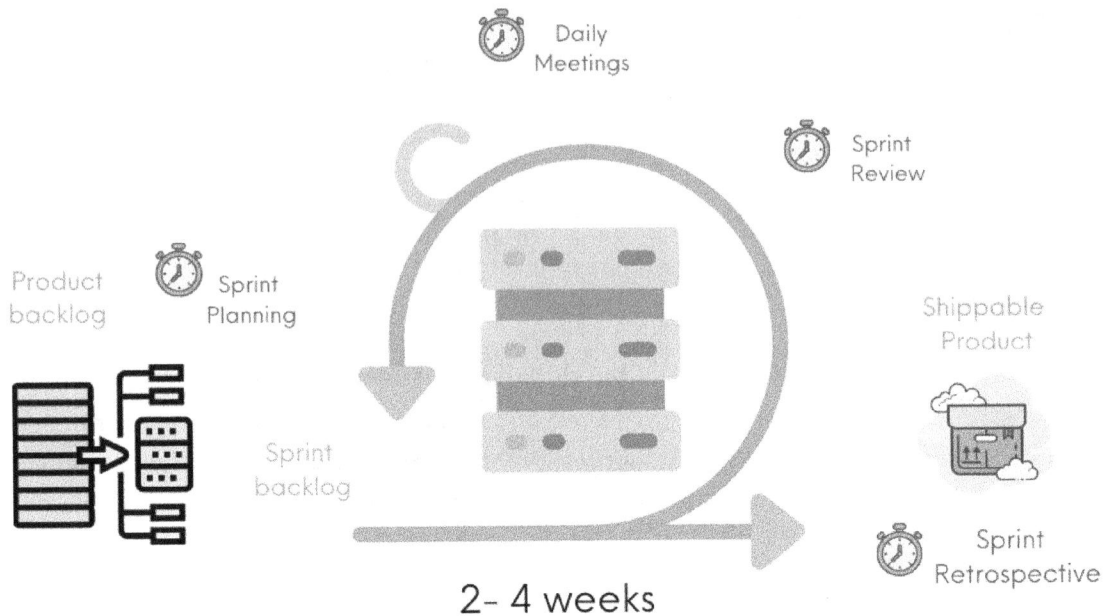

SPRINT PLANNING MEETING

The team meets before the start of the scrum/iteration and selects the PBI for the upcoming iteration. They use various prioritization methods to arrive at the selected feature. The selected PBI items are called Sprint Backlog.

DAILY STANDUPS

The team meets daily to understand the progress and discuss any issues. This is a short meeting where the team discusses the progress and issues. The agile Development Team is all that is required to be present in the meetings. For the Project Manager, also referred to here as the Scrum Master, presence in the daily meetings is to coach and help - remember servant leadership.

The Development Team can use various tools like burndown or burnup charts or Kanban to show and track the iteration progress.

SPRINT REVIEW MEETING

The team produces the deliverables by the end of the timebox. What if the timebox ends and the team has not completed the deliverables? It should not have happened if the team tracks the progress daily :)

So after the timebox, the team is ready with the deliverables. They invite a broad set of stakeholders to review the outcome. It could be the design or functionality concept or a design prototype (as per the Sprint backlog). Who should be the MUST person/role to attend the meeting?

The Product Owner

Why? Because the Product Owner was the one who worked on the product specifications and should be the one to review the outcome. The sprint review meeting will give inputs to the upcoming iterations (bugs/requirements)

SPRINT RETROSPECTIVE

After the Sprint Review meeting, the Development Team and the Scrum Master meet to reflect on the iteration. The idea is to learn from mistakes in the Sprint and enhance team productivity. The team members discuss the failures, how they could have been avoided or handled, and the good things they liked. The Product Owner is optional to be part of the meeting but can be invited.

3.12 RECAP: SCRUM EVENTS, AGENDA, AND ROLES

SCRUM Event	Timebox*	Roles to attend	The intent of the Meeting
Sprint Planning Meeting	8 Hours	Product Owner Development Team Scrum Master	Time boxed event. This is done at the start of the iteration to select the Sprint Backlog Items. The team can use prioritization methods to select the user stories for the Sprint.
Daily Stand-ups	15 Mins	Development Team	The Development Team meets daily to discuss progress and any blockers/issues and update the progress in the burndown chart.
Sprint Review Meeting	4 Hours	Product Owner Development Team Scrum Master Other Stakeholders	The Scrum Team invites stakeholders to discuss and show the Sprint deliverables. The Product Owner can release any completed functionality if they feel so.
Sprint Retrospective	3 Hours	Development Team Scrum Master Product Owner (Optional)	During a Sprint retrospective, the team discusses the top 3 questions: 1. What went well 2. What could have been better 3. Any better way of doing things

3.12.1 LET'S PLAY: MIX AND MATCH: SCRUM EVENTS

Match with the right event:

No.	Situation	Event
1	Time boxed event. This is done at the start of the iteration to select the Sprint Backlog Items. The team can use prioritization methods to select the user stories for the Sprint.	Daily Scrum
2	The Development Team meets daily to discuss progress and any blockers/issues and update the progress in the burndown chart.	Sprint Review
3	The Scrum Team invites stakeholders to discuss and show the Sprint deliverables. The Product Owner can release any completed functionality if they feel so.	Sprint Retrospective
4	During a Sprint retrospective, the team discusses the top 3 questions: 1. What went well 2. What could have been better 3. Any better way of doing things	Sprint Planning

3.13 TEAM VELOCITY

Velocity is the number of story points completed by the team in the iteration/sprint. The Team velocity is calculated at the end of the iteration by adding all the completed User Stories.

If the team has completed many iterations, then the team velocity is calculated using an average of all completed iterations.

Let's use an example to understand this: A team finished 3 iterations as below:

Q1: The story points completed by the team were 20 in Iteration one. They completed 22 story points in Iteration 2 and 24 story points in Iteration 3. What is the team velocity?

(20+22+24)/3 = 22

The team velocity is 22.

3.14 AGILE ARTIFACTS

Product Backlog	The Product Backlog contains required features, errors, or improvements. The Product Owner can compile this list from the competitor analysis, user feedback, and market demands.
Sprint backlog	The sprint backlog is the subset of the Product Backlog. The sprint backlog is the features that have been selected for the current Sprint.
Product increment	The product increment is the outcome prepared by the team in a sprint. It is called increment because it contains the older features produced by the team.

3.15 DEFINITION OF DONE (DOD):

Each individual is different, especially the development members. They have their own definition of done. Typically when I ask if the work is done? The developer may say yes, but his done means that the code is working and documentation is left. But for the team, the done means:

- Code is completed
- Unit tests are written
- Unit test results are logged
- Integration tests are successful

- Updated Manuals, if applicable
- Code is labeled and checked in
- Anything else.

A checklist is a great tool to establish a definition of done (DOD).

3.16 TESTING MINDSET FOR AGILE PRODUCT/INCREMENT
Automated tests are preferred over manual testing in agile teams.

UNIT TESTS
The developer tests the code against the features.

INTEGRATION TESTS
The different features, when integrated together, should be able to perform the functionality as a whole. For example Security module should be able to work with the buying of books. A relevant person is shown only his/her history.

SYSTEM TESTING
The whole system should work as per the intend. Typically, system tests are performed before the functionality roll out.

REGRESSION TESTS
When one feature changes, the whole system should be tested again to see if that (new update) impacts the overall functionality. For example, if you change the logo of the website, the checkout page should behave normally. Doing random checks to ensure that the system works fine is called regression testing.

ACCEPTANCE TEST-DRIVEN DEVELOPMENT (ATDD)
The tests are written first, and only then the development of the features begins. For example, in the WOOFED product, we write that the user should be able to create an account on the app. (That's the test). The code is developed later. Similarly, in construction, in a high seismic zone, the test criteria of that the building should be able to sustain an earthquake of x intensity. The tests are written first, and then the development would begin. Writing (automated) tests before developing the product helps design and mistake-proof the product.
Hardware and mechanical projects often use simulations for interim tests of their designs.

TEST-DRIVEN DEVELOPMENT (TDD) AND BEHAVIOR-DRIVEN DEVELOPMENT (BDD)
Test-driven development applies at the developer level. The developer writes the test cases before writing the code. Similarly, in other industries, BDD is developing the code based on deliverable acceptance. E.g., how a component should behave with the user. BDD is "It's using examples to talk through how an application behaves" *Wiki

Who writes them - The developer themselves. That's the reason we need T-shaped skillset individuals. Now, what was a T-shaped skilled individual?

METAPHORS

A concept from Extreme Programming (XP).

Communication is the key, and using metaphors can help efficient communication if we use good metaphors.

A good metaphor, for example, might help the developers understand and agree on the functionality of the system they are designing.

Some metaphors as used* (development of wrist camera)

PORTRAIT STUDIO

The software has the capability for transferring images from one device (e.g., PDA, PC) to another, and some image processing capabilities. It is much like a portrait studio, where a camera takes a picture, which is developed, retouched, printed, and distributed.

CITIES AND TOWNS

Larger, more capable devices are like cities, in which many services are available. Smaller, less capable devices are like small cities, or even villages, where fewer services are available. Transfer of files is like a train moving from one municipality to another.

SPIKES (TIMEBOXED RESEARCH/EXPERIMENTS)

A concept from Extreme Programming (XP). Spikes can be used to learn/prototype when we have uncertainty around various things, e.g. -

- We don't know how technology would work
- How the feature would look
- How to arrive at final estimate (new team)

An iteration can be used to establish the prototype or that risky item. This iteration where the developers work towards the concept clarity is called Spike.

3.17 AGILE PRINCIPLES

No	Principle	Implementation
1.	Our highest priority is to satisfy the customer through early and continuous delivery of valuable software.	Product Backlog and Product Backlog grooming (valuable items at top)
2.	Welcome changing requirements, even late in development. Agile processes harness change for the customer's competitive advantage.	Change-based methodology – no question on changes – shorter iterations. The Product Backlog is continuously updated
3.	Deliver working software frequently, from a couple of weeks to a couple of months, with a preference for the shorter timescale.	Timebox
4.	Business people and developers must work together daily throughout the project.	Sprint Planning and Sprint review
5.	Build projects around motivated individuals. Give them the environment and support they need, and trust them to get the job done.	T shaped Development Team. Servant leadership
6.	The most efficient and effective method of conveying information to and within a Development Team is face-to-face conversation.	Use of war rooms, Sliding window for virtual teams Collaboration tools
7.	Working software is the primary measure of progress.	Timebox and working increment
8.	Agile processes promote sustainable development. The sponsors, developers, and users should be able to maintain a constant pace indefinitely.	Team Velocity
9.	Continuous attention to technical excellence and good design enhances agility.	Dfx – Design for X is a concept you will learn in quality management

10.	Simplicity—the art of maximizing the amount of work not done—is essential.	4 events and 3 artifacts 3 roles Simple to follow
11.	The best architectures, requirements, and designs emerge from self-organizing teams.	Emphasis on Self-organizing teams with good skillsets and mindset
12.	At regular intervals, the team reflects on how to become more effective, then tunes and adjusts its behavior accordingly.	Retrospective Meetings

3.18 MODULE END QUESTIONS

1. What should be the sequence of the following activities? Put them in order.

- A. Sprint Retrospective
- B. Sprint Planning
- C. Sprint Review
- D. Team Formation

2. When multiple teams work together, each team should maintain a separate Product Backlog.

- A. True
- B. False

3. Match with the correct definition

1. A team's checklist of all the criteria must be met so that a deliverable can be considered ready for customer use.	Definition of Ready
2. A team's checklist for a user-centric requirement that has all the information the team needs to be able to begin working on it.	Acceptance Criteria
3. A set of conditions that are required to be met before deliverables are accepted.	Definition of Done
4. At or near the conclusion of a timeboxed iteration, the project team shares and demonstrates all the work produced during the iteration with the business and other stakeholders.	Variance Analysis
5. A technique for determining the cause and degree of difference between the baseline and actual performance.	Iteration Reviews

4. _____ method uses four priority groups: MUST have, SHOULD have, COULD have, and WON'T have. With this technique, stakeholders can collaboratively prioritize requirements.

- A. Moscow
- B. User Story
- C. Dot Voting
- D. Kano

5. A project is in execution, and a member is delayed on his task. What should be the next step for the team?

   A.   Discuss in the daily meeting and formulate a plan to complete the feature in the timebox

   B.   Escalate it to the Scrum Master

   C.   Escalate it to the Product Owner

   D.   Do Nothing

6. Which statement best describes the Sprint Review?

   A.   It is a review of the team's activities during the Sprint.

   B.   It is when the Scrum Team and stakeholders inspect the outcome of the Sprint and figure out what to do in the upcoming Sprint.

   C.   It is a demo at the end of the Sprint for everyone in the organization to provide feedback on the work done.

   D.   It is used to congratulate the Development Team if it did what it committed to doing or to punish the Development Team if it failed to meet its commitments.

7. What does it mean to say that an event has a time box?

   A.   The event must happen at a set time.

   B.   The event must happen by a given time.

   C.   The event must take at least a minimum amount of time.

   D.   The event can take no more than a maximum amount of time.

8. The Product Backlog is ordered by:

   A.   Small items at the top to large items at the bottom.

   B.   Safer items at the top to riskier items at the bottom.

   C.   Most valuable items at the top and least valuable at the bottom.

   D.   Least valuable items at the top to most valuable at the bottom.

9. When using agile development methodology, who is primarily responsible for making scope versus schedule trade-off decisions?

   A.   The Scrum Master

   B.   The Team

   C.   The Product Owner/Sponsor

   D.   The Project Manager

10. **How does the Agile Manifesto address planning?**

    A.   Planning is not required in an agile project, as the project is focused on the current status

    B.   Responding to change is more important than following a plan

    C.   Sign-off on the detail of Product Backlog items is mandatory before any item can be planned into an iteration.

    D.   Upfront planning and design is an integral stage before development can begin.

11. **What is the relationship between Product Backlog and Sprint Backlog?**

    A.   A Sprint Backlog is a subset of a Product Backlog

    B.   A Product Backlog is a subset of Sprint Backlog

12. **Which tools can facilitate team collaboration in a virtual environment? (Choose two.)**

    ☐ A.   Your Laptop

    ☐ B.   Facebook Connect

    ☐ C.   Team Task Boards

    ☐ D.   Team Kanban Board

13. **Your team is using planning poker, and you are given some cards. What are the most likely values in the cards?**

    A.   Random numbers as per your team's suggestions

    B.   T-shirt sizes S, M, L, XL, XXL, etc.

    C.   Fibonacci series like 1, 2, 3, 5, 8, 13, 21, 34, etc

    D.   Odd number 1, 3, 5, 7, 9, 11, etc.

14. **What are typical items discussed in the daily standup? (Select all that apply)**

    ☐ A.   What is the plan for today

    ☐ B.   Any issues hampering the progress

    ☐ C.   What did I do yesterday

    ☐ D.   Conflicts with other members, if any

    ☐ E.   How is my morale today

15. The Product Owner asked the developers to add a very important item to a Sprint that is in progress. What should be your response to it as a Scrum Master/Project Manager?

  A.   Let's add this item to the Product Backlog and revisit it in the next iteration planning meeting.

  B.   Let's do this. Adapting to change is the reason we selected the agile methodology.

16. What is the recommended size of agile teams?

  A.   5 to 10 members

  B.   5 to 9 members

  C.   4 to 11 members

  D.   6 to 9 members

17. Which of the following is the best Agile team?

  A.   An Agile team that collaborates and self-organizes continuously.

  B.   An Agile team that has no one to blame if things go wrong.

  C.   An Agile team that avoids conflicts.

  D.   An Agile team with specialists.

18. You are part of an agile team working as a Scrum Master. Which Scrum events are mandatory for you to attend? (Select all that apply)

  ☐ A.   Sprint Retrospective

  ☐ B.   Sprint Planning

  ☐ C.   Kick-off Meeting

  ☐ D.   Daily Scrum

  ☐ E.   Sprint Review

19. At the end of the iteration, the team observes that they have completed only 50% of an initially estimated story for 12 story points. How many story points from this Story would count toward the team's velocity?

  A.   Zero story point

  B.   50 story points

  C.   6 story points

  D.   12 story points

20. Since the project required a faster outcome and more work, your agile coach made three teams of 8, 9, and 6 people to perform the work in parallel using an agile methodology. Which can tool/practice help integrate the outcome? (Select two):

    ☐ A.   All Team Meet

    ☐ B.   Scrum Practices

    ☐ C.   Scrum of Scrum

    ☐ D.   Scaled Agile Practices

21. In the case of agile methodology, when does an iteration considered complete?

    A.   When the timebox is completed

    B.   When the team finishes with all Sprint backlog items

    C.   When the Product Owner decides

    D.   When the customer acceptance is over

22. Which of the following are Scrum artifacts (select all that apply):

    ☐. A.   Burndown Chart

    ☐. B.   Product Backlog

    ☐. C.   Communication Plan

    ☐. D.   Gantt Chart

    ☐. E.   Sprint Backlog

    ☐. F.   Project Backlog

    ☐. G.   Sprint Backlog

23. Team Alfa has a velocity of 25 story points, and Team Beta has a velocity of 50 story points over a 2-week iteration. What does this mean?

    A.   Velocity of two teams cannot be compared

    B.   Team Beta is more mature

    C.   Team Beta has more capacity

    D.   Team Beta is more efficient

24. In the case of agile development methodology, who should know the most about the progress toward a business objective or a release and be able to explain the alternatives?

    A.   Scrum Master

    B.   Product Owner

    C.   Project Manager

    D.   Customer

25. Who should be responsible for Product Backlog grooming

A. Product Backlog grooming is the sole responsibility of the Product Owner.

B. Product Backlog grooming is a joint responsibility of the Product Owner and Development Team.

3.19 ALL ANSWERS

ANSWERS: 3.2.1 LET'S PLAY: PRODUCT THINKING

Based on the kind of vision you have, you may have added features like:

- Payment for the dogs (Dog Listing - prices)
- Pictures of short clips of dogs
- Details and care of various dogs (Breeds)
- Healthcare/Animal shelters contacts (location-aware)
- Most important – Registration for different users. (Dog owners, Lovers, Hospitals, NGOs, etc.)

ANSWERS: 3.3.1 LET'S PLAY – PERSONA

1. Admin, who is also the Product Owner, interested to see results.
2. Rita, single, a working professional, stays away from their parents and has a dog.
3. Sam is a single sportsperson looking for pets that can help him burn calories.

ANSWERS: 3.4.1 LET'S PLAY – USER STORIES

ADMIN/PRODUCT OWNER

1. As an admin, I would like to see a list of users who enrolled today so that I can see how the app is performing.
2. As a Product Owner, I would like to see how many dogs have been adopted so that I can see the acceptance of the app
3. As a Product Owner, I would like to see the comments and interaction of people to see the value the app brings to users.

RITA

1. I would like to be reminded of my dog's vaccinations so that I do not forget them
2. I would like to meet other single dog owners to form a community
3. I would like to know the pet-care centers near me so that I can take my dog to the nearest one when needed

SAM

1. I would like to search for dogs so that I can shortlist them
2. I would be able to shortlist the required dog so that I optimize my time finding the correct species for me
3. I would like to interact with dog owners to understand the dog breed and behaviors and care required so that I'm committed and prepared.

ANSWERS: 3.5.1 LET'S PLAY – AGILE ROLES

1.   B (Harry is a team member)

Harry is responsible for working within a timeline. He attends daily team meetings to work with his peers. He is expected to call for help in case of issues beyond his control

2.   C (Ria is a Scrum Master)

She is showing the traits of servant leadership.

Ria is coaching the team on how to adopt agile. She attends the daily meetings but does not lead them. She ensures that if the team is facing some blockers, she works with management to handle them.

3.   A (Blu is a Product Owner)

Blu is working with the business to understand the requirements. He also works with the testing team to get the defects on the current product. The team comes to him for any clarity on the work under development. He does not attend the daily meetings.

4.   A (Ray is the Product Owner)

Ray is emotional to the core and is very devoted to the product's success. He checks out competitor products and works on the feature list to outrun the competition. He maintains the features list and works with the Development Team to see the outcome.

ANSWERS: 3.7.1 LET'S PLAY: PRIORITIZATION.

1. A,B,C (KANO Model)

2. A,B,C,D (Moscow model)

3. FALSE

In this technique, a list of all the User Stories in the Prioritized Product Backlog is prepared. Next, each User Story is taken individually and compared with the other User Stories in the list, one at a time. Each time two User Stories are compared, a decision is made regarding which of the two is more important. Through this process, a prioritized list of User Stories can be generated.

Not one (many)

4. A You know, Dot Voting.

ANSWERS: 3.10.1 LET'S PLAY | ESTIMATION AGILE

1. This estimation technique uses a format: 0, 0.5, 1, 2, 3, 5, 8, 13, 20, 40, 100. It may sound counter-intuitive, but that abstraction is helpful because it pushes the team to make tougher decisions around the difficulty of work.

   C. Fibonacci series

2. The team will take an item from the backlog, discuss it briefly, and each member will mentally formulate an estimate. Then everyone holds up a card with the number that reflects their

estimate. If everyone agrees, great! If not, take some time (but not too much time–just a couple of minutes) to understand the rationale behind various estimates.

D. Planning poker

3. This is one of the Story points sizing techniques to estimate user stories usually used in agile projects. It's a relative Estimation Technique. Rather than using several planning pokers, items are classified into XS, S, M, L, and XL.

A. T-shirt sizing

4. The team takes an item from the backlog, discusses it briefly, and each member will mentally formulate an estimate. Then everyone holds up a card that shows XL, L, M, and S that reflect their estimate. If everyone agrees, great! If not, take some time to understand the rationale behind various estimates. (Select two)

A. T-shirt sizing

D. Planning poker

ANSWERS: 3.12.1 LET'S PLAY: MIX AND MATCH: SCRUM EVENTS

Sprint Planning	Time boxed event. This is done at the start of the iteration to select the Sprint Backlog Items. The team can use prioritization methods to select the user stories for the Sprint.
Daily Scrum	The Development Team meets daily to discuss progress and any blockers/issues and updates the progress in the burndown chart.
Sprint Review	The Scrum Team invites stakeholders to discuss and shows the Sprint deliverables. The Product Owner can release any of the completed functionality if they feel so.
Sprint Retrospective	During a Sprint retrospective, the team discusses the top 3 questions: 1. What went well 2. What could have been better 3. Any better way of doing things

ANSWERS: 3.18 MODULE END ANSWERS

1.	**Team Formation >> Sprint Planning >> Sprint Review >> Sprint Retrospective**

2. TRUE	To avoid confusion- there is only one Product Backlog and only one owner for the Product Backlog - what's that role?

3.		
	1. A team's checklist of all the criteria must be met so that a deliverable can be considered ready for customer use.	Definition of Done
	2. A team's checklist for a user-centric requirement has all the information that the team needs to be able to begin working on it.	Definition of Ready
	3. A set of conditions that are required to be met before deliverables are accepted.	Acceptance Criteria
	4. At or near the conclusion of a timeboxed iteration, the project team shares and demonstrates all the work produced during the iteration with the business and other stakeholders.	Iteration Reviews
	5. A technique for determining the cause and degree of difference between the baseline and actual performance.	Variance Analysis

4. A	[MoScoW] this method uses four priority groups: MUST have, SHOULD have, COULD have, and WON'T have. With this technique, stakeholders can collaboratively prioritize requirements.
5. A	This is normal and should be handled at the team level. A daily meeting is the best place to discuss and take the next steps to solve the issue.
6. C	Sprint Review is a demo at the end of the Sprint for everyone in the organization to provide feedback on the work done.
7. D	A timebox is a previously agreed period of time during which a person or a team works steadily towards completing some goal. Rather than allowing work to continue until the goal is reached and evaluating the time taken, the timebox approach consists of stopping work when the time limit is reached and evaluating what was accomplished.

8. C	The Product Backlog lists any required deliverables. Its contents are ordered by business value. Backlog Item priority might change, and requirements can be added and removed - thus, the Product Backlog is a continuously maintained plan towards a growing business value.
9. C	The final decision lies with the Product Owner.
10. B	Individuals and interactions over processes and tools Working software over comprehensive documentation Responding to change over following a plan Customer collaboration over contract negotiation
11. A	A Sprint Backlog is a subset of the Product Backlog. Iteration backlog is a subset of Product Backlog. The development chooses the most valuable items for the Sprint along with the Product Owner. The list of items selected for execution in the Sprint is called Sprint or Iteration backlog.
12. C, D	Using technology can work to bring the team closer. Working together using a shared taskboard to check progress and collaboration would be a great addon. (Laptop is a piece of equipment)
13. C	Planning poker is based on a list of features to be delivered, several copies of a deck of cards, and optionally, an egg timer that can be used to limit the time spent in discussion of each item. The feature list, often a list of user stories, describes some software that needs to be developed. The cards in the deck have numbers on them. A typical deck has cards showing the Fibonacci sequence, including a zero: 0, 1, 2, 3, 5, 8, 13, 21, 34, 55, 89; other decks use similar progressions with a fixed ratio between each value, such as 1, 2, 4, 8, etc.
14. A,B,C	A. What is the plan for today B. Any issues hampering the progress C. What did I do yesterday The above questions are discussed in the daily standup.
15. A	Let's add this item to the Product Backlog and revisit it in the next iteration planning meeting. The iterations are short and should not be disturbed.
16. B	Most Agile and Scrum training courses refer to a 7 +/- 2 rule. That is, agile or Scrum teams should be of 5 to 9 members.
17. A	An Agile team is all about communication (usually daily), teamwork, problem-solving, technical development skills, and striving to improve the team's velocity

	with each iteration. ... Agile teams are composed of self-organized, cross-functional, highly effective groups of people
18 . A,B,E	The Scrum Master helps the Scrum Team perform at their highest level. They also protect the team from both internal and external distractions. Scoutmaster holds the Scrum Team accountable to their working agreements, Scrum values, and to the Scrum framework itself. The daily meeting can be held without Scrum Master
19. C	50% of 12 is 6 story point
20. C, D	Scrum of Scrum and scaled agile framework can be used in the case of more significant agile projects.
21. A	A sprint/iteration in the agile projects is timeboxed. i.e., the iteration is over when the time finishes. Usually, the timebox can be anywhere from 1 - 4 weeks.
22. A,B, E, G	Burndown Chart - Agile Artifact Product Backlog - Agile Artifact Communication Plan - NA Gantt Chart- NA Sprint Backlog - Agile Artifact Project Backlog - NA Sprint Backlog - Agile Artifact
23. A	Team story point measures can be different, and hence the team velocity of any two teams cannot be compared.
24. B	The Product Owner is accountable for maximizing the value of the product resulting from the Scrum Team's work. How this is done may vary widely across organizations, Scrum Teams, and individuals. The Product Owner is also accountable for effective Product Backlog management, which includes: → Developing and explicitly communicating the Product Goal → Creating and clearly communicating Product Backlog items → Ensuring that the Product Backlog is transparent, visible, and understood. → Ordering Product Backlog items The Product Owner may do the above work or may delegate the responsibility to others. Regardless, the Product Owner remains accountable.
25. B	Product Backlog grooming is a joint responsibility of the Product Owner and Development Team. The Product Owner owns the Product Backlog, but the PBI grooming should be a team task, and joint team sessions are conducted to classify the PBI value.

PROCESS

4. PROJECTS | BIG PICTURE

IMPORTANT TOPICS FOR THE PMP EXAM

→ Who creates the Project Charter	→ Product Roadmap
→ Performing Organization	→ Products
→ Project Plan and Document	→ Change Management
→ Measurable Business Result	→ Artifact Management
→ Change Control Process	→ Decision Making
→ Closeout procedures	→ Project Knowledge

4.1 CONTEXT

How do you start a typical workday in the office?

Most people answer that they check their emails and nowadays you may check them even before you reach the office.

Why?

The reason that we as Project Managers check our emails is because we fear:

- Someone taking any unplanned leave
- Customer escalations waiting in the inbox
- Adhoc issues etc.

Now, let's assume that you get an email from your client, and they want someone from the project team to participate in a workshop to showcase the current progress and take any questions from the audience.

The workshop is planned for early next week and is for 4 days onshore (travel expenses). How would you respond?

You can say NO, because that's not a planned activity, or you can accommodate or better negotiate. A few things to keep in mind are:

→ Availability of resources
→ Impact on schedule
→ Cost impact
→ Company policy
→ Approvals
→ Risks
→ And many other

Once you check all of the above, then you can get into a discussion with the customer about the next steps.

So what happened in the scenario?

As a Project Manager, you analyzed many aspects and then made a viable decision in consultation with your stakeholder. You used your negotiation skills (interpersonal relationship) for a better outcome with the objective of engaging the customer and ensuring that the project does not suffer (project cost, schedule, risk, timelines, quality, etc.)

This is what a Project Manager does all the time and is called INTEGRATION Management.

Remember the PDCA model? We will map the project activities with the PDCA model and process group all the time.

Now you know what the project management is at a broader level, let's dig deeper

4.2 INTEGRATION MANAGEMENT OVERVIEW

Objective: Integration Management is coordinating project planning, execution, checking progress, and taking action if required.

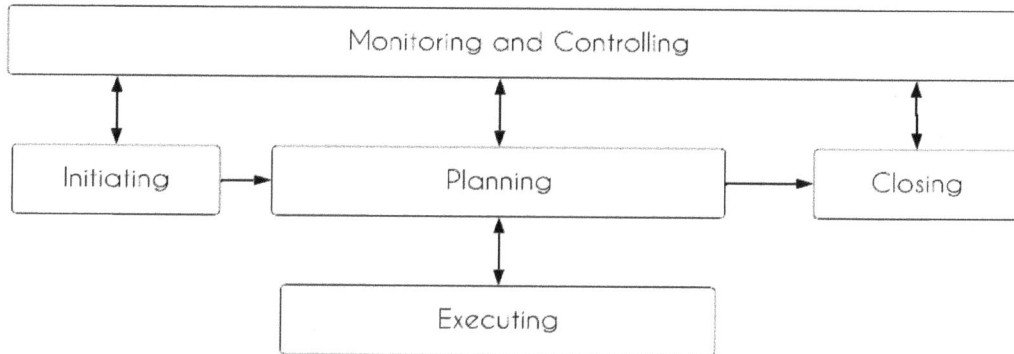

Process Name	Process Group	Major Activities
Develop Project Charter/Vision/Road map	Initiating	Allocate resources to attain a vision. Set goals and MBRs. This is an initiative by Portfolio Manager.
Develop Project Management Plan	Planning	Based on various factors, plan for project life cycle and team composition.
Direct & Manage Project Work	Executing	The team does the work and produces deliverables. Update task boards by team members.
Manage Project Knowledge	Executing	Managing Information/knowledge
Monitor & Control Project Work	Monitoring & Controlling	Understanding planned vs. actuals and actions. Update Status reports/burndown charts.
Perform Integrated Change Control	Monitoring & Controlling	Handling changes
Close Project or Phase	Closing	Formally closing the project or project phase

4.3 DEVELOP PROJECT CHARTER

The Develop Project Charter process is about developing a document that formally authorizes the project and establishes the Project Manager so the Project Manager can then use their authority to allocate organizational resources to the project.

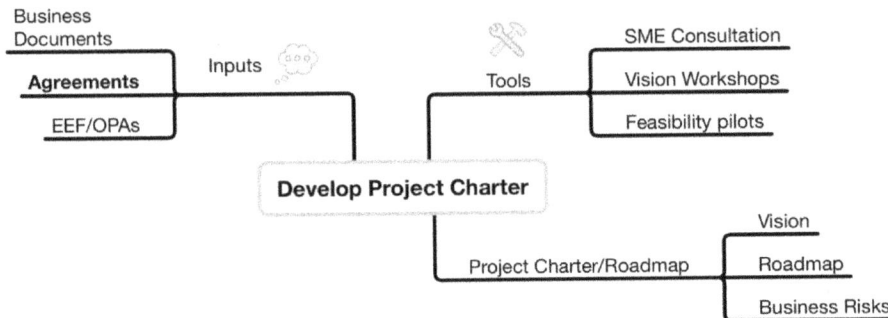

The portfolio managers are responsible for the portfolio performances. The business keeps changing. There are risks, opportunities, and compliances to meet. A project can be started to meet compliance requirements, leverage opportunities, or for any other reason by the portfolio manager. The Portfolio managers select the best project from the to-do list based on NPV (Net present value), ROI, and IRR - we have covered it in the last chapter - if you have skipped that - please do read it. That's one of the core concepts of which you should be aware.

The result of this process is that a project is started in an organization. A charter can be digital or paper-based.

The charter lists the MEASURABLE GOALS of the project, along with who (PM) is responsible for attaining it.

Someone (usually senior management) in the organization gives the go-ahead to the projects and commits resources from their group(Business Unit). **The project sponsor approves the project.**

Most Project Managers may not have seen a charter on paper, but when you think it through:
Do you submit your timesheet against a project code?

Did you get a notification that now you are a Project Manager for the XYZ project, and when you click the link, it will show you the project name, description, and project code?

A description of the project at a high level, along with project goals as envisaged by the sponsor. These are captured in the Project Charter.

Creating a charter and allocating the team resources is the first step in initiating the project. The portfolio manager controls the components in their portfolio.

For Agile projects, the portfolio manager will think of a vision and work with the Product Owner to create a long-term roadmap for the product.

4.3.1 LET'S PLAY: PROJECTS AND MBR

More than 65 million passengers pass through TANGO Airport each year. These travelers have experienced their fair share of delays. According to one report, almost a quarter of the flights both in and out of TANGO weren't on time. As TANGO traffic grew during the 1970s and 1980s, the airport's capacity couldn't keep up. Now a major modernization project, DITI is increasing the facility's efficiency and capacity to reduce flight delays. In 2008, DITI finished a new runway, extended another, and built a new air traffic control tower. Project DITI Plans to complete two more runways in 2013 and 2016. This, in turn, will increase the airport capacity by 50% and will increase runway availability by 150%.

1. Select the correct description of the project.

    A. Project DITI Plans to complete two more runways in 2013 and 2016. This, in turn, will increase the airport capacity by 50% and will increase the availability of the runway by 150%.

    B. More than 65 million passengers pass through TANGO International Airport each year, and those travelers have experienced their fair share of delays.

    C. Almost a quarter of the flights both in and out of TANGO weren't on time. As TANGO traffic grew during the 1970s and 1980s, the airport's capacity couldn't keep up

    D. A major modernization project is being undertaken to increase the facility's efficiency and capacity, which should help reduce flight delays

2. Identify the measurable business results:

    A. Project DITI Plans to complete two more runways in 2013 and 2016. This, in turn, will increase the airport capacity by 50% and will increase the availability of the runway by 150%.

    B. More than 65 million passengers pass through TANGO International Airport each year, and those travelers have experienced their fair share of delays.

    C. Almost a quarter of the flights, both in and out, wasn't on time. As TANGO traffic grew during the 1970s and 1980s, the airport's capacity couldn't keep up

    D. A major modernization project is increasing the facility's efficiency and capacity and helping to reduce flight delays

3. Project DITI is suspended due to an indefinite strike by the workers. The forecast of completion is estimated to be in the year 2021 if the strike is over by January 2018. This will also impact the project costs and current operations. The strike by the workers will be treated as _____ in the project status.

A. A change

B. An approved change

C. An issue

D. A risk

BUSINESS DIMENSION OF PROJECTS

Who creates the project charter?

A project is initiated to develop organizational capability. Understand that projects are part of a bigger organizational objective or vision, typically sponsored by the portfolio manager.

A portfolio is targeted to achieve the organization's vision through certain programs, projects, and possibly even operations. A portfolio manager evaluates all the components of the portfolio, and during this exercise, he or she may kill a component of the portfolio or initiate a new one. A component in a portfolio can be a program or project.

So, there is a portfolio manager who decides on new capabilities to be developed for the portfolio. What comes next? To decide on if the organization can develop the capability in-house or should be outsourced.

→ The organization which executes a project is called the performing organization.

→ The organization that outsources the work is called the customer.

CAPTIVE ORGANIZATION

Work is done for self. The customer is in-house (within the organization)

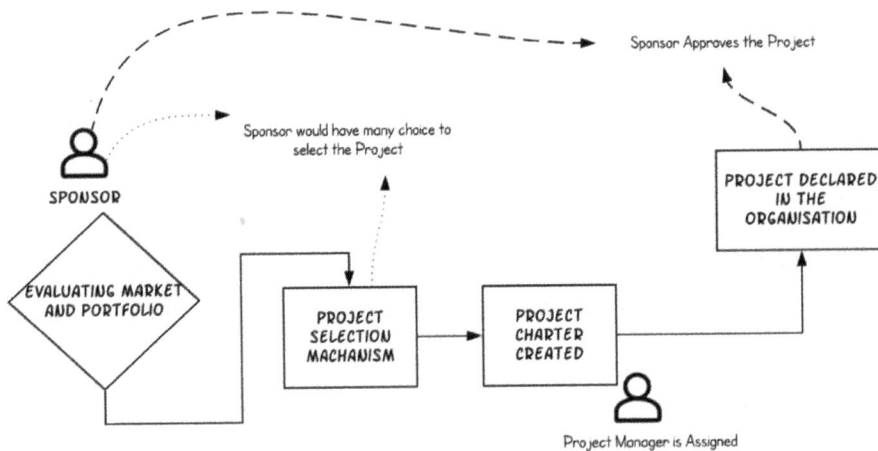

Now there are cases when the project work is outsourced. The work is performed by an external organization. Who creates the charter, then?

PERFORMING ORGANIZATION

The customer is external. You are part of the organization that does the work for the customer. So who creates a charter in the case of a performing organization?

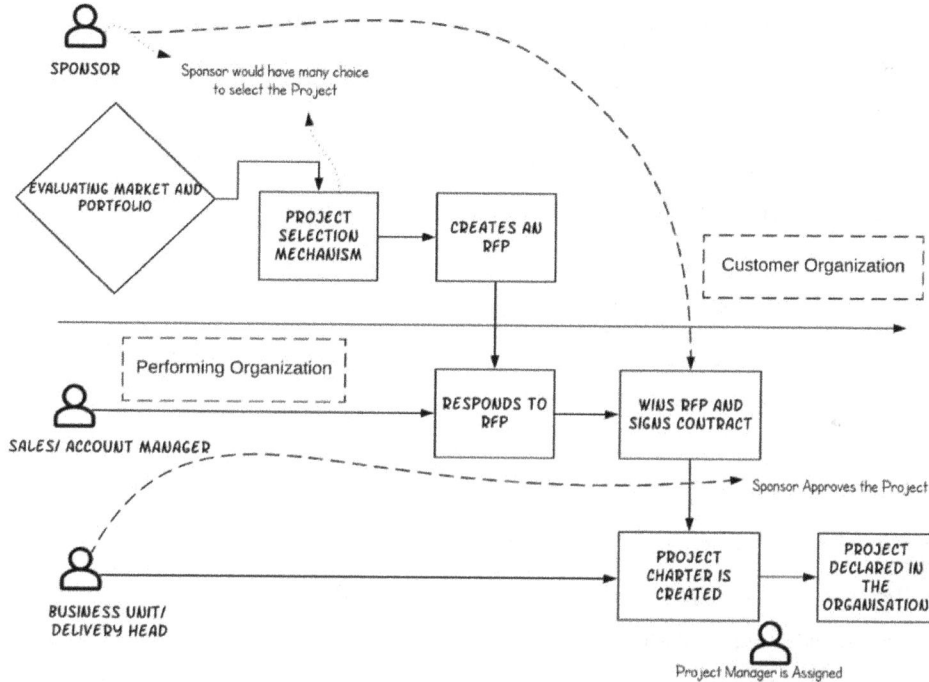

It's the senior management of the performing organization, as the business unit head/senior management commits to the work by allocating resources to the goal shared by the client.

AGILE PRODUCT ORGANIZATIONS

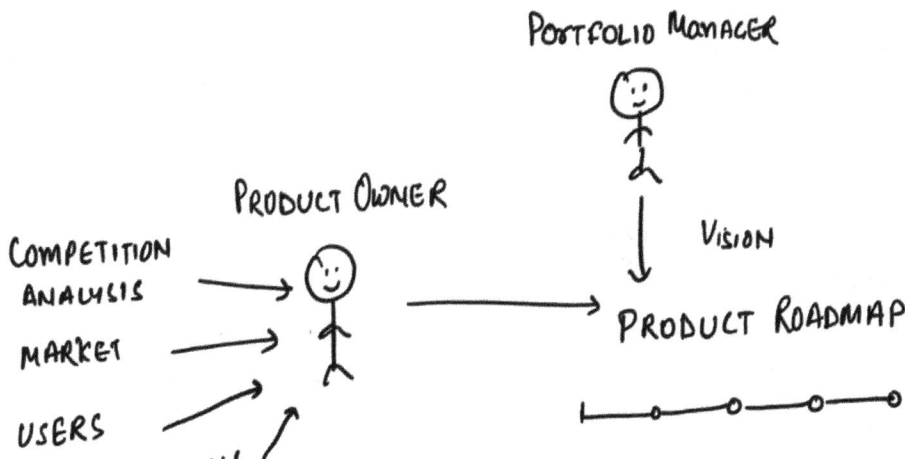

4.4 DEVELOP PROJECT MANAGEMENT PLAN

Defining all subsidiary plans and integrating them to create a comprehensive Project Management Plan.

The first thing a Project Manager does is to develop the high-level Project Plan/Product Roadmap. Development of the plan requires inputs from relevant stakeholders inputs, and hence a thorough identification of stakeholders and discussion with them is important to shape the product vision/ Project Plan.

When I was a project lead/junior Project Manager, I used to think that a schedule was the project plan. This is not correct. A project schedule is just one of the components of the overall project plan.

The project plan has many other details like:

- What is the project scope?
- What are major milestones?
- How many resources are required?
- What skill-sets are needed?
- What is the communication methodology?
- What are the risks in the project, and how to handle them?
- What are the quality requirements?
- How will you handle project changes?
- How will you manage access rights on different project phases?
- Who are all the project stakeholders, and how will you include them?
- What is the project budget? How will you ensure the project is finished within the approved budget? Etc.

There are other details to be added to the plan:

- Life cycle selected for the project
- Change Management Plan
- Configuration Management Plan
- Issues Log (Templates)
- Frequency of review by senior management
- Escalation plan, if any
- Any other details that your project needs

The integrated plan will also have a few baselines. We will learn about them soon.

The Project Charter can be the starting point in understanding what is expected out of the project to enable planning to begin.

A project plan is a LIVE document, meaning that a project plan is always changing and should be current at the time it is being reviewed.

HOW TO PREPARE THE PROJECT PLAN?

We seek the advice from Domain Experts, customers, and project teams

Also, we hold workshops or use other facilitation techniques to gather different views to create an integrated project plan.

The project team, customers, senior management, PMO, and historical data from other projects can all play a vital role in creating a better Project Management Plan.

Once the Project Management Plan is created, it should be agreed upon by the relevant stakeholders. Things like what is the scope of the project and timelines for the projects can be agreed upon and signed off.

The agreed and signed-off plan is called the project baseline. Do not get confused with benchmarking.

Remember that a baseline is an approved and agreed-on version of the plan.

When you monitor and control the project (create dashboard/status report), you compare the baseline version with the current project progress(work accomplished by your team).

A Project Management Plan varies from project to project. The details of the plan depend on the size, investment, nature, and complexity of the project.

We will learn more about the various plans in the coming chapters.

PROJECT PLAN VS. PROJECT DOCUMENTS:

What are the differences between the project plan and project documents? The plan describes HOW and WHEN, and it generally does not change. If a change is required, it goes through the change management process.

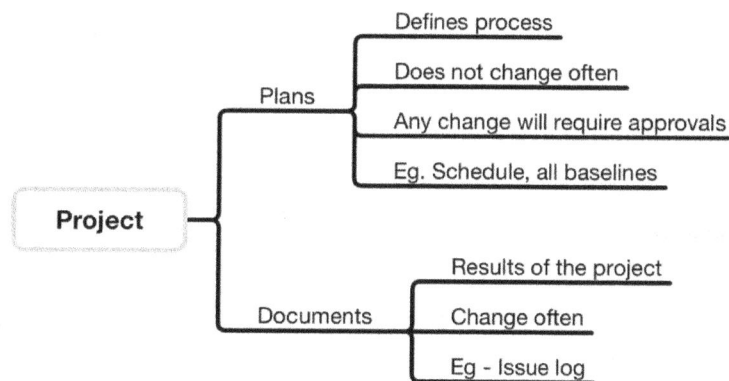

Documents, on the other hand, are documents that are supplementary to the overall plan and change often. While creating plans, You decide to put things under the plan (the things which do not change) and under documents – the things which change. While creating a stakeholder engagement plan, I will write how to manage them and what's the frequency under the plan. However, the stakeholders' names can be written in the stakeholder register as it will change often. I do not want to keep changing the names in the stakeholder plan as and when new people join the organization or leave. Rather, I will make a stakeholder register and refer to it In the plan.

Similarly, think about team detail, team meetings, issues, Change Requests, etc.

4.4.1 Let's Play: Select Project Plan or Document

ARTIFACT TYPE	SELECT THE ANSWER
1. Minutes of Meeting	A. Project Plan B. Project Document
2. Schedule Management Plan	A. Project Plan B. Project Document
3. Status Reports	A. A. Project Plan B. Project Document
4. Stakeholder Register	A. Project Plan B. Project Document
5. Stakeholder Management Plan	A. Project Plan B. Project Document
6. Issue Log	A. Project Plan B. Project Document
7. Change Management Plan	A. Project Plan B. Project Document
8. Change Request Log	A. Project Plan B. Project Document
9. Risk Management Plan	A. Project Plan B. Project Document
10. Risk Register	A. Project Plan B. Project Document

4.5 DECISION-MAKING TECHNIQUES

A group needs to agree on predefined ways to make decisions; These could change based on various situations, e.g., – you might want to use unanimity for selecting a picnic spot and may choose dictatorship if it's a decision on the client requirement. Everything is good. Here is

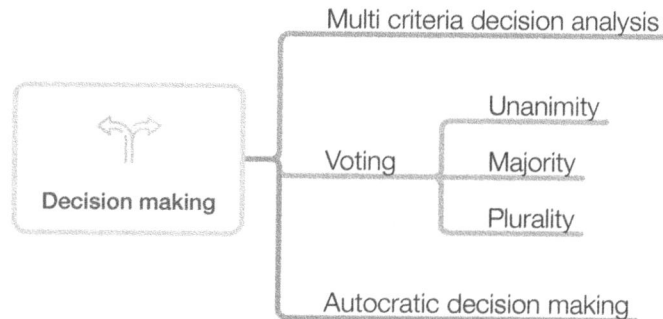

more context:

MULTI-CRITERIA DECISION MAKING

Based on the kind of decision scenario. Let's take the example of the candidate selection process for a company:

Candidates	Presentation Level (Total 10)	Skills (Total 10)	Leadership (Total 10)	Culture Fitment (Total 10) Most Crucial	Overall P+S+L+C*2
Candidate 1	5	8	5	7	32
Candidate 2	7	7	7	8	37
Candidate 3	9	7	6	6	34

The candidate who gets the most marks is selected.

VOTING
UNANIMITY

Everyone has to agree to the proposed solution; else, the decision is not taken.

MAJORITY

Support from more than 50% of the members of the group is required for the final agreement

PLURALITY

The largest set of people decides on the option. It can be less than 50%. This can be used when there are many choices to select.

AUTOCRATIC DECISION MAKING:

One individual makes the decision for the group.

4.5.1 LET'S PLAY: DECISION-MAKING TECHNIQUES

Select the correct decision-making technique in the given scenarios:

1. Some changes were suggested, and a few of them were approved as all the members of the CCB agreed. Two changes were not approved as Rob raised a question about them. There was a total of five board members in the CCB.

    A. Plurality

    B. Majority

    C. Autocratic decision making

    D. Unanimity

2. Jia, the Project Manager of project NEXT, was having difficulty finding a suitable venue for the client meeting. She suggested a few locations, but they were rejected. It seemed as if the meeting were to be canceled. However, John, the client's Supervisor, instructed everyone to meet at their headquarters.

    A. Plurality

    B. Majority

    C. Autocratic decision making

    D. Unanimity

3. A group of college students wanted to see the movie, Avengers. The movie is available in 3D, 4D, and IMAX 3D. 6 out of 10 opted for the 4D format. Hence, Ana booked the tickets accordingly.

    A. Plurality

    B. Majority

    C. Autocratic decision making

    D. Unanimity

4. Ria was in the process of selecting a book cover for her upcoming book. It was a matter of elimination rather than selection, as her choice was very specific. She asked for a general survey and selected the cover3. This cover was not liked by 52% of the people.

    A. Plurality

    B. Majority

    C. Autocratic decision making

    D. Unanimity

5. Noah is an interviewer for technical skills. A firm, SPAR, has a few open positions. There are three rounds of interviews, mainly technical, attitude and management. Each interviewer assesses the candidates and provides the rating sheet to HR (Human Resource) Representative Monika. Monika will then compile all the interviewer's scores to select the best candidate.

    A. Plurality

    B. Majority

    C. Autocratic decision making

    D. Unanimity

4.6 CONFIGURATION MANAGEMENT/ ARTIFACT MANAGEMENT

Video Available You Tube

SEARCH THIS TOPIC AT THE CHANNEL

If you work on projects and the team is at different locations, it becomes crucial to keep the information in the right place with correct security rights.

→ Your developer should be refereeing the right manual. Your stakeholders should be referring to the updated baseline plan.

→ No one should be able to delete the documents except the PM.

→ You do not want a team member to update the plan or Minutes of Meeting after circulation; instead, they should only be able to view the relevant document.

Configuration management ensures stakeholders should be able to access correct information at any point in time.

Identify the CIs and Policy	Define the access rights	Use a Tool to implement	Audit for compliance

Here are typical steps:

IDENTIFY THE CIs

→ Project plan
→ MOMs
→ Code
→ Any other document/physical asset

DEFINE THE ACCESS RIGHTS

→ Which team members should have the right to access
→ Document that
→ Define naming convention and version policy

USE A TOOL TO IMPLEMENT

→ Using SharePoint or dropbox
→ A role Configuration Incharge can be assigned to one of the team members who can implement the defined rights
→ For physical products, a physical lock and key or access card can be used

AUDIT FOR COMPLIANCE

→ It is recommended to check if the right permissions are implemented or not
→ To check if people are using correct naming and version norms

IDENTIFY THE CIs

Starts with deciding on the Configurable Items (CIs), i.e., project plan, MOMs, user manuals, etc. In a construction context (including materials), you do not want unauthorized personnel to have access to this data/product/service/document. These are the CIs.

DEFINE THE ACCESS RIGHTS

Once you've identified the CIs, then you need to control the access to CIs. This is where tools like VSS, Remedy, File system access, or Share Point may come in handy. **These CIs that you control are called CONTROLLED CIs.**

There are other documents that may undergo revision, such as software codes, project plans, and user manuals. These are the version document, and you want the authorized people to view the CORRECT version at any point in time.

Think of a situation where you are referring to the project plan Version 4, and your team is referring to Version 3. That could be chaotic. Even worse, in the case of a user manual for a controller(a system software used to control the underlying hardware), you may be referring to a different version. The development of the system program will not work if you are referring to a wrong, outdated manual.

The CIs that undergo versions are called Managed CIs.

These are controlled as well.

MANAGE AND CONTROL

Audits are important to ensure the right access is given to the right people on the selected CI. Audits also ensure CIs are correctly configured.

4.6.1 Let's Play: Identify The Correct Category of CI

Identify if the item should fall under control CI or managed CI

ARTIFACT	CI CLASSIFICATION
1. Project Plan	A. Controlled B. Managed
2. Minutes of Meeting	A. Controlled B. Managed
3. Training Recordings	A. Controlled B. Managed
4. Issue Log	A. Controlled B. Managed
5. Stakeholder Register	A. Controlled B. Managed
6. Code	A. Controlled B. Managed
7. Status Report	A. Controlled B. Managed
8. Task Boards	A. Controlled B. Managed
9. Test Results	A. Controlled B. Managed

4.7 DIRECT AND MANAGE PROJECT WORK

Direct and Manage Project Work is doing the work as per the plan and implementing the approved changes.

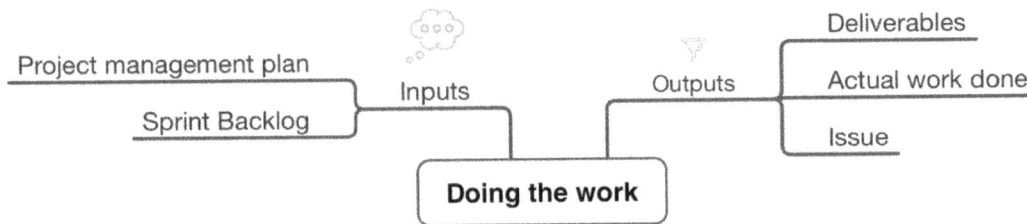

Project management plan
Sprint Backlog
Inputs
Doing the work
Outputs
Deliverables
Actual work done
Issue

What happens here?

My team started working on the assigned work as per the plan and work assignments.

In many projects, I have successfully used whiteboards for daily meetings. My team would meet (daily stand up meetings) and discuss topics like:

- What did I complete yesterday?
- What is my plan for today?
- Discuss issues
- Discuss and allocate any interdependency

ACTUAL WORK DONE/ WORK PERFORMANCE DATA/ ACTUAL STATUS

Actual work completed by the team is noted and compiled. A software or whiteboard information radiators (Charts) can be used. The team gives information on:

→ Actual hours spent,
→ Actual money spent,
→ Actual work completed
→ % of tasks completed
→ % of money spent
→ Work start status

DELIVERABLE

Tangible or intangible results produced at the end of a process, phase, or project are referred to as a deliverable. A deliverable is to be tested first before customer acceptance.

CHANGE REQUESTS

A change request is a formal proposal to modify a process, deliverable, or baseline.

Most people think of a change request as a change in scope sought by the client, but that's an incomplete view.

A change request is any deviation from the plan.

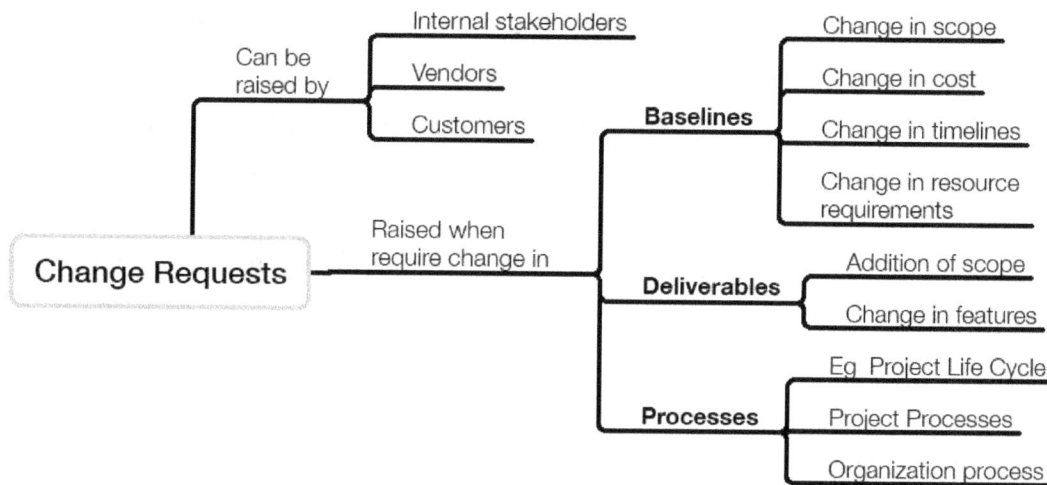

Change Requests

Can be raised by
- Internal stakeholders
- Vendors
- Customers

Raised when require change in
- **Baselines**
  - Change in scope
  - Change in cost
  - Change in timelines
  - Change in resource requirements
- **Deliverables**
  - Addition of scope
  - Change in features
- **Processes**
  - Eg. Project Life Cycle
  - Project Processes
  - Organization process

WHO CAN RAISE A CHANGE REQUEST?

Who can ask for it? A customer, a team member, or maybe senior management when they are preparing to take away your resource.

Most of you are not even aware that when you use a RED status in the status report, you actually are asking for a change. This change request could be changed in the baselines. Significance of colors:

- Green – In control
- Yellow – A warning sign
- Red color – Out of control (Issue – needs management intervention)

The red color in a status report is a change request in the project. A red status shows that your project is delayed or overspent and hence may need more time or resources, or money. That's a deviation from the plan and hence is a change request which was raised by you.

4.7.1 LET'S PLAY: IDENTIFY THE CORRECT CATEGORY

Mia is remodeling her friend Emma's villa. Emma lives with her son S and daughter D. This is a tricky task, as the requirements are unclear. Emma wants a breezy look with wooden furniture. However, when Mia started decorating the study, the teenage daughter, D, requested the slim copper furniture that is very popular right now. The painting was completed in two days. Mia has spent ten days, as of now, on the task. According to how the work has been going, it looks like Mia may have to spend the next 60 days on the remodeling project. The kitchen and two other bedrooms are not started yet. The objective is to redo all the bedrooms, the kitchen, and the study.

1. **Emma wants a breezy look with wooden furniture.**

    A.   Deliverable

    B.   Actual Work Status

    C.   Change Request

2. **The teenage daughter, D, has requested slimmer copper furniture that is very popular.**

    A.   Deliverable

    B.   Actual Work Status

    C.   Change Request

3. **The wall color was completed in two days.**

    A.   Deliverable

    B.   Actual Work Status

    C.   Change Request

4. **Mia has spent ten days as of now on the tasks.**

    A.   Deliverable

    B.   Actual Work Status

    C.   Change Request

5. **The kitchen and two 0bedrooms are yet to be started.**

    A.   Deliverable

    B.   Actual Work Status

    C.   Change Request

6. **The objective is to redo all the bedrooms, the kitchen, and the study.**

    A.   Deliverable

    B.   Actual Work Status

    C.   Change Request

4.8 MANAGE PROJECT KNOWLEDGE

A project, while underway, creates much knowledge that can be preserved to help other projects, and thus the organization, tremendously.

The knowledge categories:

TACIT KNOWLEDGE

The knowledge is personal, i.e., a belief system, know-how, insight, or experience. It's not documented. You learn while you are working with the team. For example, if you check any office manual or instruction manual, you would not know where the cafeteria is. But when you join the office, you find out. This is an example of tacit information

EXPLICIT KNOWLEDGE

This is the documented knowledge. For example – what is the employee vacation policy, etc. In a project, it's easy to get and document the explicit knowledge but ensuring the tacit information is also documented for future projects or for the success of an ongoing project is a great challenge.

There are various tools suggested to help manage knowledge:

- Networking
- Informal discussions
- Communities of practice
- Shadow and reverse shadow
- Knowledge fairs
- Interactive training etc.

Tools to document knowledge are information management tools:

- Lessons learned
- Recording training sessions
- Discussion of records (Minutes)
- Creating new processes using the knowledge of experienced personnel

4.8.1 LET'S PLAY: TYPE OF KNOWLEDGE

1. **The knowledge that can be easily documented**

    A.   Tacit Knowledge

    B.   Explicit Knowledge

2. **Usual mechanism to share this knowledge is forums, informal interactions, and observations**

    A.   Tacit Knowledge

    B.   Explicit Knowledge

3. **This type of knowledge can be found in the OPAs**

    A.   Tacit Knowledge

    B.   Explicit Knowledge

4. **Belief systems, Know-how is a type of:**

    A.   Tacit Knowledge

    B.   Explicit Knowledge

4.9 MONITOR AND CONTROL PROJECT WORK

The process of reviewing the project by creating Project Progress Reports that compare the current progress with the baseline.

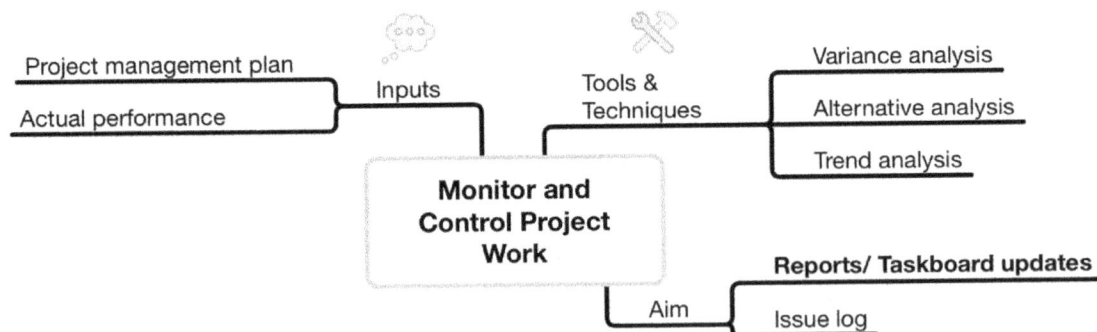

A report Is called a WORK PERFORMANCE REPORT and can be referred to as a status report or dashboard in normal project discussion.

Data analysis techniques, like variance analysis, 'What-if Analysis,' Earned Value Analysis, and Trend Analysis, are used to control the project.

In the case of Agile teams, the daily meeting is the place where the burndown charts are plotted to see the variations. Instead of creating a report, an agile team updates the progress charts/tasks boards so that information can be available to all stakeholders.

4.10 CHANGE MANAGEMENT

While executing the project, a change may be requested by a stakeholder. A team member might want a change to the timeline. The client may need to add a few new items to the scope, or the PM may want to make a change to a milestone date.

THE CHANGE MANAGEMENT PLAN ADDRESSES QUESTIONS LIKE:

→ What would be classified as a change?

→ Where would it be documented?

→ Which Impact Analysis template be used?

→ Are there any change management tools available?

→ Who decides if the change Is implemented or rejected?

→ Who is on the Change Control Board (CCB)?

→ How will approved changes be implemented?

A CCB/ authorized person makes the decision to approve or reject each and every change request.

This results in an Approved Change Request.

CHANGE MANAGEMENT PROCESS

Change Control Board (CCB) Meetings are required to understand the nature of the change and the impact. The CCB can decide to look at the plan, schedule, and or the overall business outcome. The CCB can make a decision to approve or reject the change. They can also request more information or that changes be implemented in a later phase. These meetings should be pre-planned meetings as laid out in the change management plan. The CCB should be identified at the time of planning and informed of their roles as well.

All the changes should be documented so that the origin of the change and what happened to the change can be understood along with the impact analysis. The change control tool should have the ability to log the changes and trace them.

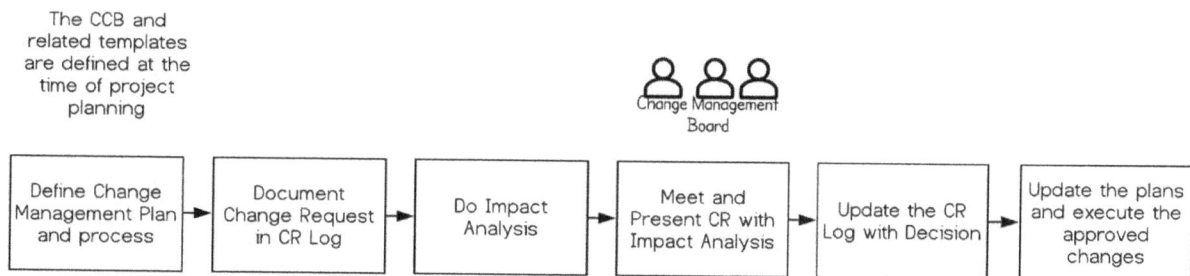

The CCB and related templates are defined at the time of project planning

Change Management Board

| Define Change Management Plan and process | → | Document Change Request in CR Log | → | Do Impact Analysis | → | Meet and Present CR with Impact Analysis | → | Update the CR Log with Decision | → | Update the plans and execute the approved changes |

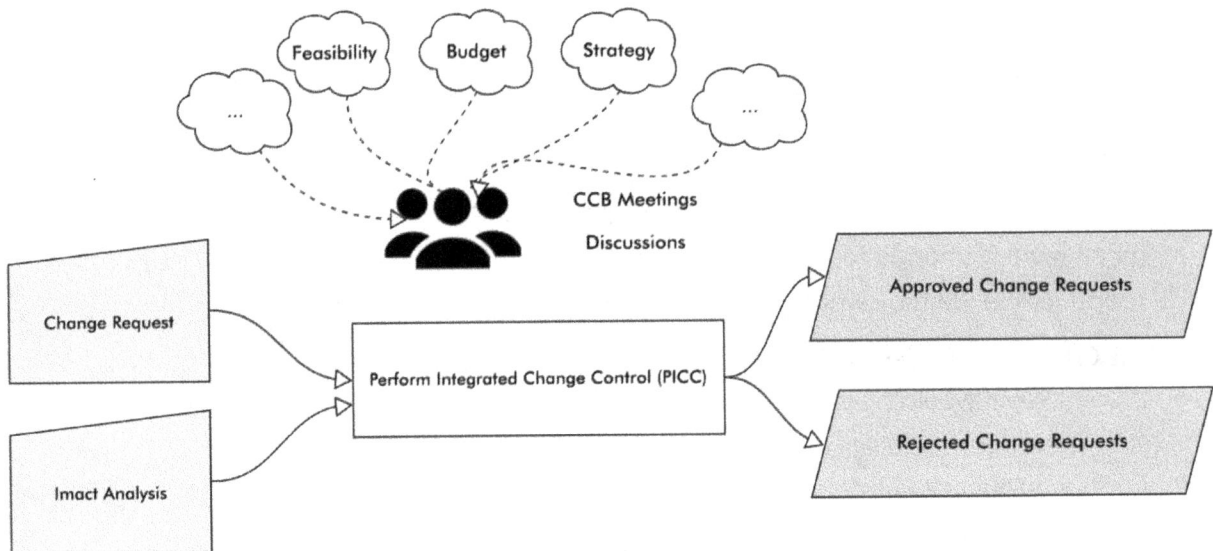

Approved changes will undergo planning and execution again. The project baselines will generally change when the approved changes are incorporated into the plan, resulting in changes in the baselines.

A TYPICAL CHANGE MANAGEMENT PROCESS:

Perform Integrated Change Control is one of the processes under the monitoring & controlling process group and is part of the Integration Management Knowledge Area. You can expect many questions on change management in the PMP exam.

A FEW SCENARIOS:

- A team member comes to you and proposes changes to a high-level design for security module interfaces. He feels confident that introducing those changes will lead to less effort and more secure and decoupled interfaces.
- You (Project Manager), along with a few senior team leads, are having a meeting with the customer to get the prototype signed off. The customer feels that the screen is too bland and needs a better UI (User Interface).
- Your senior manager informs you that the interrelated BPO project has a few changes in the process, and so the current project (under you) needs to change to match the updated workflow.

What do you think of the given situations? Are these change requests? Would you implement them?

According to PMBOK, all of the above scenarios can induce changes to the project plan and, therefore, should be considered change requests. These changes may impact the schedule/quality/scope/risk of the project and should follow the Integrated Change Control process.

REAL-LIFE

Real-life may not perfectly align with PMBOK theory, but a change request is never implemented immediately until and unless you are using agile methodology.

Typically, the process as advised by PMBOK is:

1.   Document the CR in the Change Request Register.

2.   Assign the CR to an SME (Subject Matter Expert) for an Impact Analysis

3.   Present the cumulative Impact Analysis forms to CCB (Change Control Board)

4.   CCB meetings need to be periodic and interactive.

5.   The CCB accepts or rejects the CRs

6.   The approved CRs go back for planning.

7.   The PM revises plans and gets approvals. A new baseline is in place now.

KEY TAKEAWAYS

→ There is always a CCB.

→ There is always a Change Management Plan.

→ Any change, even a reduction of scope, must go through the Change Management process, which means:

→ The Change Request documentation is added to the Change Request Register.

→ The change is executed according to agreed-upon plans.

→ Never implement unapproved changes, however small they seem. (Remember this for the exam.)

AGILE PROJECTS AND CHANGE REQUESTS

Agile is change based project life cycle. Iterations are timeboxed and are of a small time frame (Typically 1-4 weeks). The Product Owner keeps evaluating the requirements and keeps changing the priority using the Product Backlog Grooming. This would ensure that the high-value specifications are discussed and implemented in the upcoming iterations.

In case a change is advised to a developer while they are working on the Sprint/Iteration, The developer should redirect the request to the Product Owner. The product owner has the ultimate authority to make any changes in the Product backlog.

In an urgent case, if, due to some ad-hoc regulations or business requirements, a change is required in the ongoing iteration, the Product Owner can request the development team to stop working on the PBI item. The team and the Product Owner can then take a call to replace the PBI with another user story or terminate the ongoing iterations. Buts that is an exception scenario.

4.11 CLOSE PROJECT OR PHASE

Administrative closure occurs when a project or phase is complete.

After the customer accepts all the due deliverables, a formal process to close the project starts.

This process is NOT about acceptance testing. The deliverables as per the agreements have been created, tested, and accepted. The process is kicked off when all of that is achieved or when the customer request to terminate the agreement. Yes – The process is also followed for pre-mature project closures.

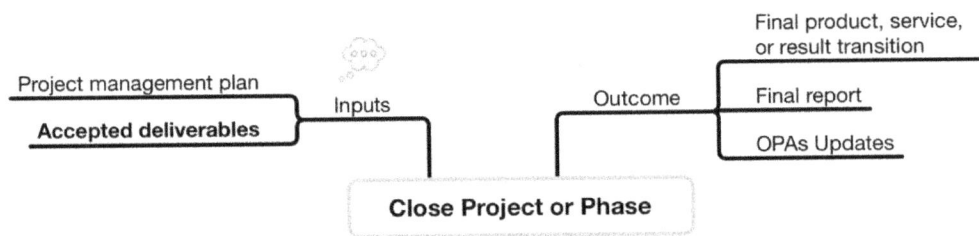

It is critical to achieving two things in this process:

→ One: Hand over the deliverable to the customer or the operations team

→ Two: Create a project final report to document the project's performance.

In addition, you will get all the updated documents from the project team (manuals, help files, etc.), And conduct a retrospective meeting to ensure you capture the lessons learned in the completed project/phase. Why is this necessary? So that other Project Managers can take precautions to avoid certain pitfalls or do things better.

Activities involved in administrative closure are:

- Verify agreement details with the customer
- Get FINAL formal acceptance by the customer
- Create and circulate the final project performance report
- Close the procurements
- Communicate the project's final status to required stakeholders
- Conduct a retrospective meeting to gain insights from the team
- Update lessons register
- Update and archive all project documents
- HANDOVER
- Release project resources (possibly conduct formal feedback sessions)
- Celebrate a job well done.

4.12 MODULE END QUESTIONS - PMP STYLE

1. You work as a team member in an agile project developing a next-gen team collaboration platform. One of the key stakeholders requested an urgent feature in the current iteration. How would you handle this request?

   A. The person is a key stakeholder, so you start working on the request.

   B. You bring up the request in the daily meeting the next day.

   C. You tell the stakeholder to talk to the Product Owner

   D. You ask the stakeholder to talk to the Project Manager and log it as a change request

2. You work as a team member in a construction project developing a high-end mall in the town. The floor layout and blueprint have been signed off, and construction has started. One of the key stakeholders requested an urgent change in one of the layouts of a floor plan. How would you handle this request?

   A. The person is a key stakeholder, so you start working on the request.

   B. You bring up the request in the daily meeting the next day.

   C. You tell the stakeholder to talk to the Product Owner

   D. You ask the stakeholder to talk to the Project Manager and log it as a change request

3. You work as a team member in a construction project developing a high-end mall in the town. You are in the initial phases of the project. The final floor plan is under discussion. One of the key stakeholders requested an urgent change in one of the layouts of a floor plan. How would you handle this request?

   A. The person is a key stakeholder, so you start working on the request.

   B. You write the request as a suggested feature in the requirements.

   C. You tell the stakeholder to talk to the Product Owner

   D. You ask the stakeholder to talk to the Project Manager and log it as a change request

4. You are working as a Project Manager on a hybrid project. The projects aim to develop a drone controller software. There are various functions that can be achieved by the drone as per the drone manufacturing firm. They provide you with the controller software and manuals. And they told you that the latest software could be downloaded from their website. Your team downloaded the wrong manual and wrong controller modules. This caused a lot of reworks in the past. What would you do to avoid such mistakes?

   A. Implement a configuration management system and make the manuals and controller software a controlled Configuration Item

B.   Implement a change management system and make the manuals and controller software a controlled Item

C.   Send an email to all team members to use the right controller software

D.   Change to a new drone hardware manufacturing firm

5.   A Project manager is like the conductor of a large orchestra. The roles of the Project Manager and the conductor are alike, except for:

A.   They should be knowledgeable and experts in the project domain

B.   They provide the team with leadership, planning, and coordination through communication

C.   They should be responsible for the final outcome of the team

D.   They should interpret the mission, vision, and objectives of the product

6.   Your project is expected to take about two years to complete. Six months into the project, the customer informs you that the project needs to be scrapped. What would you do?

A.   Start with the closing activities, including handover and final reports

B.   Meet with the customer to understand the issue and take it from there

C.   Start blaming your team for the early termination

D.   Ask your functional head to meet with the customer's senior management

7.   You work in a hybrid project to automate one process of the supply chain management process. There are many vendors working with you in the current process. Where will you list the vendor details?

A.   Vendor List

B.   Stakeholder register

C.   Stakeholder Management Plan

D.   Vendor Management Plan

8.   You work on an agile project. Your team meets daily and updates their progress using tracking software. The software also plots a burndown based on the status updates. One of the senior stakeholders asked you about project progress. You will:

A.   Create a status report and send it to him over email

B.   Tell that he should talk to the Product Owner to get status

C.   Enable the burndown chart view for the stakeholder

D.   Enable the task progress view for the stakeholder

9.   A project is considered complete only when:

A.   The acceptance testing is signed off

B.   Quality control is achieved

C.   The customer has taken the handover of deliverables

D.   The handover is completed, and the final report is circulated

10.   **The following are examples of deliverables, EXCEPT:**

A.   The planning team submitting the Project Management Plan

B.   The software development team developing the application software

C.   Team member Zena updating the activity-Z start date in the project management information system

D.   Portfolio Manager creating the Project Charter

11.   **What should be the aim of the Project manager wrt Knowledge Management?**

A.   Keep the knowledge to self as this will help him progress on the career ladder

B.   Foster an open and collaborative environment where people share knowledge

C.   Have a mandatory information sharing session every week

D.   Create a Key Performance Areas (KPA) for sharing knowledge for all members

12.   **Select the typical Agile events from the given list: (Select 3)**

☐. A.   Retrospective meeting

☐. B.   Daily standup Meeting

☐. C.   Project kick-off meeting

☐. D.   Team building meeting

☐. E.   Release Planning meeting

☐. F.   Workshop meeting

13.   **Knowledge can be split into two types. Tacit and explicit. Tacit knowledge can be managed and used in projects through:**

A.   Communities of practice, networking, and storytelling

B.   Formal training and documentation

C.   User manuals and instructions updates

D.   Lesson learned register and retrospective meetings

14. A change control board is:

    A.   A formally chartered group to support the project by establishing change management protocols

    B.   A formally chartered group responsible for reviewing, evaluating, approving, or rejecting changes to the project

    C.   An informal group responsible for reviewing, evaluating, approving, or rejecting changes to the project

    D.   A formal or informal group to provide management oversight to an ailing project

15. The client asked for a business-critical change at the last minute. The change seems to be minor at the outset. You are convinced that your team should be able to accommodate the change within the given timelines. What is the BEST thing to do?

    A.   Compress the schedule

    B.   Accept the change and start implementing

    C.   Consult the sponsor before taking any action

    D.   Ask the subject matter expert to analyze the impact of change

16. You joined a meeting where you discussed individual task status, issues, and next steps. Which meeting was this?

    A.   Project Steering meeting

    B.   Daily stand-up meeting

    C.   Escalation meeting

    D.   Release Planning meeting

17. Select all that will qualify as information radiators: (Select 3)

    ☐. A.   Project Plan

    ☐. B.   Team task board

    ☐. C.   Change management process

    ☐. D.   Project Burndown chart

    ☐. E.   Team holiday lists

    ☐. F.   Team ground rules

4.13 ALL ANSWERS

ANSWERS: 4.1 PROJECTS MBR

1. D	A major modernization project is being undertaken to increase the facility's efficiency and capacity, which should help reduce flight delays
2. A	MBR should focus on the business results of the project. The business results should be measurable and time-limited. Choice A is the best answer.
3. C	The strike has happened and caused an impact. Understand that this issue is current, and risks have a probability of occurrence (in the future). Strikes are not a change request; change requests may arise because of strikes.

ANSWERS: 4.4.1 LET'S PLAY: SELECT PROJECT PLAN OR DOCUMENT

	ARTIFACT TYPE	THE ANSWER
1.	Minutes of Meeting	Project Document
2.	Schedule Management Plan	Project Plan
3.	Status Reports	Project Document
4.	Stakeholder Register	Project Document
5.	Stakeholder Management Plan	Project Plan
6.	Issue Log	Project Document
7.	Change Management Plan	Project Plan
8.	Change Request Log	Project Document
9.	Risk Management Plan	Project Plan
10.	Risk Register	Project Document

ANSWERS: 4.5.1 LET'S PLAY: DECISION-MAKING TECHNIQUES

Question	Correct Answer	Why?
1.	Unanimity	100% agreement
2.	Autocratic decision making	One person took the decision
3.	Majority	The decision was liked by more than 50%
4.	Plurality	The decision was liked by less than 50%
5.	Multi-criteria decision analysis	A decision matrix is used. Check the keywords.

ANSWERS: 4.6.1 LET'S PLAY: IDENTIFY THE CORRECT CATEGORY OF CI

Artifact	CI Classification	Why
1. Project Plan	Managed	Project Plan has versions. You manage and control the access
2. Minutes of Meeting	Controlled	No versions. Just one. Access is controlled
3. Recording of a training	Controlled	No versions. Just one. Access is controlled
4. Issue Log	Controlled	No versions. Just one. Access is controlled
5. Stakeholder Register	Controlled	No versions. Just one. Access is controlled
6. Code	Managed	Has versions to roll back or refer to.
7. Status Report	Controlled	No versions. Just one. Access is controlled
8. Task Boards	Controlled	No versions. Just one. Access is controlled
9. Test Results	Controlled	No versions. Just one. Access is controlled

ANSWERS: 4.7.1 LET'S PLAY: IDENTIFY THE CORRECT CATEGORY

1.	Emma wants a breezy outlook with wooden furniture:	Deliverable	A breezy outlook with wooden furniture is the project scope. The scope is further divided into smaller deliverables.
2.	The request from the teenage daughter, D, was to get slim copper furniture that is popular	Change Request	Deviation from the original request.
3.	The wall color took two days to complete	Actual work status	Took 2 days to complete is information about the task. This is schedule data
4.	As of now, Mia has spent ten days on the task	Actual work status	Ten days. Work reported and the time spent on that is actual data on the task
5.	The kitchen and two other bedrooms are yet to be started.	Work Status	Report on work completion status
6.	The objective is to redo all the bedrooms, kitchen, and study	Deliverable	At the end of the project, all of the given work is to be completed and hence forms the deliverable of the project.

ANSWERS: 4.8.1 LET'S PLAY: TYPE OF KNOWLEDGE

Question	Answer
1. The knowledge that can be easily documented	Explicit Knowledge
2. Usual mechanism to share this knowledge is forums, informal interactions, observations	Tacit Knowledge
3. This type of knowledge can be found in OPAs	Explicit Knowledge
4. Belief systems, Know-how is a type of:	Tacit Knowledge

ANSWERS: 4.12 MODULE END QUESTIONS - PMP STYLE

1. C — In Agile projects, additional change is welcomed. However, since the iterations are small and timeboxed, it's not advisable to change the scope of the iteration. Also, the Product Owner is accountable for accepting or evaluating the value of the feature. In this scenario, Let the Product Owner decides.

2. D — Understand this is a project which follows the waterfall model. Any change will is to be evaluated as per the Change Management Plan. Notice that the specifications are signed off. This request is to be taken and processed as per the change management plan.

3. B — Waterfall or predictive life cycle. However, you are in the requirement phase. You can log the request as one of the requirements for further analysis and execution.

4. A — A configuration management system will help the team to find the correct controller software and manuals at the correct locations. Errors of which version to look at will be minimized. Think of a file server with controlled access or a dropbox or SharePoint server to implement a pull-based system for your team.

5. A — Use an elimination technique for EXCEPT-type questions. The FALSE one is the right answer.

A. They should be knowledgeable and expert in the project domain: FALSE, they can use the domain experts for the required job.

B. They provide the team with leadership, planning, and coordination through communication: TRUE

C. They should be responsible for the final outcome by the team: TRUE

D. They should interpret the mission, vision, and objectives of the product: TRUE

6. B	Its always recommended to have an interactive meeting to understand the issue or the causes of terminations. Next steps like informing the seniors or closing the project can happen after the discussion and root cause analysis.
7. B	A vendor is a stakeholder. It will be a good idea to store them in excel or software for easy retrieval. A vendor list is not a recognized document in the PMBOK.
8. C	It is assumed that the stakeholder is authorized to view/ask about the status. Instead of creating any report, it's a good idea to route the stakeholders to the project war room to see information radiators. The information radiators can be digital in the current era of virtual teams. The task progress view will not provide the right information to the stakeholders and can be very detailed. The best tool to see the project's progress is the Burndown chart.
9. D	The project is considered complete and closed only after completion of the process close project/ phase. Two main tasks in the project closure are handover and creation of the final report along with OPA updates.
10. C	Using the process of elimination: A. Project Management Plan: Deliverable B . Application software: Deliverable C . Team member Zena updating the activity-Z start date in the project management information system: WPD D . Project Charter: Deliverable
11. B	A PM should focus on creating an environment where people help each other and share knowledge. This is an environment of trust. Policies can be implemented, but they may not be effective if the team does not trust each other.
12. **A, B, E**	A. Retrospective meeting B. Daily standup Meeting E. Release Planning meeting The above are typical agile meetings/events

13. A   Tacit knowledge can be managed and used in projects by using Communities of practice, networking, and storytelling

14. B   Using the TRUE/FALSE technique:

A.   A formally chartered group to support the project by establishing change management protocols: FALSE, CCB does not establish change management processes.

B.   A formally chartered group responsible for reviewing, evaluating, approving, or rejecting changes to the project: TRUE, CCB does review the changes and approves or rejects them

C.   An informal group responsible for reviewing, evaluating, approving, or rejecting changes to the project: FALSE, CCB is not an informal group

D.   A formal or informal group to provide management oversight to an ailing project: FALSE. This is just some random sentence.

The best answer is B.

15. D   Even if you think that changes have minimum impact, you need to know the impact. You are a PM and not an SME. A good practice is to understand the impact of the change, always. This is the change management process. Follow it.

16. B   It is a daily stand-up meeting where the team discusses the task progress and shares any issues/risks.

17.
B, D, E   Information radiators are Kanban board that shows the project progress information for all the team/stakeholders to view. These can be manual boards in the team area or can be digital using an application. A static policy does not qualify as a Kanban board.

A.   Project Plan – Not changing and is not a radiator

B.   Team task board - Yes – Shows team task progress

C.   Change management process - NO

D.   Project Burndown chart - Yes

E.   Team holiday lists – Yes – people refer to it for planning

F.   Team ground rules – No – Static mostly

5. SCOPE AND DELIVERABLES

Topics we cover in this chapter

→ Deliverable Journey	→ Delphi Technique
→ Scope Management Plan	→ Nominal Group Technique
→ Requirement Collection	→ Affinity Diagram
→ Requirement Traceability Matrix	→ Work Breakdown Structure
→ Requirements Dimensions	→ Terms under WBS
→ Prototype	→ What is 100% rule of WBS
→ Context Diagram	→ Validate Scope

A project starts with a need. It could be a need by your customer or by your senior management or market demand.

It is of utmost importance that we understand what customers want, what is most valuable for them, and how the project delivers it. **It's as simple as this. Projects exist to fulfill the demands of the sponsor.**

Let's understand a few projects and their requirements:

1. A noodle company wants to try a new flavor of the project and wants to launch an advertising campaign to launch the product.

2. There is a need to develop a residential complex for a senior citizen living space.

3. A website is to be developed to streamline the order management system. Currently, the orders are handled using manual processes, and it has become difficult to manage them seamlessly since the orders have grown extensively.

All the above scenarios show that there is some work that should be completed to enable the business to work better. That's where Projects come into the picture and are initiated.

5.1 Scope Management Overview

Objective: Complete all the work required, and only the work required.

Process Name	Process Group	Why
Plan Scope Management	Planning	Creating the plan to collect requirements and delivery
Collect Requirements	Planning	Gathering what needs to be done
Define Scope	Planning	Defining boundaries of work
Create WBS	Planning	Decomposing to smaller controllable work
Control Scope	Monitoring & Controlling	Planned Vs Actual and Action
Validate Scope	Monitoring & Controlling	Customer acceptance

PROCESS FLOW

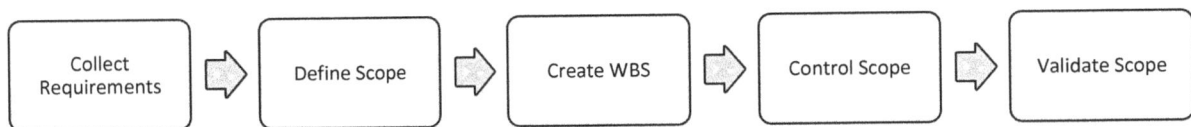

Collect Requirements → Define Scope → Create WBS → Control Scope → Validate Scope

5.2 PRODUCT SCOPE AND PROJECT SCOPE

One of the automobile manufacturing units took a strategic decision to design a future car. The features required in the car were:

- The car should run on water.
- The car should have a mileage of 100 miles per gallon.
- The car should be sleek enough to park in very crowded areas.
- The car will be launched in developing regions like Asia and Africa, and hence the cost should be less than $10,000.

PRODUCT SCOPE

These are the features and functions that characterize a product, service, or result.

For future car projects, the **product scope is - the car that runs on water.** Everything that customer wants.

The customer owns the product scope and product specification.

PROJECT SCOPE

The **work** that needs to be accomplished to deliver the specified features and functions (Product scope).

The project scope for the future car will be - everything that needs to be done. This will involve the following work (at a high level):

- Design of the car
- Cutting job to make the car body
- Painting
- Testing

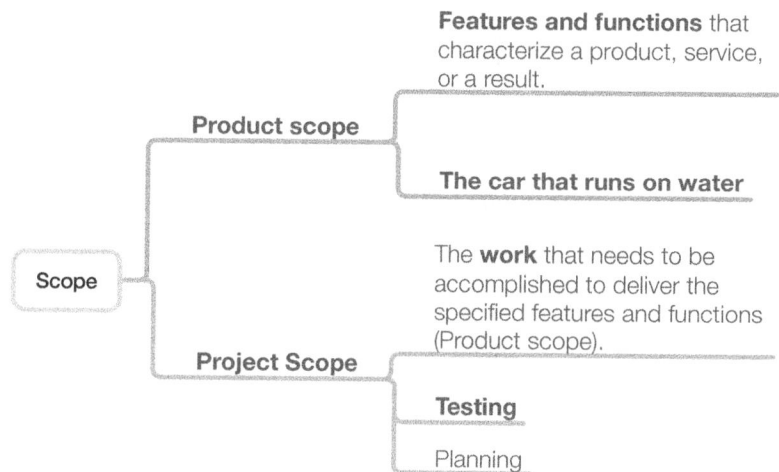

Features and functions that characterize a product, service, or a result.

Product scope

The car that runs on water

Scope

The **work** that needs to be accomplished to deliver the specified features and functions (Product scope).

Project Scope

Testing

Planning

5.2.1 LET'S PLAY: PRODUCT VS. PROJECT SCOPE

James is managing the project ACADEMY for an academic institute. The project is to develop collaboration software for teachers, students, and parents. To get the requirements, James conducted a focus group. The top requirements listed by the focus groups were:

1. Announcement board
2. Email and SMS notifications
3. Homework discussion forum
4. Events calendars
5. Online surveys

To get started on the project, the team needs to create a prototype and conduct a focus group to get an initial understanding from the user group. The project team will also need to identify the right solution platform to develop the required solution.

Select if the item in the description falls under product scope or project scope:

Description	Scope Type
1. Announcement board	A. Product Scope B. Project Scope
2. Conducting focus group	A. Product Scope B. Project Scope
3. Email notification	A. Product Scope B. Project Scope
4. Identifying the solution platform	A. Product Scope B. Project Scope
5. Planning for entire project activities	A. Product Scope B. Project Scope

5.3 PLAN SCOPE MANAGEMENT

Plan Scope Management describes how the project scope will be defined, validated, and controlled.

The aim of the Plan Scope Management process is to create:

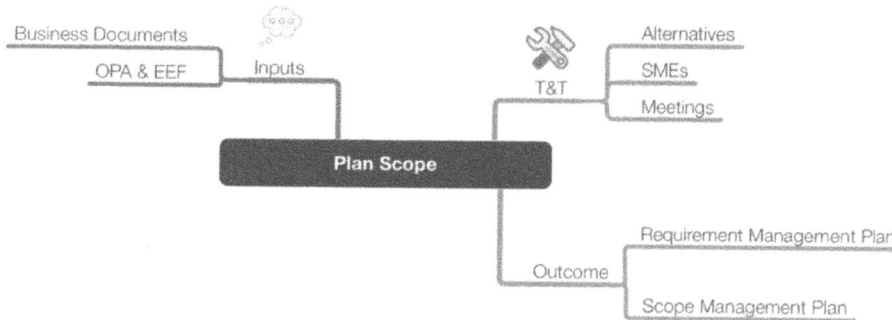

REQUIREMENT MANAGEMENT PLAN

The Requirement Management Plan is a component of the Project Management Plan. This can be a section in the document or could be a separate document that is referred to in the Project Plan. This plan describes how requirements will be collected, analyzed, documented, and managed.

SCOPE MANAGEMENT PLAN

The Scope Management Plan is a component of the Project Management Plan. This can be a section in the document or could be a separate document that is referred to in the Project Plan. It describes how the scope will be defined, developed, monitored, controlled, and verified with the client.

This is a good time to discuss the requirement agility with the team and customer and arrive at or suggest the right delivery methodology.

If case requirements are clear and the industry is matured, and/or changes are costly, you may lean towards a predictive project life cycle.

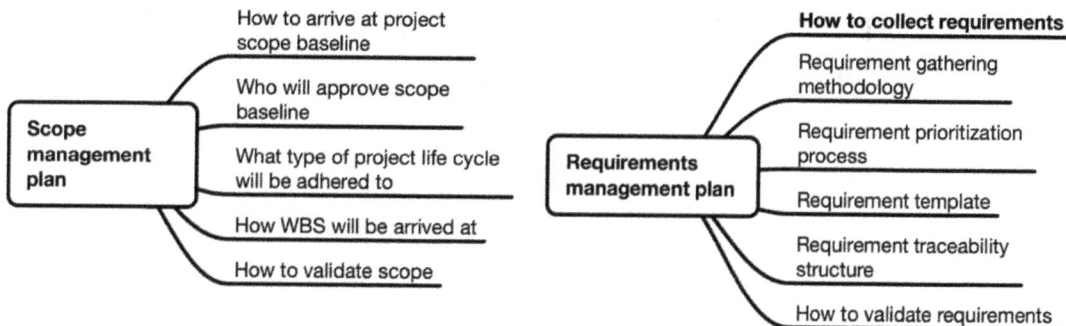

If the requirements are changing, the customer is unclear, or the overall industry is evolving, then you may lean towards change based methodology like agile.

5.4 COLLECT REQUIREMENTS

Collect Requirements is about gathering and documenting stakeholder needs and establishing the mechanism to cross verify the deliverables.

There are different templates and methodologies/techniques to collect requirements. A good requirement has an owner and is complete and testable.

One of the key functions of collecting requirements in projects is getting a clear set of requirements and establishing the value of the features/requirements to prioritize them.

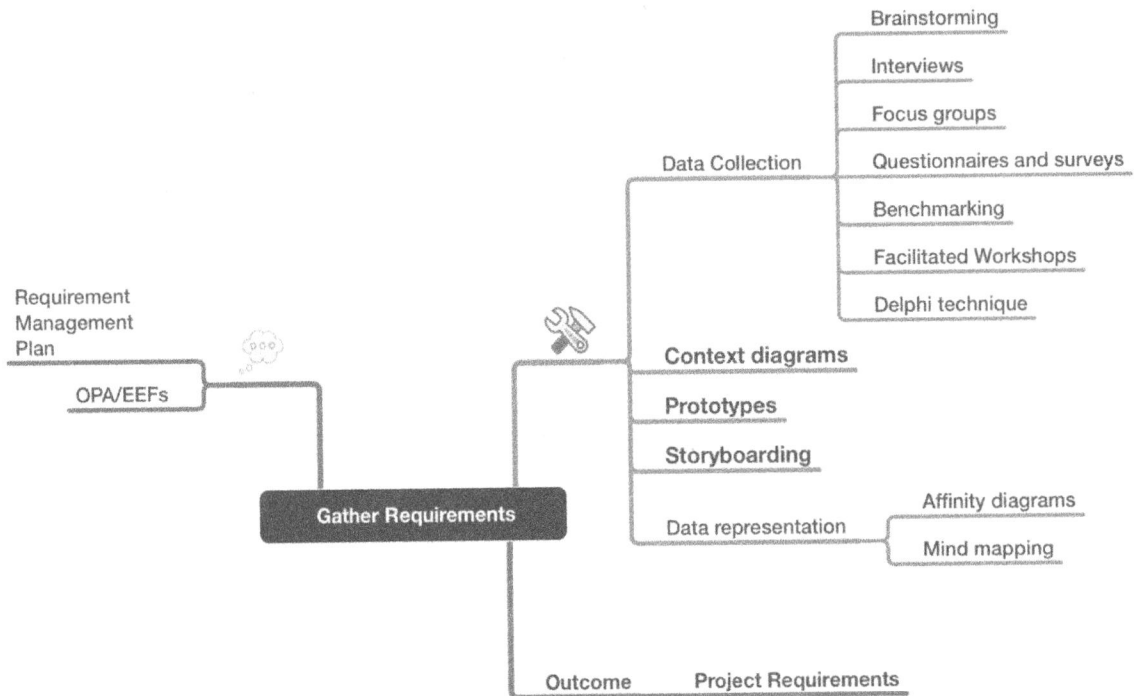

PROJECT REQUIREMENTS CATEGORIES:

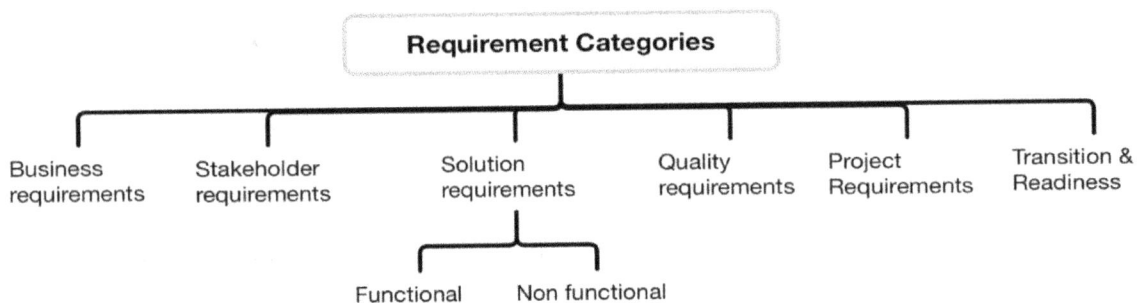

BUSINESS REQUIREMENTS:

High-level organization needs come from portfolio management.

STAKEHOLDER REQUIREMENTS:

Different groups of stakeholders may have different requirements.

SOLUTION REQUIREMENTS:

The term is mostly used in software projects. The requirements of the requested solution can be further categorized as FUNCTIONAL (Interaction, data, workflow, etc.) And NON- FUNCTIONAL (reliability, security, safety, etc.) These are supplementary requirements.

TRANSITION AND READINESS REQUIREMENTS:

The term is mostly used in business process outsourcing projects describing data conversion, as if, and future states.

PROJECT REQUIREMENTS:

The specific conditions or processes which the project needs to meet, e.g., constraints (milestones or costs), agreement specifications, etc.

QUALITY REQUIREMENTS

Processes to test the requirements, e.g., test cycles, process certifications like ISO or CMMI.

5.5 TECHNIQUES TO GATHER INFORMATION

BRAINSTORMING

Think of working with your customers or team to generate various ideas on a few ways to develop the new housing blueprint or process flow. Brainwriting is when you ask your team to prepare before the meeting and come up with ideas.

THE KEYWORD IS IDEAS.

INTERVIEWS

Predefined questions are asked to the stakeholders in an interview, and responses are collected. The mode of conducting an interview can be a one-to-one discussion or a meeting.

Interviews can be used for gathering information on complex scenarios and from very important stakeholders like senior management or SMEs (Subject Matter Experts). It requires your time and the other person's time and hence is a very expensive tool. You can use it to gather information from the KEY stakeholders

EFFECTIVENESS: HIGH, TIME REQUIREMENT: HIGH

When to use:

→   For important stakeholders, to gather information.

→   For complex requirements, which require two-way discussions.

QUESTIONNAIRES AND SURVEYS

Can be used when the target audience is vast
and geographically dispersed. These are termed
a passive information exchange to reach out to a
broad respondent base in a short span of time.
The technique comes in handy when the
respondent base is geographically dispersed.

Effectiveness: Low

Time Requirement: Low

Geo Spread: High

When to use:

→ To reach out to larger participants.

→ For an easier set of requirements that can be expressed simply.

FOCUS GROUPS

A broad agenda is prepared to get people from **similar
backgrounds** or similar domains to discuss requirements, views,
and perceptions to get more information. In a focus group, a
group of people is asked about their perceptions, opinions,
beliefs, and attitudes towards a product, service, concept,
advertisement, idea, or packaging.

Focus groups are two-way, interactive, and a very effective
technique to gather thoughts around focused requirements or
domains.

EFFECTIVENESS: HIGH

TIME REQUIREMENT: HIGH

When to use:

→ To get multiple viewpoints.

→ For complex requirements, which require two-way discussions.

DOCUMENT ANALYSIS

To collect the requirement, a project team can refer to various documents like:

→ Agreements

→ Business case

→ Issue logs

→ Request for proposal

→ SOPs (Standard operating processes, etc.)

FACILITATION/FACILITATED WORKSHOP

Facilitated workshops are two-way, interactive, and a very effective technique to gather thoughts around cross-functional requirements or domains.

Since people from different backgrounds participate in the group discussion, a facilitator is required to control and modulate the discussion. Joint Application Development Sessions (JAD) and Quality Function Deployment (QFD) used in the manufacturing industry are a few examples of the facilitated workshop.

What is the difference between a focus group and a facilitated workshop? The keyword is cross-domain participation. So if people are from various backgrounds, they may have a different viewpoints, and you need facilitation techniques like a parking lot to get the meeting going.

NOMINAL GROUP TECHNIQUE

How many times have you brainstormed and then selected the top 3 ideas? Many times. The technique which you used at that time is called the nominal group technique. See, you have been doing it all along. You just did not know the name.

The nominal group technique enhances brainstorming with a voting process used to rank the most useful ideas for further brainstorming or prioritization.

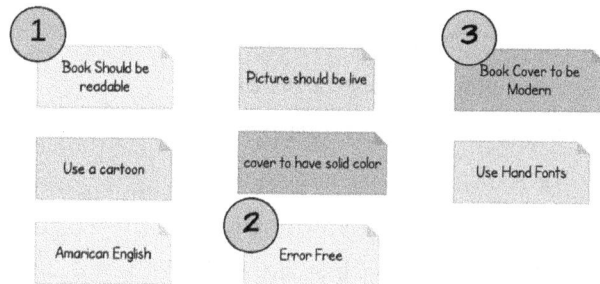

KEYWORDS: RANKING/RATING OF IDEAS

DELPHI TECHNIQUE

Suppose you want to gather unbiased opinions from experts/SMEs or user groups. Let's take an example. You created two book covers and want to know the feedback firsthand. You also do not want your users to talk to each other and create biases (They are in the same room). So, you give them a yellow sticky and ask them to rate the covers on a scale of 1-5, 5 being the best liked. The participants don't have to write their names. This way, you can compile honest feedback on both the covers and select the one which got better ratings.

KEYWORDS: UNBIASED AND ANONYMOUS.

BENCHMARKING

Used to compare the planned products or features with the comparable organizations to identify the best practices and generate ideas for improvements. Benchmarking helps in getting the implicit requirements (Assumed or non-spoke.

One of the BEST ways to ensure that you do not miss out on requirements.

OBSERVATIONS

Also known as work/job shadowing.

Observations can be used in scenarios when the process is very complex, language exchange is difficult, or when there is a verbal or mental block to exchanging information. An observer observes the people performing their job or process and collects the requirements.

CONTEXT DIAGRAMS

A great way of depicting the system visually and showcasing how other people or systems interact with the new upcoming product. System Context Diagrams represent all external entities that may interact with the system in consideration. **A context diagram shows the system at the center, with no details of its interior structure, surrounded by all its interacting systems, environments, and activities.**

The objective of the system context diagram is to focus attention on external factors and events that should be considered for the project under development.

IDEA/MIND MAPPING

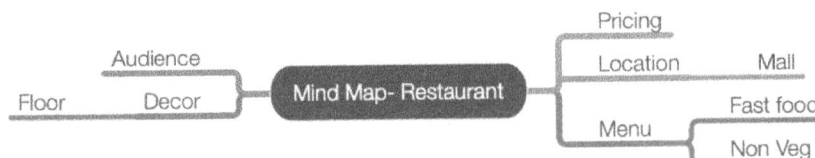

You have been seeing mind maps in the book. The idea mapping also referred to as mind maps, uses free flow danglers to showcase related ideas.

KEYWORDS: PICTURE, RELATED IDEAS

AFFINITY DIAGRAM

As the name suggests, similar ideas are clubbed together. You can use sticky notes to write the ideas and then rearrange them to form groups. Very useful to categorize the requirements in groups.

KEYWORDS: CATEGORY, BUCKETS

PROTOTYPES

One of the MOST effective methods to get requirements verified at the start of the project.

A prototype will help the project group to get early confirmation of the requirements, thus, reducing the overall rework time.

Storyboarding is a type of prototype where various frames are shown with the overall action steps in visual design.

A prototype can be a small miniature model that can be reused or a throwaway. It is made to gather feedback on requirements from stakeholders. Examples of prototypes are wireframes in IT projects.

Storyboarding is a visual prototype for advertisement or visual industries

KEYWORDS: MINIATURE/MODEL, CUSTOMER SIGNOFF

SUMMARY – DATA GATHERING TECHNIQUES

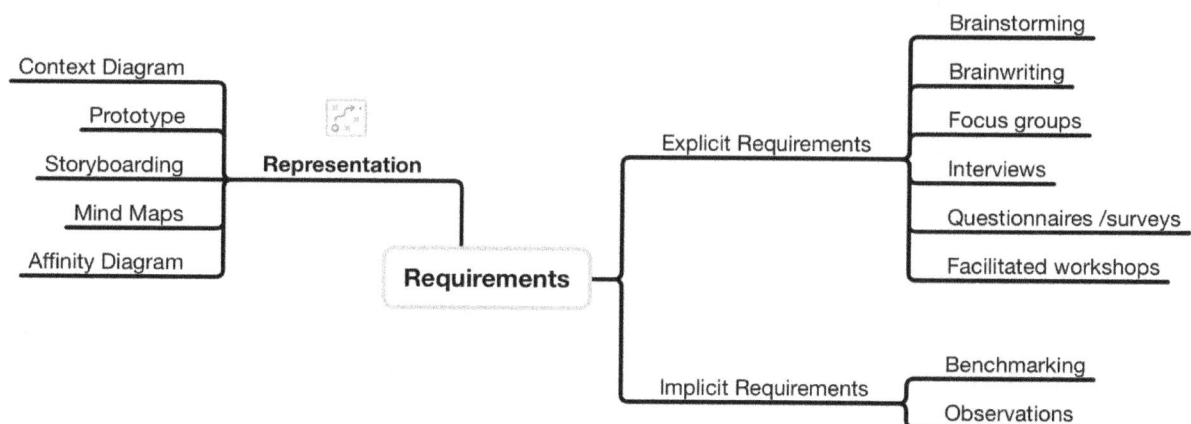

5.5.1 LET'S PLAY: REQUIREMENT GATHERING TECHNIQUES
Select the appropriate technique for given scenarios:

1. The marketing team met to generate ideas for a new product advertisement. The team leader grouped ideas into relevant categories.

    A. Facilitated workshop

    B. Context diagram

    C. Delphi technique

    D. Affinity diagram

2. The training manager sought responses from the participants on how the workshop went. They used yellow sticky paper, and the participants were asked NOT to write their names. The training manager did this to get unbiased feedback.

    A. Facilitated workshop

    B. Context diagram

    C. Delphi technique

    D. Affinity diagram

3. The business analyst put together a diagram that showed the system interaction with all the users and old systems.

    A. Facilitated workshop

    B. Context diagram

    C. Delphi technique

    D. Affinity diagram

4. To start collecting a general idea of the new process and process gaps, the manager called a meeting with all of the vendors and buyers, along with the finance team. This could be chaotic, so a seasoned transition manager controlled the discussion.

    A. Facilitated workshop

    B. Context diagram

    C. Delphi technique

    D. Affinity diagram

5.6 DEFINE SCOPE

Once the project team gets the requirements, they sit with each other, brainstorm, and describe the IN SCOPE and OUT of SCOPE work. This will help the project team to set clear expectations for the team and customers.

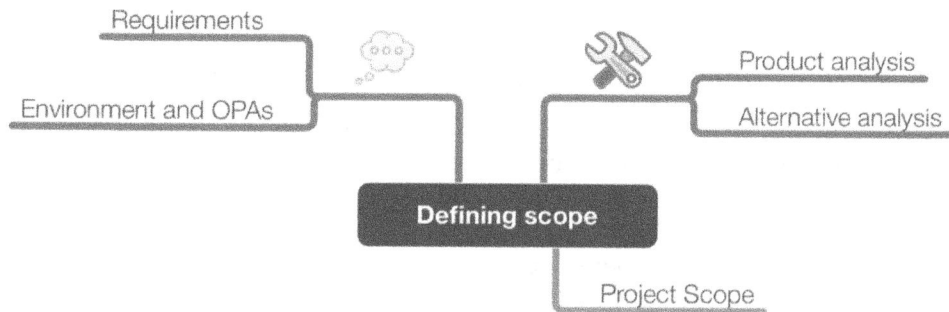

PROJECT SCOPE STATEMENT CONTAINS:

→ Product scope (Features required by customer)

→ Project scope (Work to be performed to achieve the desired features)

→ Major deliverables

→ Acceptance criteria of the product

→ Out of scope items/requirements

→ Assumptions

→ Constraints

Do agile projects have a scope or Project Scope Statement? What are the 3 artifacts which we discussed for agile teams? Go back and come up with an answer...

One of the agile project artifacts is Product Backlog. The Product Backlog contains the features/list of work that should be completed in the upcoming iterations. A product owner can define the overall vision and product roadmap (Hmm, a new word – we learn more about it in Business Environment) to create and visualize the product in the long run. The Product Owner, along with other senior stakeholders, may decide to keep a few features always out of the Product backlog or may define some guiding principles. This can be loosely compared with Project Scope. For example, WhatsApp founders discussed and have one principle that they would never want the advertisement to appear for users in the WhatsApp applications. **Agile is used where changes are frequent; hence creating scope boundaries is neither required nor desirable.**

PRODUCT ANALYSIS

This needs to be done to understand and develop the project features.

The first task in product analysis is to become familiar with the product! What does it do? How does it do it? What does it look like? All these questions and more need to be asked before a product can be analyzed. As well as considering the obvious mechanical, electrical, or any other requirements, it is also important to consider the ergonomics, such as how the design was made user-friendly, and any other marketing issues. These all have an impact on the later design decisions.

Let's take an example of a bike to understand product analysis:

→ What is the function of a bike?

→ How does the function depend on the type of bike (e.g., racing, about-town, or child's bike)?

→ How is it made to be easily maintained?

→ How much should it cost?

→ What should it look like (colors, etc.)?

→ How has it been made to be comfortable to ride?

→ How do the mechanical bits work and interact?

ALTERNATIVES GENERATION

This is a technique used to discover different methods or ways of achieving the work of the project. For example, if you do not have a particular type of resource, such as C++ developers, can you use Java developers, or are there any other self-made products that can be used to get the work done?

5.7 CREATE WORK BREAKDOWN STRUCTURE

Create Work Breakdown Structure (WBS) is the process of subdividing project work into smaller, more manageable units.

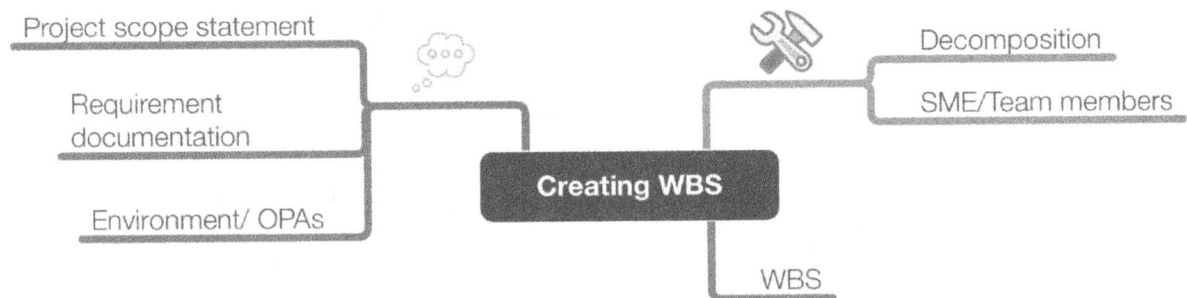

A project can never be completed by a single person. Hence, the overall work needs to be broken into smaller, manageable units to allocate it to a team/vendor/department or a team member.

The main outcome expected from this process/activity is the work breakdown structure (WBS). We start from IN-SCOPE items and decompose them into smaller work packages/deliverables to create a WBS.

The approved scope is called SCOPE BASELINE. A baseline can be changed only through formal change control procedures and is used as a basis for comparison with actual progress to manage the project.

DECOMPOSITION

Decomposition is a technique to divide and subdivide the project deliverables into smaller, manageable units called work packages.

Based on the complexity, project size, and urgency, you may want to decide on the ideal WBS size. Depending on the project, a work package can be one month long or as small as 6 hours of work. PMBOK does not specify the ideal WBS size.

In the case of agile projects, you would see the decomposition of 1-2 days of work because the overall phase (feature drop/Timebox) is of 1 – 4 weeks long.

WBS IN DETAIL

WBS is a deliverable-oriented hierarchical decomposition of the work to be executed by the project team to accomplish the project objectives.

It organizes and defines the total scope of the project. Each descending level represents an increasingly detailed definition of the project work.

A Work Breakdown Structure is the foundation of project planning. It is a tool for breaking down a project into manageable parts and then detailing the specific tasks and activities required to create each of these parts (also called a work package).

Can you think of an Agile artifact that can be compared to WBS?

PRODUCT BACKLOG.

A Product Backlog contains the overall scope of the work to be delivered in the upcoming iteration. Product Backlog grooming uses decomposition so that the agile team can estimate and deliver the Iteration backlog. What are the decomposition criteria for PBIs? INVEST. You can also apply INVEST to WBS Items. Works perfectly.

Let's take an example of WBS so that we can understand the terms associated with WBS
The WBS can be represented in a variety of ways, including graphical, textual, or tabular views. Regardless of the representation used, the WBS enables the project team to predict and forecast costs, schedules, resource requirements, and allocations more accurately.

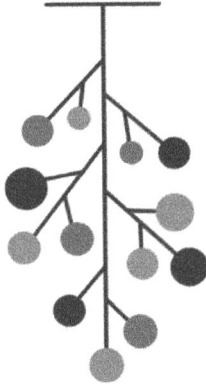

A project WBS starts with the highest levels of work in the project. Each lower level breaks the work into smaller chunks. The breakdown continues to as many levels of detail as you need. There is no fixed number of levels for "proper" decomposition. Think of a tree. You invert it, so you get the trunk as the main parent, then branches and subbranches, and the last leaf can be equated as a work package or deliverable.

DELIVERABLE:

Any unique and verifiable product, result, or capability to perform a service must be produced to complete a process, phase, or project.

DECOMPOSITION:

A planning technique that subdivides the project scope and project deliverables into smaller, more manageable components until the project work associated with accomplishing the project scope and providing the deliverables is defined in sufficient detail to support executing, monitoring and controlling the work.

```
                        55 Dinner
                          Party
       ┌──────────┬──────────┼──────────────┐
   55.1 Food   55.2 Drinks  55.3 Music    55.4
                                         Planning
       │                                    │
   55.1.1 Veg                          55.4.1 Team calls
      Food                                  │
       │                               55.4.2 Status
   55.1.2 Non Veg                         Reports
      Food                                  │
                                      55.4.3 Project Plan
```

CODE OF ACCOUNT:

Each component in the WBS hierarchy, including work packages, is assigned a unique identifier called a code of account identifier. These identifiers can then be used in estimating costs, scheduling, and assigning resources to identify the component.

55.1 is a unique identifier that refers to food.

CONTROL ACCOUNT:

Think of a cost code. When you travel, you fill out a reimbursement report and write the cost code so that your reimbursement can be allocated to a particular project/department. A cost code later can be analyzed by senior management to understand the cost-benefit etc. A project is a cost code, also called a control account. If you or your senior management want to watch the spending on a particular WBS item, then that can also be mapped as a cost code. For example, 55.4 is mapped as a cost code so that management can see the efforts and spending on the planning activities. A management control point where scope, budget (resource plans), actual cost, and schedule are integrated and compared to earned value for performance measurement. Control accounts are placed at selected management points (specific components at selected levels) of the work breakdown structure. Each control account may include one or more work packages, but each work package may be associated with only one control account.

WORK PACKAGE:

A Work Package is a deliverable or project work component at the lowest level of each branch of the work breakdown structure.

55.4.3 is a deliverable – Project Plan.

THE 100% RULE:

The 100% rule is a core characteristic of the WBS. This rule states that the WBS includes 100% of the work defined by the project scope and captures ALL deliverables—internal, external, and interim—regarding work to be completed, including project management work.

It makes sense as we started from the total IN scope and divided it to reach the WBS items

The work outside the WBS is considered out of scope.

Think of Product backlog. Any feature which is required by the Product Owner, if not included in the Product Backlog, will never be developed.

5.8 CONTROL SCOPE

PDCA, We planned the scope to be completed and allocated it to the team to perform the work. In agile, The team signs up for the work as per Sprint/Iteration backlog and starts doing the work. The work is never allocated in agile teams. Rather, the team members discuss the work and take the responsibilities to complete the PBIs or smaller tasks.

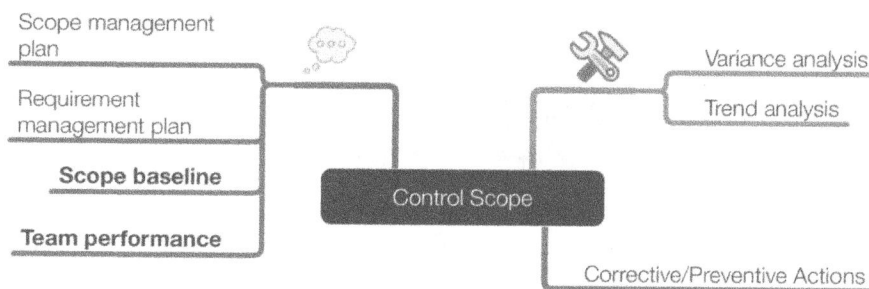

The Control arm of PDCA is when the PM creates the status reports (every week/ month). In the case of agile, it's Daily, and the ownership belongs to the team members.

The goal of Control Scope is to find out the differences between the planned scope and the actual scope and take corrective actions if applicable.

VARIANCE ANALYSIS

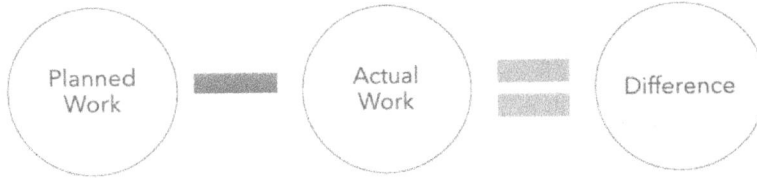

Variance analysis, in simple terms, means planned vs. actuals. If the result is zero, i.e., the actual results are equal as per the plan. You are a happy Project Manager because your team gave you the planned output. If not, then you may take corrective or preventive action to correct the situation.

The actual work can be retrieved from the team at the time of creating the project status report and can be compared with the Planned Scope.

In agile projects, the variance analysis is performed every day in the stand-up meeting.

5.9 VALIDATE SCOPE

Validate Scope is the process of formalizing acceptance of the completed project deliverables. You can map it with ACCEPTANCE TESTING.

The goal of Validate Scope is to drive acceptance from the client and get sign-off on accepted deliverables.

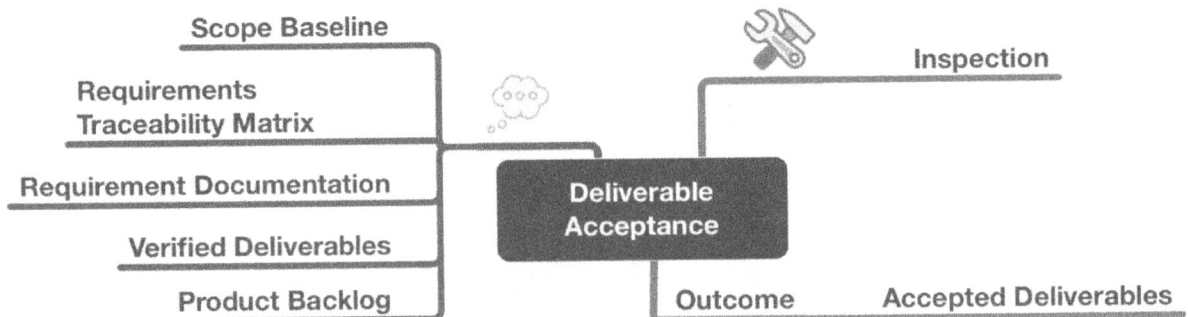

Upon completion of the Validate Scope process, if everything goes well, the client accepts the deliverables and provides a sign-off on the deliverables. In case the client does not accept the deliverables, changes have to be made. This results in Change Requests.

Validate Scope process is performed by the customer/Sponsor.

Which meeting in agile is equivalent to validate scope process? Who accepts the deliverables?

INSPECTION

The client/sponsor/Product Owner will run acceptance test cases that are either written by their team or provided by you to them. As a best practice, it's always good to have the Acceptance Test Criteria defined right at the time of getting requirements and put them as part of the deliverable testing criteria.

5.10 THE DELIVERABLE JOURNEY

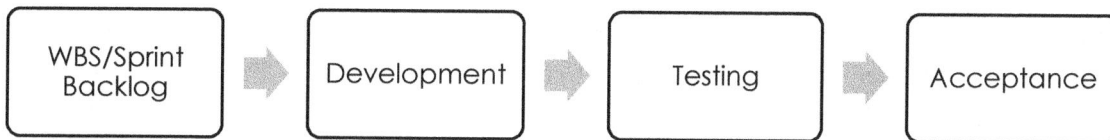

WBS/Sprint Backlog ➡ Development ➡ Testing ➡ Acceptance

A deliverable is planned at the time of planning from the IN SCOPE items. The team works on it and develops it. Before we show this deliverable to the customer, It should be reviewed for errors (Who does it? QA/Testers)

In the case of predictive teams, you can have another set of testers in agile the development team typically tests the work themselves and ensures that the deliverable meets the DOD. What is DOD? Refer Agile section if you do not know the full form of DOD.

5.11 REQUIREMENT TRACEABILITY MATRIX

The requirement traceability matrix, as the name suggests, is a tool to trace the requirements from their origin and trace it to all the project stages until the requirement is finally delivered. A typical IT requirement traceability matrix is given:

Requirement ID	Requirement Description	Business Need/Origin	Design Document	Code	Test Case	Acceptance Test Case
1.0 Use case no 1.0	Transformation of process1	XYZ	Design doc para 1.1	Page – abc.as px Xyz.asp	TestCase1 Scenario 3.0	AT1 AT3 AT5
1.1 Use case 1.1	Transformation	The sponsor	DD para 1.4			
2.0	Requirement 3	ABZ	DD para 2.0			

5.12 MODULE END QUESTIONS

1. Emily was in the process of creating WBS along with her team. The team thinks that WBS and deliverables are interchangeably used. Which of the following BEST describes the distinction between Work Breakdown Structure and deliverables?

    A.   The work breakdown structure contains deliverables.

    B.   The deliverables contain work breakdown structure.

2. Noah, the senior manager, was most concerned about customer acceptance for the project MOON. MOON is a huge construction project and has been going on for the last five years. Ana is managing the project MOON. While speaking with Ana, Noah asked her to ensure the complete delivery of the requirements at project closing. Which choices would help Ana the most, to make sure that all the needs have been met by the project team and to get a hassle-free sign-off from the client?

    A.   Project Plan

    B.   Scope Statement

    C.   Requirement Traceability Document

    D.   Scope Management Plan

3. There have been delays in the project due to changes in features requested by the customer. What's worse is that the changes are raised at the time of customer acceptance. It looks like the customer is not able to firm up the features of the product. Which tool can help the project team to firm up the requirement in the early phases of the project?

    A.   Interviews

    B.   Surveys

    C.   Document Analysis

    D.   Prototype

4. Ethan is working on the redesign of the collaboration platform for the firm FXA. His team works with all the stakeholders to get company-specific policies and information around all business units. Today, he is meeting with team members from the marketing department to shortlist the collaboration feature list from the marketing group. Which information gathering technique applies to the given scenario?

    A.   Delphi

    B.   Focus Group

    C.   Interviews

    D.   Facilitation

5. To get unbiased and anonymous feedback or suggestions, the event management team kept a suggestion box at the reception. The inputs will help the event management firm to plan the next bigger event in a better manner. Select the technique used by an event management firm.

   A.   Delphi

   B.   Focus Group

   C.   Interviews

   D.   Facilitation

6. Sophie is one of the oldest and most experienced Project Managers that the company, "Lion Airways," has ever had. Recently, the company has faced a few challenges managing the lead to revenue process. There were revenue leakages due to major issues in the process. The CIO authorized Sophie to suggest process optimization changes aiming to decrease revenue losses by 10% in the next six months. Sophie called a meeting to get ideas on how to go about doing this with a few of the experts. The ideas were ranked, and she chose three of the most rated ideas to check for feasibility. Which technique did Sophie use?

   A.   Brainstorming

   B.   Nominal group technique

   C.   Interviews

   D.   Facilitation

7. In which meeting of an Agile project a deliverable signoff is achieved?

   A.   Sprint Planning

   B.   Daily Stand-up

   C.   Sprint Review

   D.   Sprint Retrospective

8. A different number is given to each WBS item. This unique identifier is also known as:

   A.   Control account

   B.   WBS

   C.   Code of account

   D.   Deliverable

9. Ana is the most charismatic person you will ever meet. She is dynamic and gets the work done. Ana called for a meeting to get input on a recent project issue. The issue would cause major havoc if not contained early. The meeting included the project team members, user groups, and the senior managers. Ana facilitated the meeting where she used the drawing board to write the idea in a picture format and brainstormed on related ideas. At

the end of the meeting, she could get a picture where all the related ideas were captured in a picture format. Which technique is used in the scenario?

    A.   Brainstorming

    B.   Nominal group technique

    C.   Affinity diagram

    D.   Idea/mind mapping

10. In case of MOSCOW requirement prioritization technique W stand for _____. Fill in the blank.

    A.   Would have

    B.   Won't have

    C.   Wise to have

    D.   Will not have

11. Jack was given a project to develop the CIO dashboard. The CIO dashboard will be refreshed every day at 11 am to showcase governance, performance, and efficiency Key Performance Indicators. The work required was to understand the CIO's expectations on reporting format and system capabilities to integrate and run batch update queries. The CIO dashboard can be considered as:

    A.   Product scope

    B.   Project scope

    C.   Assumption

    D.   Constraint

12. You are working on a creative project to design a new product. You had several mock-ups and wanted to get opinions from the team. Your team voted and then, based on the voting, shortlisted a few ideas to be explored further. Which tool is used in the scenario?

    A.   Nominal group technique

    B.   Focus group

    C.   Facilitated workshop

    D.   Brainstorming

13. You are developing a cost-effective mechanism for bullet practice for the defense department. The team has put in a lot of effort, and now the software is ready. However, the client is not happy with the features which your simulation provides. What could you have done to avoid this gap in requirement understanding?

    A.   You should have held more workshops

    B.   You should have created a requirement traceability matrix

    C.   You should have created a prototype to get your customer onboard

    D.   This is normal and is part of any project acceptance phase

14. Joe, a marketing manager at a bike manufacturing company, is working on the launch of new super-fast blue bikes, set to release on the eve of Christmas. This means that they need to be ready for market by October for the annual trade fair, where dealers and consumers interact. Joe is in the process of ensuring that the bike meets federal safety standards, which it does, but the product has problems with additional non-federal safety issues that are only now being uncovered. Identify the assumption, constraint, and product description:

    A. Assumption: Federal safety regulations are sufficient for the bike. Constraint: The product must be market-ready by October. Product Description: The vehicle is a bike.

    B. Assumption: The product must be market-ready by October. Constraint: The product should be fast. Product Description: The vehicle is a motorcycle. Risk: Federal safety regulations are sufficient for the bike. Issue: The product is facing non-federal-related issues.

    C. Product Description: The vehicle is a fast bike with a blue theme. Constraint: The bike should be ready by October. Assumption: Federal safety standards are sufficient to launch the bike.

    D. Product Description: The vehicle is a super-fast bike with a blue theme. Assumption: The product must be market-ready by October. Constraint: The product must be fast.

15. You are in a requirement gathering workshop with Jack and Emma. James asked for better color combinations and has a strong opinion on the user interface of the system. At the same time, Emma had some other requirement which was much more urgent than this. And these are only two people so far. Your team needs to meet with 5 more stakeholders to gather further requirements. A time constraint is already mentioned in the contract. What should you do?

    A. Implement all the requirements

    B. Use requirement traceability matrix

    C. Develop requirement priority matrix

    D. Just ignore a few requirements to meet the timelines

16. Decomposition may not be possible for a deliverable or subcomponent that will be accomplished far into the future. The project team usually waits until the deliverable or subcomponent is agreed to, so the details of the WBS can be developed. This technique is sometimes referred to as _____. Fill in the blank.

    A. Decomposition
    B. Reserve Analysis
    C. Alternative Analysis
    D. Rolling Wave Planning

17. What do I stand for in the INVEST criteria?

    A. Individual
    B. Interesting
    C. Independent
    D. Informal

18. The formal acceptance of the deliverables should be taken from?

    A. The senior manager of the performing organization
    B. The PMO
    C. The head of sales of the customer organization
    D. The sponsor

19. The requirements may change at any point in time as the customer get to know what all is achievable. What should be the Project Manager's approach toward frequent requirement changes?

    A. Reject them
    B. Analyze the requirements and select the predictive life cycle
    C. Accept them
    D. Analyze the requirements and select the right project life cycle

20. You are working with an international client. The client's native language is not English. While you discuss the requirements, you are not sure if the customer understands them fully. Which requirement gathering tool could help the most?

    A. Interviews
    B. Focus Group
    C. Facilitated Workshop
    D. Observation

5.13 ALL ANSWERS

ANSWERS: 5.2.1 LET'S PLAY: PRODUCT VS. PROJECT SCOPE

Description	Scope Type	Why?
1. Announcement board	Product Scope	Part of customer requirements
2. Conducting focus group	Project Scope	Project activity
3. Email notification	Product Scope	Part of customer requirements
4. Identifying the solution platform	Project Scope	Project activity
5. Planning for entire project activities	Project Scope	Project activity

ANSWERS: 5.5.1 LET'S PLAY: REQUIREMENT GATHERING TECHNIQUES

Question	Correct Answer	Why?
1. The marketing team met to generate ideas for a new product advertisement. The team leader grouped ideas into relevant categories.	Affinity Diagram	Grouping of ideas
2. The training manager sought responses from the participants on how the workshop went. They used yellow sticky paper, and participants were not asked NOT to write their names. The training manager did this to get unbiased feedback.	Delphi technique	Unbiased feedback
3. The business analyst put together a diagram that showed the system interaction with all the users and old systems.	Context Diagram	System interaction
4. To start collecting a general idea of the new process and process gaps, the manager called a meeting with all of the vendors and buyers, along with the finance team. This could be chaotic, so a seasoned transition manager controlled the discussion.	Facilitated workshop	Controlling discussions

ANSWERS: 5.4 MODULE END QUESTIONS - PMP STYLE

1. A — The work breakdown structure contains deliverables that is TRUE

2. C — The requirements traceability matrix links product requirements from their origin to the deliverables. The implementation of a requirements traceability matrix helps ensure that each requirement adds business value by linking it to the business and project objectives. It provides a means to track requirements throughout the project life cycle, helping to ensure that requirements approved in the requirements documentation are delivered at the end of the project.

3. D — Prototyping is a method of obtaining early feedback on requirements by providing a working model of the expected product before actually building it. This can be used in scenarios when the requirements are a little fuzzy or the customer is not an expert on the domain.

4. B — Check the keyword "same department." Focus groups bring together pre-qualified stakeholders and subject matter experts from similar domains to learn about their expectations and attitudes about a proposed product, service, or result.

5. A — Anonymous and unbiased are the keywords for the Delphi technique. The Delphi technique helps reduce bias in the data and keeps any one person from having undue influence on the inputs.

6. B — Ranking is the keyword for Nominal Group Technique. The team did brainstorming first and then ranked the ideas. The Nominal Group Technique fits better than brainstorming. What is Nominal Group Technique? A technique that enhances brainstorming with a voting process is used to rank the most useful ideas.

7. C — A Sprint Review meeting is the meeting where the deliverables/sprint outcome is inspected by the Product Owner, and the necessary action is taken.

8. C — The WBS is finalized by assigning each work package to a control account and establishing a unique identifier for that work package from a code of accounts. Code of Accounts is the numbering system used to uniquely identify the component of the WBS.

9. D — Check the keywords PICTURE and IDEAS and RELATIONSHIP. Idea/mind mapping is the technique in which ideas created through individual brainstorming sessions are consolidated into a single map to reflect commonality and differences in understanding and generate new ideas.

10. B — Won't have is the correct answer

11. A — CIO Dashboard is a client requirement and is classified as Product scope.

12. A	The nominal group technique is where the ideas are ranked by voting.	
13. C	A prototype helps in getting the requirement verification in the early phases of the project and helps in arriving at final requirements.	
14. C	We keep looking until we get the best answer:	
	Option A seems good but let's see if we get a better fit.	
	Option B, the assumption is wrong.	
	Option C, by far, is a better answer than option A. Selecting it and checking if D is a better choice.	
	Option D, Assumption is wrong. It's a constraint.	
	Option C is the best answer.	
15. B	A requirement priority matrix will help the project team prioritize the requirements to achieve a defined timeline.	
16. D	Rolling wave planning is an iterative planning technique in which the work to be accomplished in the near term is planned in detail, while they work in the future is planned at a higher level.	
17. C	In INVEST, I stand for Independent.	
18. D	The sponsor of the project would be the ultimate authority to formally initiate a go-ahead to the handover process.	
19. D	If requirements are changing too frequently and you are struggling, maybe you selected the wrong project life cycle. Work with experts and customers, check the process maturity of the project domain, and then select the right project life cycle so that you can stay ahead of the curve. A few changes are OK, but a lot of changes, if a predictive life cycle is selected, maybe the wrong option to go for. Maybe agile works better in your project. Analyze and select the right methodology to execute and deliver the project work. The project scope baseline is the output of Create WBS. Do not get confused with the process Define Scope. Check the outputs of both of these processes to be sure :).	
20. D	Observations as a requirement gathering tool could be helpful in case of language issues or mental biases.	

6. TIME MANAGEMENT

TOPICS WE COVER IN THIS CHAPTER

→	Agile planning	→	Iteration Burndown chart
→	PDM - Drawing PDM and analyzing it	→	Critical Path Method
→	Leads and lags	→	Critical chain method
→	Estimation techniques	→	Resource optimization techniques
→	Dependency Type – FF, SS, FS, SF	→	Crashing, Fast-tracking
→	Mandatory and Discretionary Dependency	→	Iteration Burndown chart

6.1 SCHEDULE MANAGEMENT OVERVIEW

Objective: Project Schedule Management is managing the project completion ON TIME.

Process Name	Process Group	Why
Plan Schedule Management	Planning	Defining how
Define Activities	Planning	Decomposing WBS further to the activity level
Sequence Activities	Planning	Defining relationships between activities, if any
Estimate Activity Durations	Planning	Estimating time requirements for activities
Develop Schedule	Planning	Applying constraints and arriving at a baseline schedule
Control Schedule	Monitoring & Controlling	Planned Vs. Actual and Action

6.2 PLAN SCHEDULE MANAGEMENT

The purpose of planning is to develop an approach to create the project schedule.

The WBS items become the starting point to start planning for the next step of action. Similarly, in Agile projects, the Sprint Backlog becomes the key starting point.

AGILE ROADMAP

The Product Owner, as per the vision, creates a high-level product roadmap/plan. This is shown below. The product roadmap is high-level planning using swim lanes. The agile team selects the PBIs as the iteration/sprint backlog based on the product roadmap and develops the increments. I have covered the agile release and planning in the Agile section - kindly refer to for details.

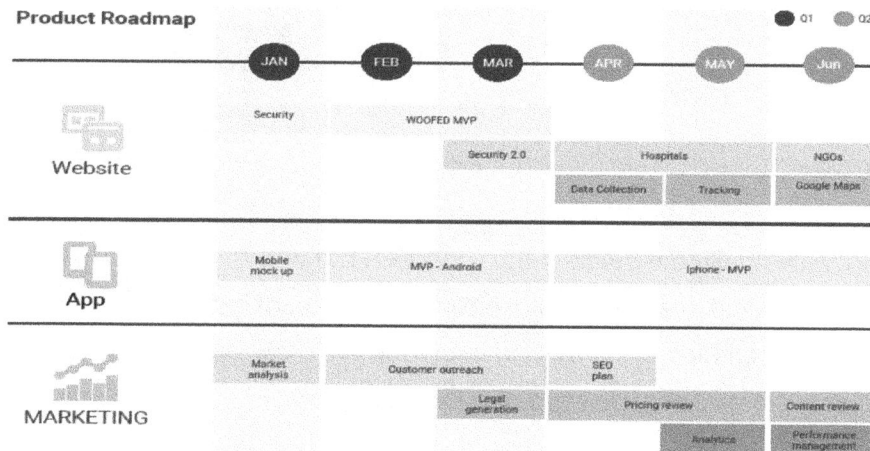

Since Agile projects have a shorter delivery cycle – typically 1-4 weeks and the teams are self-organizing, i.e., the work is not allocated. Rather the team chooses the work, and the planning and monitoring for the Sprint/Iterations happen in the daily meetings.

Predictive projects, on the other hand, may require a lot of planning and estimation efforts since the team is of various skill sets, and the delivery delay/cost overruns can cause serious issues in the project.

Let's think of Predictive projects (complex ones) while we think of planning activities.

The first thing to keep in mind is that WBS is the starting point of all project planning activities. If a scope item is missed from WBS, then it would never be planned and delivered.

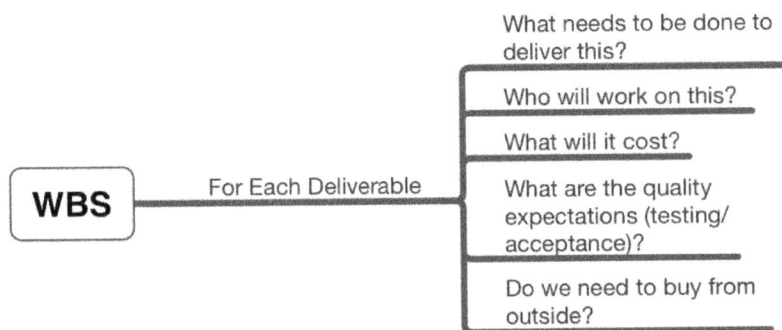

6.3 DEFINE ACTIVITIES
The goal of defining activities is to have the entire activity list and any additional information listed (i.e., activity attributes). Also, we list all the milestones.

ACTIVITY LIST
We define the actions required for each WBS Item.

MILESTONE:
A milestone is a significant point or event in the project. At the time of identifying all the activities, you want to identify **significant points** in the schedule, but why?

A milestone makes communication easier for all stakeholders. Instead of reporting 1000 tasks, you can mention a milestone completion status, and everyone will know. Many times, a millstone may be attached with payments in case of a fixed bid project.

DECOMPOSITION

Decomposition means subdividing. This technique can be used whenever we need to go modular, like creating WBS or Product Backlog Grooming.

ROLLING WAVE PLANNING
Rolling wave planning is an iterative planning technique where the work to be accomplished in the near term is planned in detail, while the work in the future is planned at a high level. **It is also called progressive elaboration.**

The best example of rolling wave planning is that, in your plan, you would have detailed down the overall work for the current phase along with the resource name, hours allocated along with all the leaves, and the work calendar. But, for the next phase, you might have broad-level activities that have no mention of resources because you don't know what type of resources you would get and when.

DINNER PARTY
You are planning a party at home for the first time. Few of your friends are coming over (A total of 5 families with kids). There are demands:

→   Pizza for kids

→   Wine for women

→   Beer for a few folks

→   Cold drinks for few

→   Food should have vegetarian options along with non-vegetarian appetizers to go with drinks

→ Special demand from kids for new age music

A typical WBS for a dinner party is:

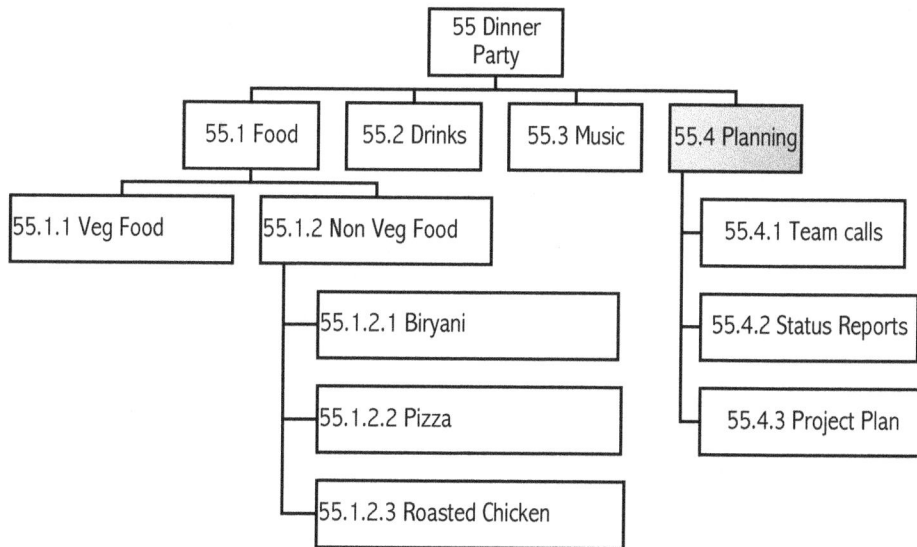

One of the WBS items 55.1.2.1 is biryani as the non-veg option as the main course. You planned to make the biryani at home.

The ACTIONS to produce biryani are:

1. Buy raw ingredients like chicken, masala, and rice

2. Wash and prepare ingredients

3. Cook

4. Serve.

5. Clean

Once we have identified the activities, we may want to see if any relationship exists between them. For example, I cannot cook biryani until the ingredients are not washed and prepared. There is a finish-to-start relationship(FS). Let's learn more about relationships:

Before we start understanding dependencies, let's understand a few more terms:

6.4 SEQUENCE ACTIVITIES

Identifying relationships amongst activities, if any.

ACTIVITY DEPENDENCIES

Before we understand the different types of dependencies, let us understand the key terms:

PREDECESSOR

A predecessor activity is an activity that logically comes before a dependent activity on a schedule.

SUCCESSOR

A successor activity is a dependent activity that logically comes after another activity on a schedule.

In the given picture, A is the predecessor, and B is the successor. This means that activity B will start only after activity A finishes.

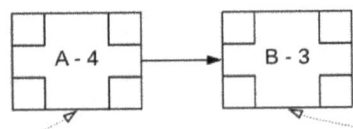

Activity A is for 4 days, and B will last for 3 days. This is an FS relationship. What are other types of relationships?

There are typically 4 types of activity dependencies:

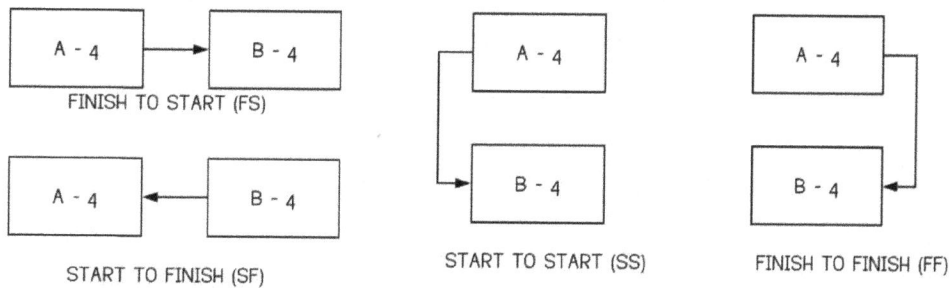

FINISH TO START (FS)

START TO FINISH (SF)

START TO START (SS)

FINISH TO FINISH (FF)

FINISH-TO-START (FS):

Successor activity cannot start until a predecessor activity has finished.

Example: The awards ceremony (successor) cannot start until the race (predecessor) has finished.

FINISH-TO-FINISH (FF):

Successor activity cannot finish until a predecessor activity has finished.

Example: Writing a document (predecessor) is required to finish before editing the document (successor) can finish.

START-TO-START (SS):

Successor activity cannot start until a predecessor activity has started.

Example: Level concrete (successor) cannot begin until pour foundation (predecessor) begins.

START-TO-FINISH (SF):

Predecessor activity cannot finish until the successor activity has started.

Example: The first security guard shift (predecessor) cannot finish until the second security guard shift (successor) starts.

There are other dimensions of action/node dependency:

MANDATORY DEPENDENCIES:

Mandatory Dependencies are contractual or physical limitations. They are also called Hard Logic dependencies. One has to wait for them. You cannot Fastrack (we learn this soon) the dependent activity if need be.

Example: In a construction project, it is not possible to erect the superstructure until after the foundation has been built.

DISCRETIONARY DEPENDENCIES:

These are "Best practices" within a particular application area. They are also called preferred logic, preferential logic, or soft logic.

These are the type of activities that can be executed in parallel if you face a shortage of time in the schedule.

Example: In a software project, it is advisable that you do not start development work until and unless you get a sign-off from the architect. But, in case you, as the Project Manager, think that the developers are free and you want to optimize time, then you can make a call and start the development activities.

EXTERNAL DEPENDENCIES:

External Dependencies involve relationships between project activities and non-project activities. They can be regulatory dependencies.

Example: In the case of telecom roll-out projects, you cannot start deployment until the government grants you the licenses. The team cannot control them, and hence they have to plan accordingly.

INTERNAL DEPENDENCIES:

These are internal between the team and can be controlled. The plan can be changed/managed if there are internal dependencies.

Example: In your team, one of the modules is dependent on the other module's output.

LEADS AND LAGS
LEAD

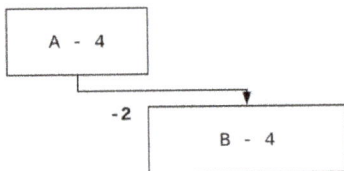

Lead is the amount of time whereby a successor activity can be advanced with respect to a predecessor activity. In the above picture above, Activity B has a LEAD or 2 Days.

LAG

Lag is the amount of time whereby a successor activity will be delayed with respect to a predecessor activity.

In this picture, Activity B has a LAG of 5 Days.

To avoid confusion, Map the Lead with the minus, and Lag with the plus.

Lead means that you would be doing the successor activity ahead of time, i.e., – X days. Lag means that you would WAIT for X time, i.e., + X days.

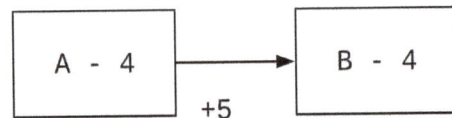

PRECEDENCE DIAGRAMMING METHOD

The precedence diagramming method (PDM) is a technique used for constructing a schedule model where activities are represented by nodes and are graphically linked by one or more logical relationships to show the sequence in which the activities are to be performed.

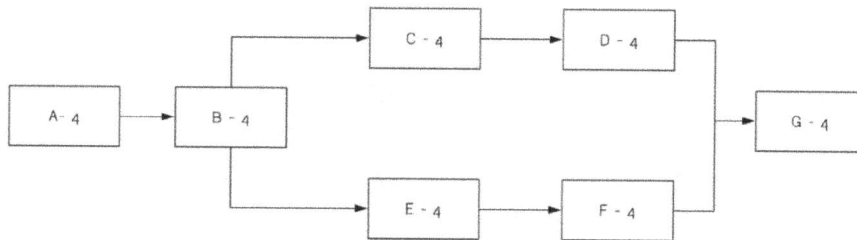

Activity-on-node (AON) is one method of representing a precedence diagram.

6.5 ESTIMATE ACTIVITY DURATIONS

Estimate Activity Durations is the process of estimating the number of work periods needed to complete individual activities.

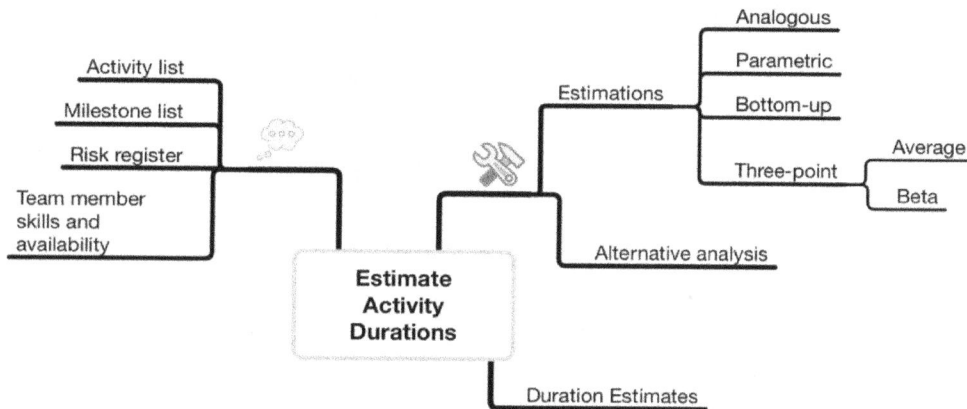

6.6 ESTIMATIONS

Now since activities are identified, we estimate how much time they need to complete them. Now, you can fill up the next column of MSP or primavera or the excel sheet. Different ways to estimate are:

ANALOGOUS ESTIMATING

Similar or Top-down estimates are the keywords for it. You look at similar activities from a similar type of project and base your estimates on this information. This method is most useful when you don't have enough information about the current activity/project.

Analogues estimation is also called quick and dirty estimate just because it's not accurate enough.

Keyword: Similar

PARAMETRIC ESTIMATING:

If 10 * 10 sq. feet takes 2 mins to paint, how much time would it take to paint 100* 100 sq. feet of the wall?

This is an example of parametric (calculations) estimation. Any estimate that is arrived at using calculation is a parametric estimate. The function point estimate is one of the examples in the software industry.

The parametric estimate accuracy is as good as the underlying data on which the estimations are based.

Keyword: Calculations

THREE-POINT Estimations

What if your boss comes over to your desk and asks you, "How much time would you take to complete XYZ task?"

What do you do?

You calculate the task duration in your mind, add some buffer time, and then give him some hours or days. You did the right thing. However, if in case there were dependencies and you had an optimistic view, then you probably would not be able to give results on a required day. Would it have been better if you had told him:

Boss, it will take ten days to complete if everything goes well (optimistic scenario). It will take 15 days if something goes wrong (pessimistic scenario), and most likely, I should be able to deliver something by the 12th day (a most likely scenario).

This is called a 3-point estimate.

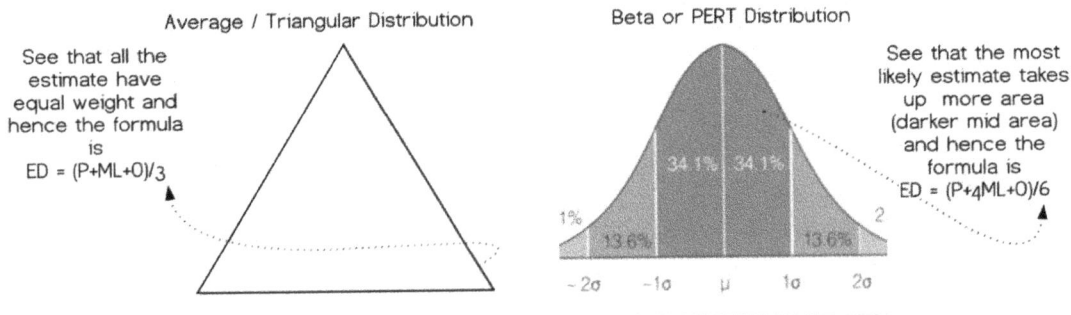

Average / Triangular Distribution

See that all the estimate have equal weight and hence the formula is $ED = (P+ML+O)/3$

Beta or PERT Distribution

See that the most likely estimate takes up more area (darker mid area) and hence the formula is $ED = (P+4ML+O)/6$

TRIANGULAR DISTRIBUTION

Triangular distribution is also called the Average Distribution

Expected Duration = (O + ML + P) / 3

BETA DISTRIBUTION

Beta distribution is also called PERT Expected Duration = (O + 4ML + P) / 6.

Where:

O is the Optimistic estimate, ML is the Most Likely estimate and P is the Pessimistic estimate

6.6.1 LET'S PLAY: ESTIMATION TECHNIQUES

Identify the Estimation techniques

1. You started to work on the dinner menu. Keeping the last party in mind, you ordered the raw material for this one.

    A. Top-down Estimates

    B. Bottom-up Estimates

    C. Parametric Estimates

    D. Three-Point Estimates

2. You allocated 3 resources to a particular activity. The reason 3 resources were allocated is that you wanted to finish the activity within the next four days. It was assumed that 1 resource could complete the activity in 12 days.

    A. Top-down Estimates

    B. Bottom-up Estimates

    C. Parametric Estimates

    D. Three-Point Estimates

3. While estimating the project timelines, you estimated the most optimistic and the most pessimistic scenario along with the most likely conditions to arrive at the expected duration and then shared the time estimates with the senior management

    A. Top-down Estimates

    B. Bottom-up Estimates

    C. Parametric Estimates

    D. Three-Point Estimates

4. Sam detailed each activity with the project team. He discussed and finalized the activity-wise estimates and then combined all the days together to arrive at the final effort for the project.

    A. Top-down Estimates

    B. Bottom-up Estimates

    C. Parametric Estimates

    D. Three-Point Estimates

6.7 DEVELOP SCHEDULE

The process of analyzing activity sequences, durations, resource requirements, and schedule constraints to create the Project Schedule Baseline.

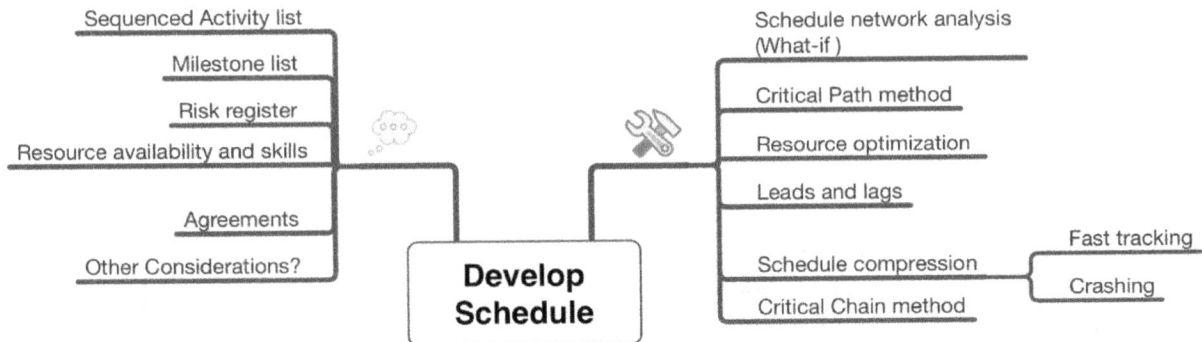

So far, we have decomposed the project to get the activities to achieve deliverables. We added dependencies if any, and durations for each activity. However, we have not set the constraints until now.

→ There can be a time constraint. For example, the client may want to go live on X Date.

→ A resource constraint. For example, you cannot get more than five architects for a week.

→ Cost constraints or other constraints like quality etc.

All the constraints, especially time constraints, are applied at the time of arriving at the final schedule. Because a formal sign-off is taken in this process. A schedule baseline is the result of the process. The baseline schedule is established and circulated.

SCHEDULE NETWORK ANALYSIS

While applying the constraints, one would analyze the effects of each input on the entire project. It could be a simple analysis like:

→ What if I add another resource in activity C?

→ What if I do the activity in parallel

CRITICAL CHAIN METHOD

Adding project end buffers and feeding buffers before a critical activity so that any delays can be absorbed. You tell your team that the project is only for 7 days, and keeping a buffer of 3 days is the live example of using the Critical Chain Method.

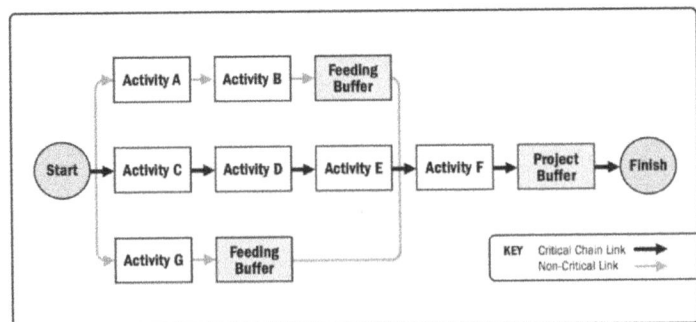

RESOURCE OPTIMIZATION:

If a resource is not available on the allocated time period of the activity or allocated to more than the predefined limit (say more than 8 hours per day), then you need to ensure that the resource allocation of the project is aligned and optimized.

SCHEDULE COMPRESSION

Video Available You Tube

SEARCH THIS TOPIC AT THE CHANNEL

Schedule compression techniques are used to shorten the schedule duration without reducing the project scope, to meet schedule constraints, imposed dates, or other schedule objectives.

Days	1	2	3	4	5	6	7	8	9	10	11	12	13	14	15	16	17	18	19	20	21	22
Normal																						
Crashing																						
Fast tracking																						

CRASHING

A technique used to shorten the schedule duration for the least incremental cost by adding resources. Examples of crashing include approving overtime, bringing in additional resources, or paying to expedite the delivery of activities on the critical path. Crashing works only for activities on the critical path where additional resources will shorten the activity's duration. Crashing does not always produce a viable alternative and may result in increased risk and cost.

FAST-TRACKING

A schedule compression technique where activities or phases that are normally done in sequence are performed in parallel for at least a portion of their duration. An example is constructing the foundation of a building before completing all of the architectural drawings. Fast-tracking may result in rework and increased risk. Fast-tracking only works if activities can be overlapped to shorten the project duration.

6.7.1 LET'S PLAY: SCHEDULE COMPRESSION TECHNIQUES

Identify the schedule compression technique used in the given scenarios:

1. The Project Manager starts coding before the requirements are signed off by the customer.

    A.   Fast Tracking

    B.   Crashing

2. Ryan asked the project team to spend extra hours on weekends to complete the identified activity on time.

    A.   Fast Tracking

    B.   Crashing

3. The book publishing team started working on the format of the book while the academic team was in the last stage of editing the content.

    A.   Fast Tracking

    B.   Crashing

4. Due to a few issues, the project was behind schedule. To meet timelines, you asked the team to work overtime.

    A.   Fast Tracking

    B.   Crashing

6.8 CONTROL SCHEDULE

Control Schedule is the process of analyzing planned vs. actual schedules and taking action. Once the schedule baseline is achieved, plans are in place. The project team executes the work. Meanwhile, you keep on monitoring and controlling the schedule.

The most important aspect of the Control Schedule is to determine whether the project is ahead of schedule or behind schedule, or at par so that you can take appropriate action accordingly.

The planned vs. actual schedule is established here, and you arrive at the difference ex ahead of schedule or behind schedule.

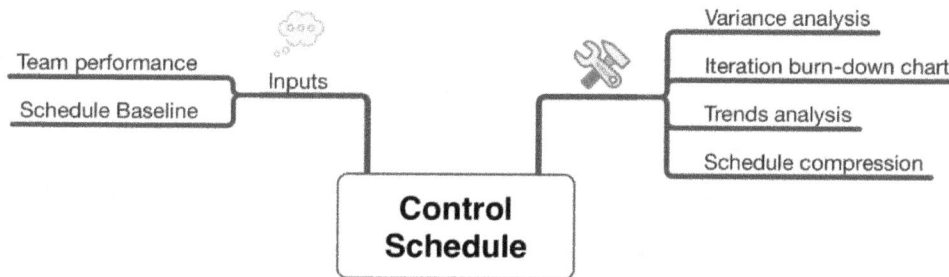

The forecasts (how much more time is required to complete) are established, and change requests, if any, are identified and worked upon.

VARIANCE ANALYSIS

Variance analysis is PLANNED VS ACTUALS, Always. This is used to understand the schedule performance as what was planned to be achieved in said time and how much work is achieved.

ITERATION BURN-DOWN CHART

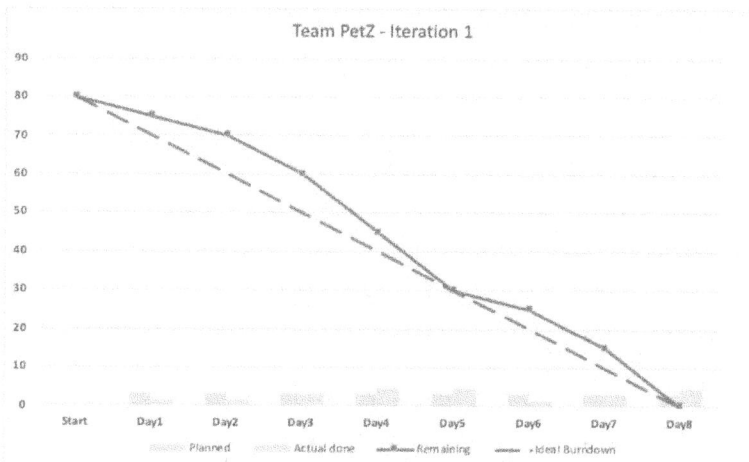

The iteration burndown chart shows the planned effort along with how much is already spent and how much remains on the project. This may show the actual effort along with the planned efforts.

TREND ANALYSIS

Trend analysis checks the trend of project performance over a period of time to check if the project schedule performance is improving or deteriorating. A visual graph will help analyze the trends.

TEAM VELOCITY

Velocity is a measure of the amount of work a Team can complete within a Sprint. Velocity is calculated at the end of the sprint/iteration by adding all the story points completed in the sprint.

This can help with the overall forecast for the project roadmap.

Let's understand team velocity using an example:

A team has the following historical data:

→ Iteration 1: Completed story points 38

→ Iteration 2: Completed story points 29

→ Iteration 3: Completed story points 38

→ Iteration 4: Completed story points 39

What is the final team velocity?

We take an average of all the completed story points. That will give us the team velocity.

In this case, the team velocity is: (38+29+38+39) / 4 = 36

Can we compare the team velocity of two different teams? No. Why? Because for each team, a story point value can be different, and hence the comparing team velocity may not give any perspective.

ON-DEMAND SCHEDULING

The concept is based on lean and Kanban methodologies. Team members "pull" work from a queue when available. Provides incremental business value with limited resources. Let us take an example to understand:

Think of an assembly line. There are 3 stages. In the first stage, which is assembly, 8 cars can be assembled at a given point. The second stage is painting. The capacity is 8 cars. However, in the last stage, which is testing and inspection, due to a shortage of resources, the capacity is 6 cars. Does it make sense that stage 1 and stage 2 work with full capacity and keep the unfinished goods at stage 3? No (until and unless we are thinking of increasing the stage 3 capacity). So a Kanban board will help. It can show the capacity and the available capacity. The work will be pulled from a previous stage rather than pushing the work.

Testing Job	Painting Job	Assembly Job
Capacity 5, in 4	Capacity 6, in 5	Capicty 8, In 8

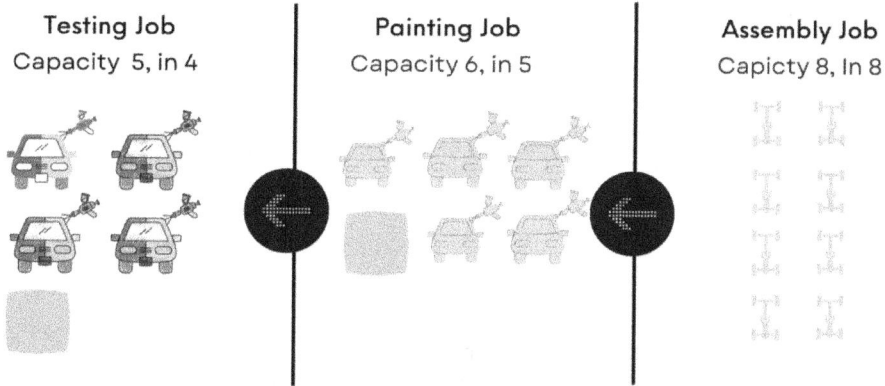

Similar way, an agile team can create Kanban boards like the one shown below:

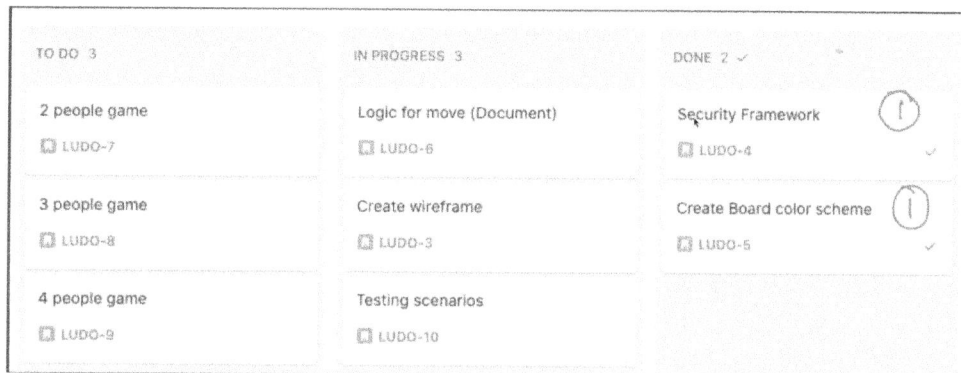

TO DO 3	IN PROGRESS 3	DONE 2 ✓
2 people game LUDO-7	Logic for move (Document) LUDO-6	Security Framework LUDO-4
3 people game LUDO-8	Create wireframe LUDO-3	Create Board color scheme LUDO-5
4 people game LUDO-9	Testing scenarios LUDO-10	

6.9 CRITICAL PATH METHOD

Video Available YouTube

SEARCH THIS TOPIC AT THE CHANNEL

Defined as the longest path of activities that must be completed on time for the project to be completed by its due date. A project schedule network diagram is the base to arrive at the critical path of the project. Why should we calculate the critical path? So that as a Project Manager, I can understand the most crucial activities with zero tolerance for delay (zero slack). These should be paid attention to start and complete on time because if they get delayed, then the whole project will be delayed.

(It is observed that the CPM questions in the new PMP exam after 2nd Jan 2021 are far fewer. You may want to practice CPM to understand the concepts in detail. However, from the PMP exam perspective, expect less calculation, so fewer CPM and EVM questions.)

→ A critical path is the longest path in the network. Each node that falls under the critical path has either zero or a negative Float (Slack).

→ Why should I bother?

→ Because if any of the activity in the critical path is delayed, we will miss the project end date. Not a good thing.

→ How to calculate CPM?

→ So, we start by understanding a sample node first:

→ A sample node has a name, duration, and relationship arrow. The early start (ES), early finish (EF), late start (LS), and late finish (LF) will be calculated by us while we calculate the critical path.

SAMPLE NODE

Early Start		Early Finish
	Task Name - Duration	
Late Start		Late Finish

A PDM Node

THE APPROACH:

The work starts on day zero. The early start and early finish date is calculated using a forward pass (STEP 1). The late start and late finish are calculated in backward pass (STEP 2). Then we calculate the float (STEP 3).

A SAMPLE PROBLEM

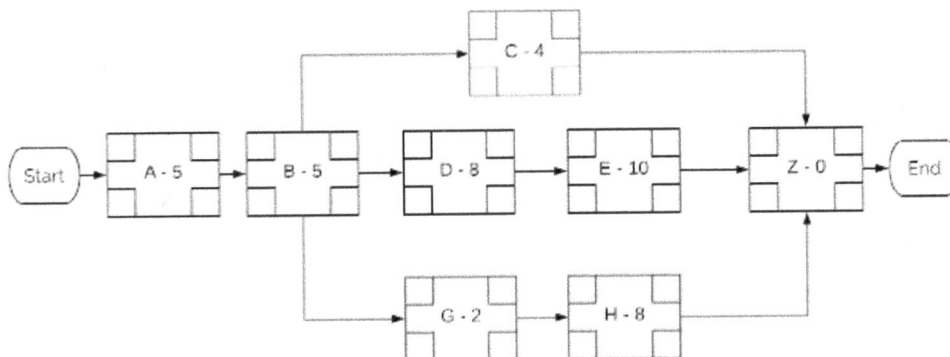

Let's start:

THERE ARE 3 STEPS TO CALCULATE CPM:

1.   Forward Pass - To calculate the Early Start (ES) and Early Finish (EF) of the node.

2.   Backward Pass - To calculate the Late Start (LS) and Late Finish (LF) of the node.

3.   Calculate Float and thus CPM.

STEP 1 - THE FORWARD PASS:

- o   We start from the first node (Start node).

- o   The work begins on day 0.

- o   We'll fill up the information in the highlighted boxes:

- o   In the forward pass, we calculate the Early Start and Early Finish date of activities.

NODE A:

- o   The activity starts on day zero. Since the duration for Activity A is 5 days, the early finish will take Early Start and duration; i.e.:

- o   A(EF) = A(ES) + Duration A (EF)= 0 + 5 = 5

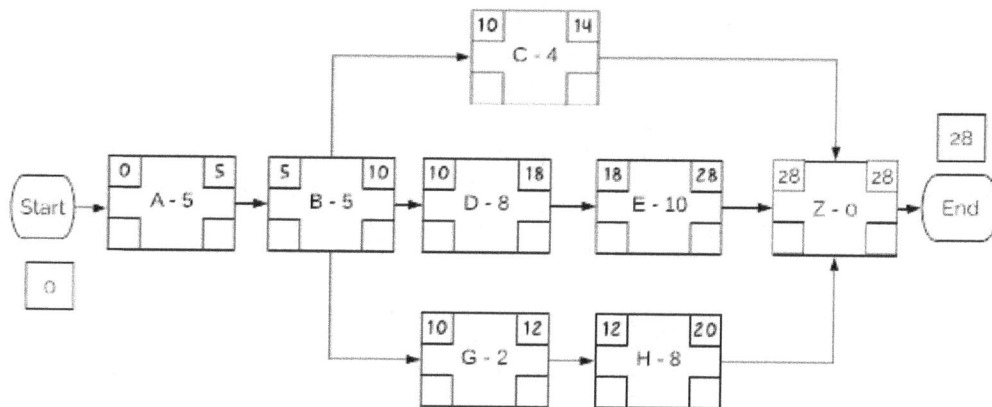

STEP 1 - Forward Pass

NODE B:

- o   Since there is only one node which precedes activity B, the relationship is F->S. That means the activity B can start only when activity A ends. Hence:

- o   B (ES) = A (EF) = 5

- o   B(EF) = B(ES) + Duration = 5+ 5 = 10

ACTIVITY C:

- o   C(ES) = B(EF) = 10

- o   C(EF) = C(ES) + Duration = 10+ 4 = 14

NODE Z:

- o   Now, node C leads to node Z, but can we calculate the Z(ES)??

177

- o No, we cannot since it has to wait for two more activities for it to start.
- o Node Z cannot start until activities C, E, and H are complete. So, let's complete the calculations of all activities before Z.

ACTIVITY D, E, G, H

- o The calculations are pretty simple (same as B) since they have only one predecessor.

BACK TO ACTIVITY Z:

- o Since this is a merging node (i.e., many activities have to end before we begin activity Z), Z has more than one predecessor.
- o Z can start only when all the activities which are merging into Z are complete; hence, Z can only start when the last activity is complete.
- o $Z(ES) = Max \mid C(EF) \text{ or } E(EF) \text{ or } H(EF) \mid$
- o $Z(ES) = Max \mid 14 \text{ or } 28 \text{ or } 20 \mid Z(ES) = 28$
- o $Z(EF) = 28 + 0 = 28.$

STEP 2 - THE BACKWARD PASS:

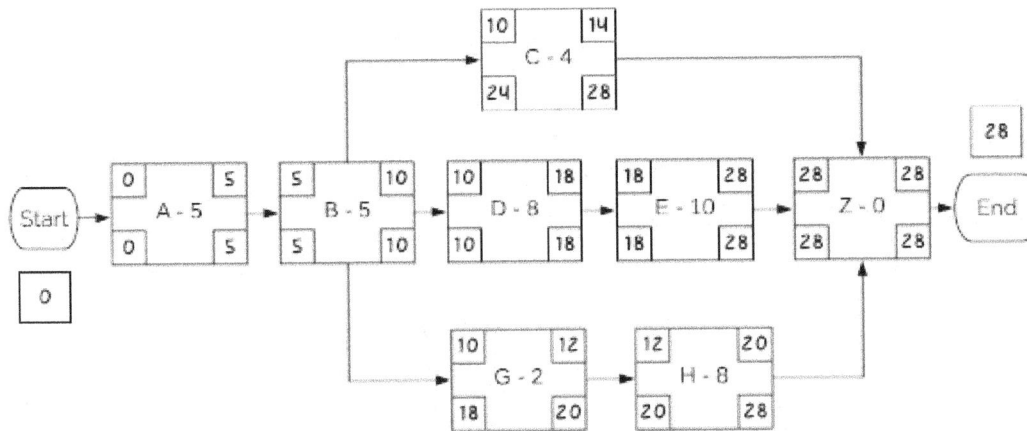

STEP 2 - Backward Pass

- o Here we'll start from the last node, i.e., Z,
- o We calculate the bottom 2 squares (Late Start and late finish)

NODE Z:

- o As this is the last node, Z's last finish date would be equal to the earliest finish date of Z, i.e., $Z(LF) = Z(EF) = 28$
- o $Z(LS) = Z(LF) - \text{Duration } Z(LS) = 28 - 0 = 28$
- o Node H
- o Node H has only one node preceding it in the backward pass (node Z). Hence $H(LF) = Z(LS) = 28$
- o $H(LS) = H(LF) - H(Duration) = 28 - 8 = 20$

178

NODE E

o   Node E has only one node preceding it in the backward pass (node Z). Hence E(LF) = Z(LS) = 28

o   E(LS) = E(LF) – E(Duration) = 28 – 10 = 18

NODE C

o   Node C has only one node preceding it in the backward pass (node Z). Hence C(LF) = C(LS) = 28

o   C(LS) = C(LF) – C(Duration) = 28 – 4 = 24

o   Node G calculations are exactly as simple node calculations

NODE B

o   Since Node B is where most of the activities are merging in the backward pass, i.e., C, D, and G, this is where we need to pay more attention. In backward pass, the node B's Latest Finish (LF) would be the earliest or all the nodes Late Start i.e.

o   B(LF) = Least | C(LS) or D(LS) or G(LS) | B(LF) = Least | 24 or 10 or 18 |

o   B(LF) = 10

o   B(LS) = B(LF) – B(Duration) = 10 -5 = 5

o   Node A

o   A(LF) = B(LF) = 5

o   A(LS) = A(LF) – A(Duration) = 5 - 5 = 0

STEP 3 - CALCULATING TOTAL FLOAT:

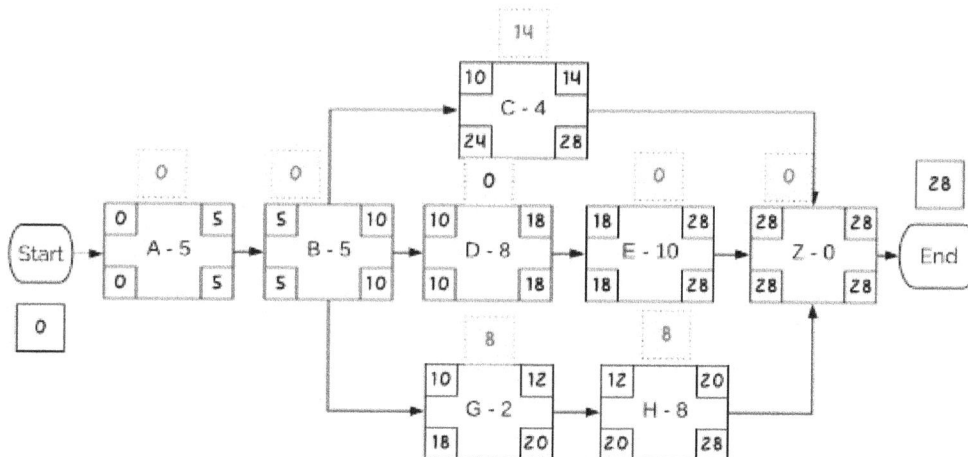

STEP 3 - FLOAT & CPM

TOTAL FLOAT

o   The total amount of time that a scheduled activity may be delayed by its early start date without delaying the project finish date or intermediary milestone. It is calculated using:

- o Activity (ES) – Activity (LS) or activity (EF) Activity (LF) – Both will give you the same results.
- o C (Total Float) = C (LS) - C(ES) = 24 – 10 = 14

FINDING THE CRITICAL PATH

Calculate the total float for all activities as per the formula.

All nodes which have zero or negative float/slack form the CRITICAL PATH.

Here we can see that:

→ Nodes A, B, D, E, and Z form the critical path.

6.9.1 LET'S PLAY: CPM1 (OPTIONAL)

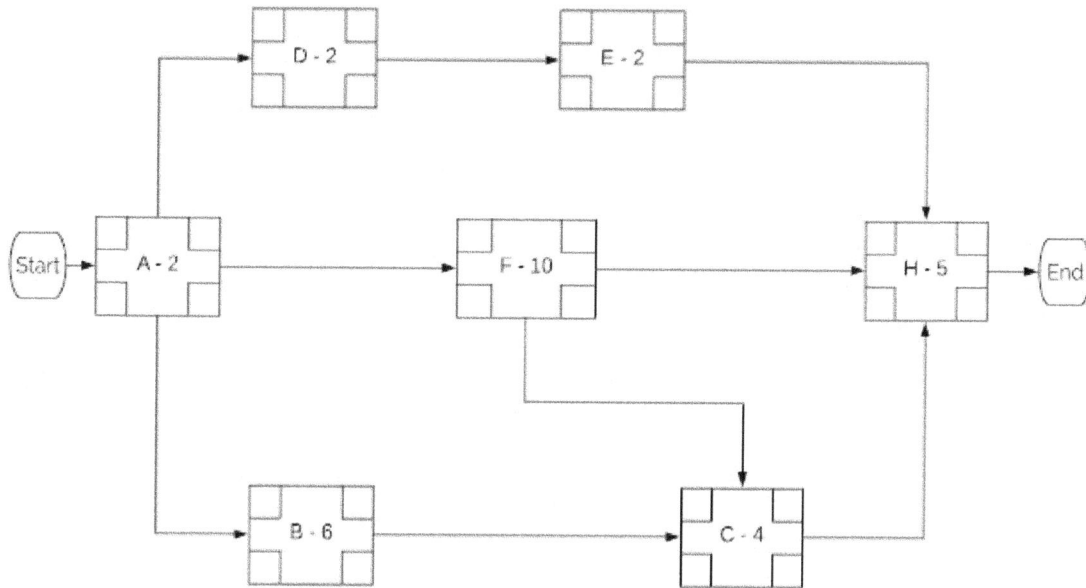

1. What is the CPM for the given PDM?

   Answer _____

2. Find the Float for the node B

   Answer _____

3. Find the Float for node D

   Answer _____

4. Find the Float for node F

   Answer _____

6.9.2 LET'S PLAY: CPM2 (OPTIONAL)

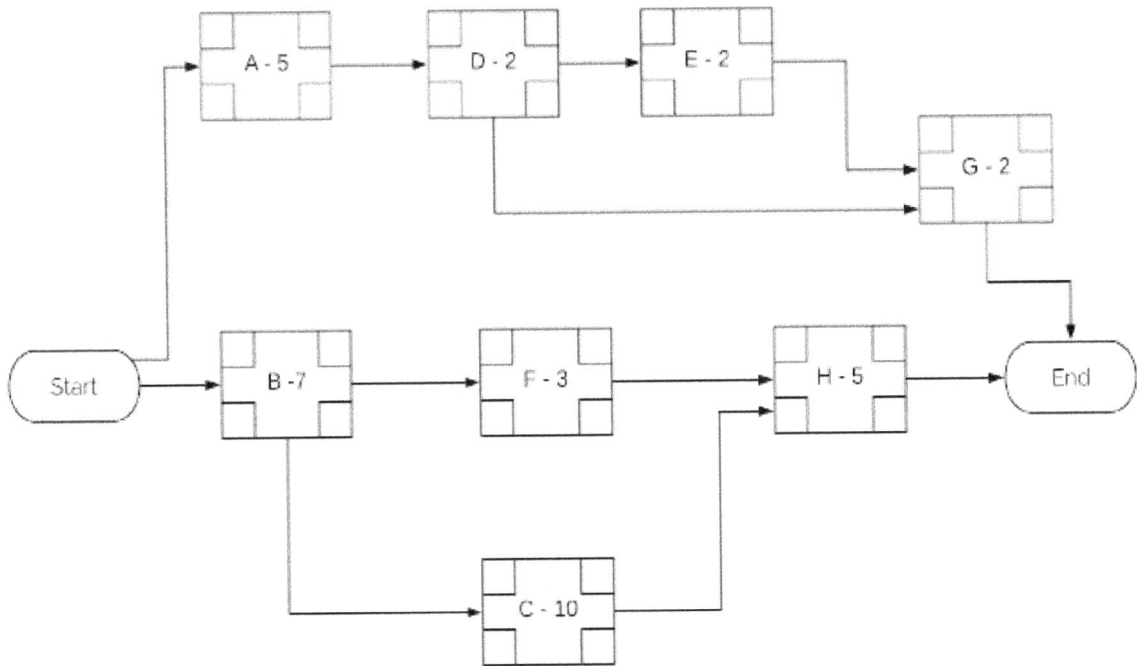

1. Find the critical Path

   Answer _____

2. Float for F

   Answer _____

3. Float for H

   Answer _____

4. Float for E

   Answer _____

6.9.3 LET'S PLAY: CPM3 (OPTIONAL)

You are midway, and you have completed activities A and B on time. Activity D started after a delay of 11 days, And activity F started after a delay of 5 days.

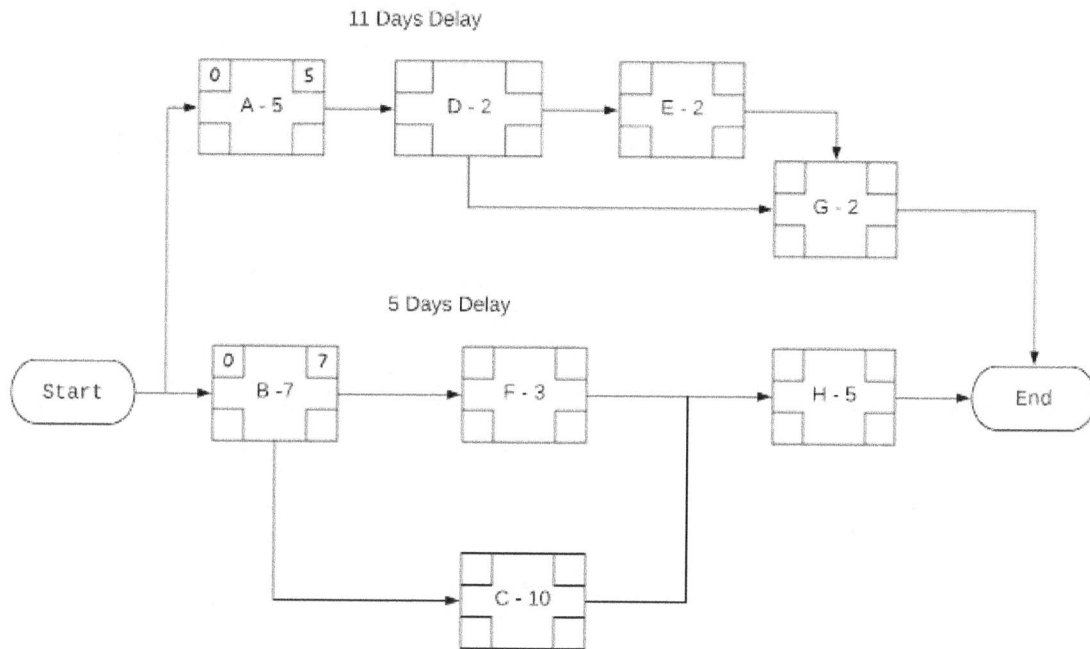

1. Calculate the new critical path

   Answer _____

2. Calculate the Float for node C

   Answer _____

3. Calculate the Float for node D

   Answer _____

4. Calculate the Float for node E

   Answer _____

6.9.4 LET'S PLAY: CPM4 (OPTIONAL)

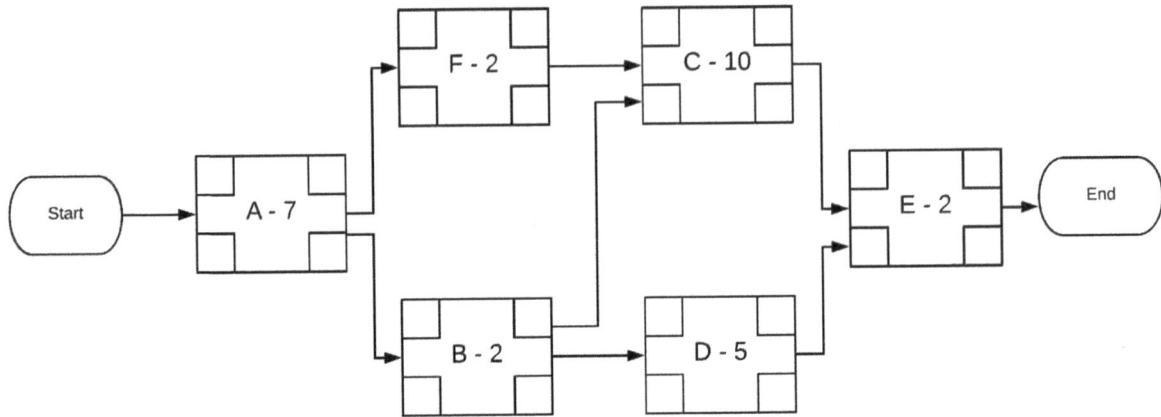

1. **What is the CPM for the given PDM?**

Answer _____

2. **Find the Float for the node E**

Answer _____

3. **Find the Float for node D**

Answer _____

4. **Find the Float for node F**

Answer _____

6.9.5 LET'S PLAY: CPM5 (OPTIONAL)

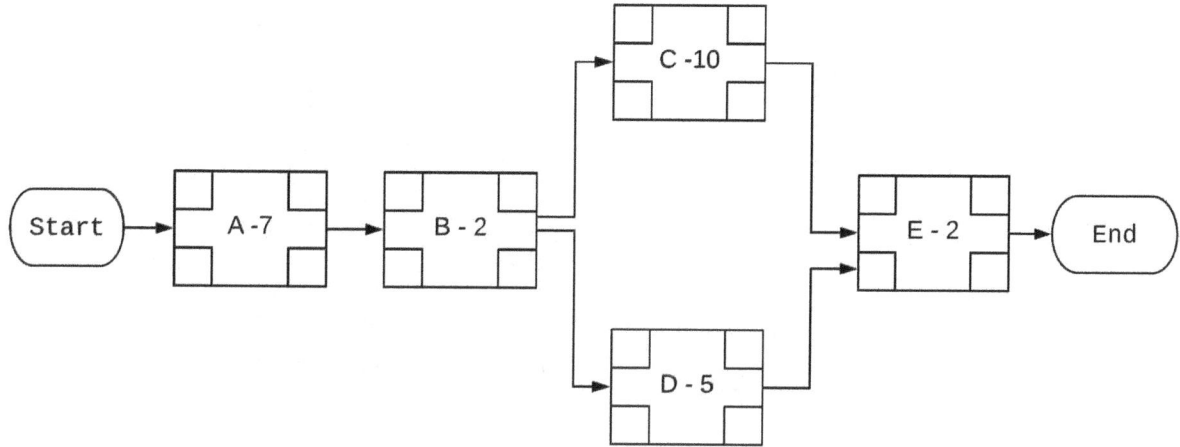

1. What is the CPM for the given PDM?

Answer _____

2. Find the Float for the node E

Answer _____

3. Find the Float for node D

Answer _____

4. Find the Float for node B

Answer _____

6.9.6 LET'S PLAY: CPM6 (OPTIONAL)

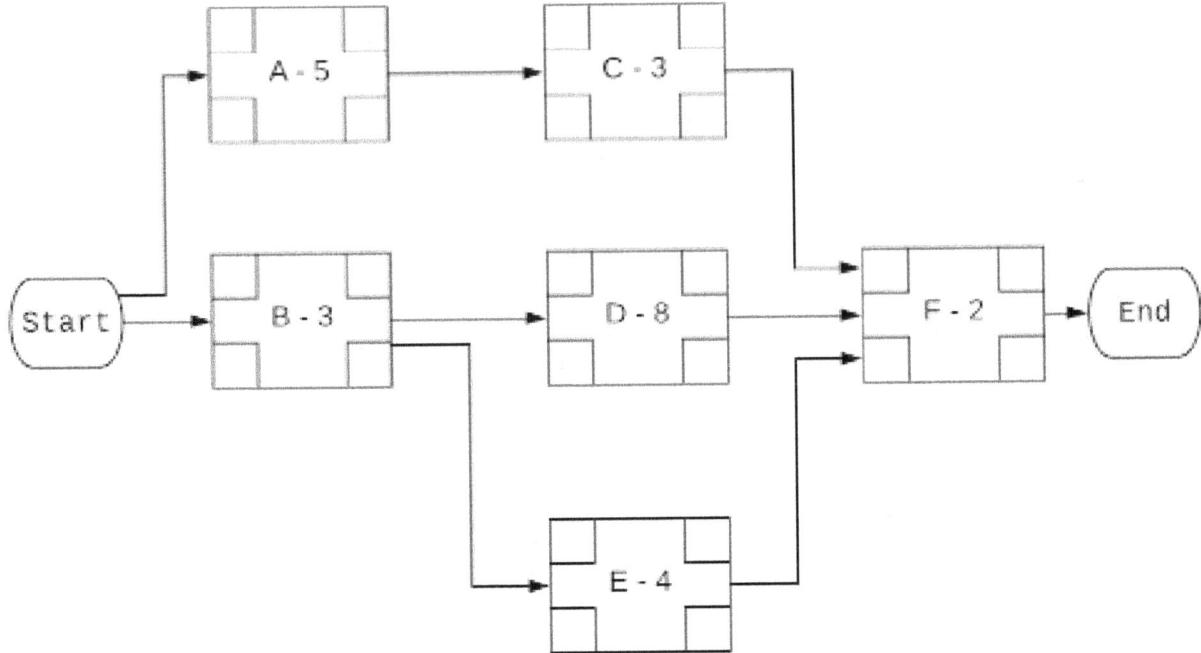

1. What is the CPM for the given PDM?

Answer _____

2. Find the Float for the node E

Answer _____

3. Find the Float for node D

Answer _____

4. Find the Float for node C

Answer _____

6.10 MODULE END QUESTIONS - PMP STYLE

1. You are in the process of creating the project schedule and found that a few resources are over-allocated beyond their committed hours. As the next step, you analyzed the activities and trimmed down the required hours for over-allocation. Which technique did you use?

    A. Crashing

    B. Fast Tracking

    C. Resource optimization

    D. What-if analysis

2. You are a Project Manager in an IT firm. You received several calls in the past 2to 3 days inquiring whether any of the resources can be released from the project. There were 3 more calls today. Your project appears to be going at a good pace, people appear to be happy, and the project risk rating is low. Activity A has an early start date of 4 and a late start date of 2. Activity B has a float of 3 days. Activity R has an early start date of 5 and a late start date of 15. The CPI of the project is 1.2. Most of the stakeholders appear to be fine with the project's progress. The procurement has been kicked off per the plan. What should you do?

    A. Crash Activity A

    B. Crash Activity R

    C. Think of ways to reduce the impact of phone calls

    D. Plan procurement in detail

3. Which of the following indicates a negative float?

    A. The early finish date is equal to the late finish date

    B. The late start date is earlier than the early start date

    C. Crashing results in a negative float

    D. Fast-tracking results in a negative float

4. To overcome a critical delay, you allocated three more resources to a critical activity. Which technique did you use?

    A. Fast Tracking

    B. Crashing

    C. Analyzing Schedule

    D. Control Schedule

5. Each activity requires a minimum of 3 days to complete. If your management asks you to reduce the project by two days, which of the following activities is MOST likely to change?

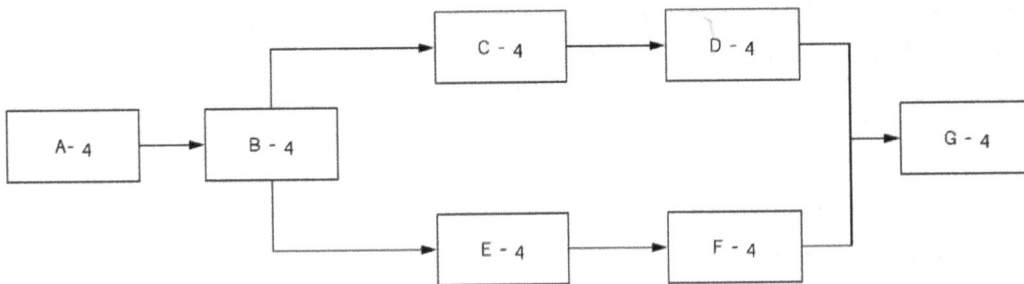

```
                          ┌────────┐        ┌────────┐
                      ┌──▶│ C - 4  │──────▶ │ D - 4  │──┐
                      │   └────────┘        └────────┘  │
┌────────┐   ┌────────┐                                 │   ┌────────┐
│ A- 4   │──▶│ B - 4  │                                 ├──▶│ G - 4  │
└────────┘   └────────┘                                 │   └────────┘
                      │   ┌────────┐        ┌────────┐  │
                      └──▶│ E - 4  │──────▶ │ F - 4  │──┘
                          └────────┘        └────────┘
```

   A.   C and D
   B.   E and F
   C.   G and F
   D.   A and G

6. In your project, activity A has an Early Start (ES) on day 5 and a Late Start (LS) on day 5. This activity is preceded by R, which has an Early Finish (EF) on day 11 and a Late Finish (LF) on day 21. The Activity A:

   A.   Is on the critical path
   B.   Has a lag
   C.   Is progressing well
   D.   Is not on the critical path

7. Team A has a velocity of 35, and Team B has a velocity of 30. What does it translate to?

   A.   Team A is performing better than Team B
   B.   Team B is performing better than Team A
   C.   Team velocity cannot be compared with others
   D.   More information required

8. What happens if the Development Team is delayed and cannot complete the sprint backlog within the iteration timebox?

   A.   The team should adjust the timebox for futures
   B.   You can adjust the current timebox to complete the development
   C.   Work with the Product Owner to discuss if the feature can be rescheduled for the next sprint
   D.   Scrum Master should act as a team member to complete the work in the given timebox.

9. **What is a milestone?**

    A. Milestones are marked for payments.

    B. Milestones are similar to regularly scheduled activities, with the same structure and attributes.

    C. Milestones depict a significant point or event in a project.

    D. The schedule should always have milestones.

10. **You realize that you cannot start one of the activities without getting the requisite approval from a government regulatory body. What type of dependency is described in the scenario?**

    A. Mandatory - Internal dependency

    B. Mandatory - External dependency

    C. Discretionary - Internal dependency

    D. Discretionary - External dependency

11. **A project has a velocity of 20. What does this information convey?**

    A. Project team can deliver 20 features in one iteration

    B. There are 20 people on the team

    C. The development team can finish 20 story points in one iteration

    D. The development team can finish 20 days of work in one iteration.

12. **Select the INCORRECT statement**

    A. Leads are used in limited circumstances to delay a successor activity with respect to the predecessor activity.

    B. Lags are used in limited circumstances to delay a successor activity with respect to the predecessor activity.

13. **One of the activities is delayed beyond recovery days. If the project goes with the same plan, it will get delayed by at least a few weeks. Your management has told you that no delay is acceptable and that arranging new resources for the project will take substantial time and is not a valid option. Also, the organization policy is no overtime and no work on weekends. No employee can be asked to do more than 40 hours of work. What is the best option you are left with?**

    A. Do work in parallel

    B. Put more resources into the project

    C. Analyze the schedule to see if a few activities can be shortened or can be overlapped

    D. Reduce the scope

14. ABC Expressway is a 6-lane, 165 km long, controlled-access expressway. It connects City A with City B. You are managing the project to set up the toll booths. Setting up the toll booths with toll charges requires getting approvals from the government before you proceed with setting up the cabin. The contract, which was sanctioned, approves you to set up the booths; however, the final discussions about toll charges are yet to happen. Can you fast-track the activity of setting up the booths?

   A. Yes. This project is entitled to set up the booths along with tool tickets. We will do it as per the plan.

   B. No. Government approval is always mandatory

   C. Yes. After checking the contract, work can start on the setting up the booth while the toll charges approval takes place

   D. No. Paperwork is a MUST before we carry out any activity

15. Crashing is preferred over fast-tracking when:

   A. Project SPI < 1

   B. Project CPI is <1

   C. Project CPI is >1

   D. Project SPI >1

16. Activity A has a duration of 2 weeks with a 20% probability of exceeding the timelines. What does it convey?

   A. It is certain that activity A will be finished in 2 weeks.

   B. It is only 20% possible that activity A can finish within 2 weeks

   C. It is 80% probable that activity A will finish within 2 weeks

   D. Activity A will finish within 2 weeks with a plus or minus of 20%

17. Select the INCORRECT statement

   A. Leads are employed in limited circumstances to advance a successor activity on the predecessor activity

   B. Lags are used in limited circumstances to delay a successor activity on the predecessor activity.

   C. Crashing shortens the schedule duration for the least incremental cost by adding resources.

   D. Fast tracking is a technique used to shorten the schedule duration for the least incremental cost by adding resources.

6.11 ALL ANSWERS

ANSWERS: 6.6.1 LET'S PLAY: ESTIMATION TECHNIQUES

1. You started to work on the dinner menu. Keeping the last party in mind, you ordered the raw material.	Analogues estimate	Keyword: Similar
2. You put 3 resources into a particular activity. The reason 3 resources were allocated is that you wanted to finish the activity in the next Four days. It was assumed that 1 resource could have completed the activity in 12 days.	Parametric estimate	Keyword: Calculation
3. While estimating for roll-out date for your project, you estimated the Most optimistic scenario and most pessimistic along with the most likely conditions and then gave your estimates to senior management	3-point estimates.	Keywords: Optimistic, Pessimistic, and Most likely
4. Sam detailed each activity with the project team. He discussed and finalized the activity-wise estimates and then combined all the days together to arrive at the final effort for the project.	Bottom-up estimates	Keyword: Detailed out

ANSWERS: 6.7.1 LET'S PLAY: SCHEDULE COMPRESSION TECHNIQUES

1. The Project Manager starts coding before getting the requirement sign-off from the customer.	FAST-TRACKING	(Work in Parallel)
2. Bond got his team to put in extra hours to complete an activity on time.	CRASHING	(Extra Hours/team within an activity/activities)
3. The book publishing team started working on the format in parallel while the academic team was reviewing the content.	FAST-TRACKING	(Work in Parallel)
4. Due to a few issues, the project was behind schedule. To meet timelines, you asked the team to work extra hours.	CRASHING	(Extra Hours/team within an activity/activities)

ANSWERS: 6.9.1 LET'S PLAY: CPM1

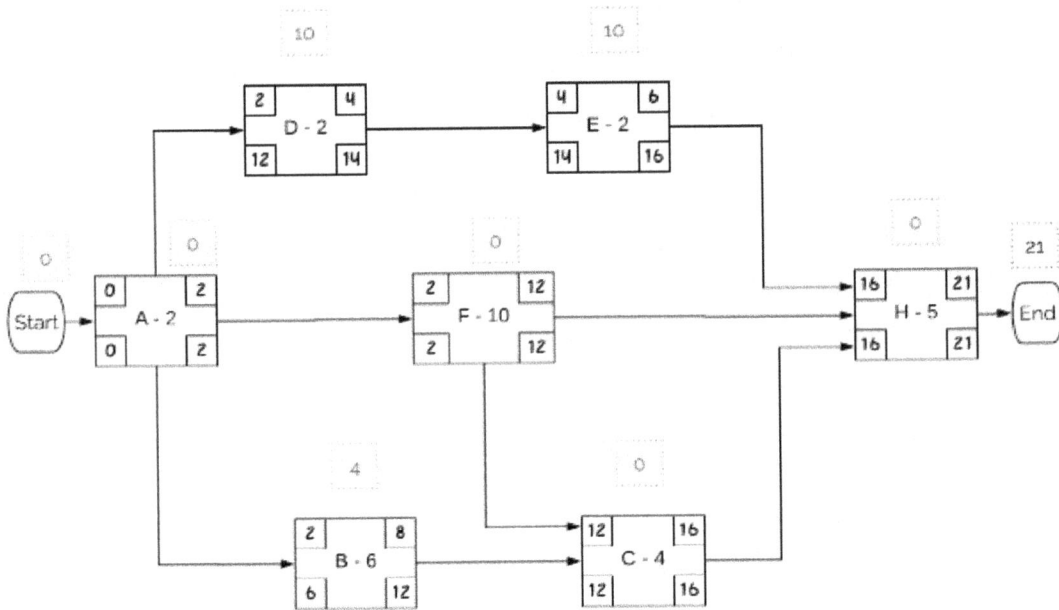

ANSWERS: 6.9.2 LET'S PLAY: CPM2

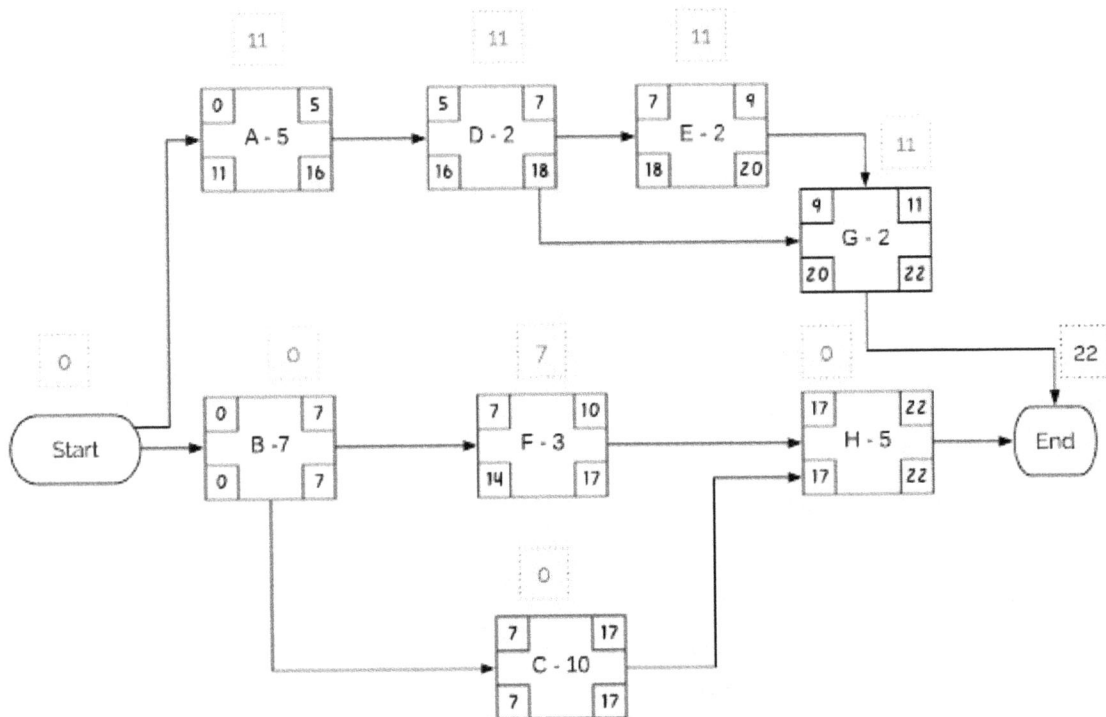

ANSWERS: 6.9.3 LET'S PLAY: CPM3

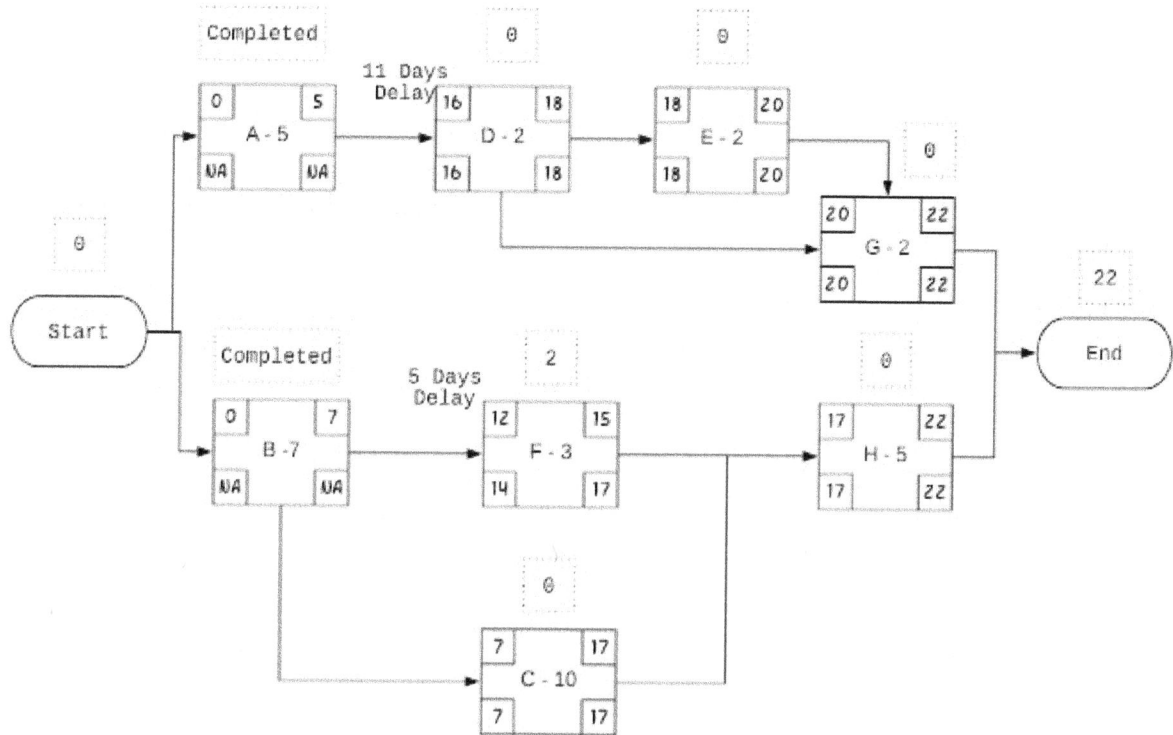

ANSWERS: 6.9.4 LET'S PLAY: CPM4

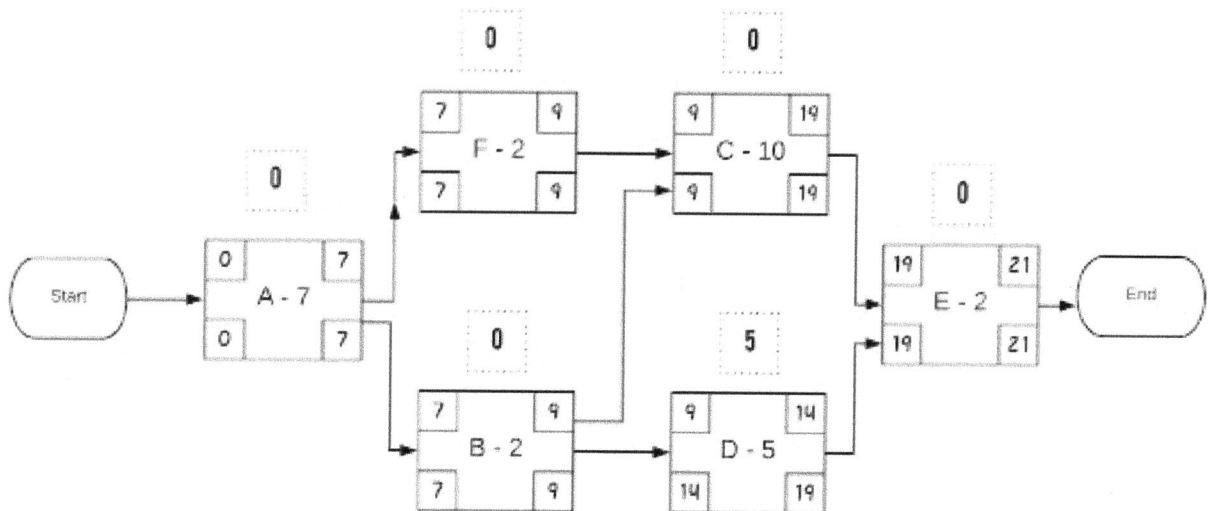

ANSWERS: 6.9.5 LET'S PLAY: CPM5

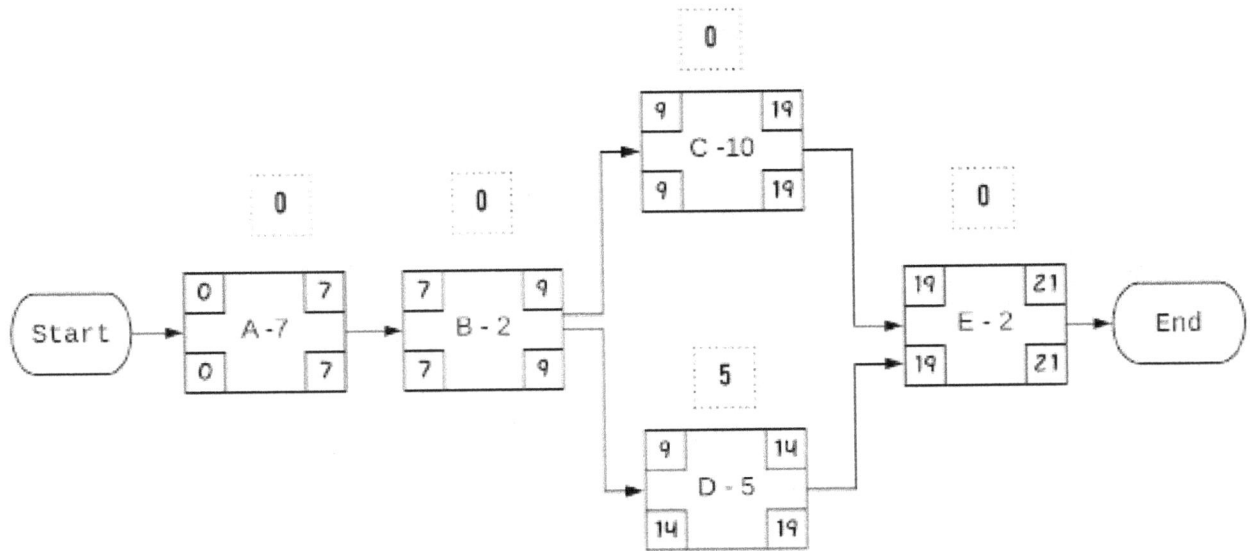

ANSWERS: 6.9.6 LET'S PLAY: CPM6

ANSWERS: 6.10 MODULE END QUESTIONS - PMP STYLE

1. C	Resource optimization is a technique that adjusts the activities of a schedule model such that the requirements for resources on the project do not exceed certain predefined resource limits.
2. A	A Lot of information is given in this question. Activity A is delayed and has a negative float. Activities B and R have a positive float, so the most important thing to do is crash Activity A.
3. B	Float = Late Start – Early Start
4. B	Adding resources to shorten an activity is crashing
5. D	Only A and G are common nodes. Crashing them will help achieve the desired results for sure.
6. A	Activity A is on the Critical path as the float for A is zero. Draw activities A and R with all the data, and then you will be able to find the answer quickly.
7. C	Each team has a different measure of story points, and hence the team velocity of different teams can not be compared.
8. C	Agile/Scrum Guide is pretty clear on this: you don't extend sprints. At the end of a sprint, if there is incomplete work: "All incomplete Product Backlog Items are re-estimated and put back on the Product Backlog." This does not mean that the sprint was unsuccessful As per the Scrum Guide: "If the Development Team determines it has too much or too little work, it may renegotiate the selected Product Backlog items with the Product Owner." During a sprint: "Scope may be clarified and renegotiated between the Product Owner and Development Team as more is learned."
9. C	"A milestone is a significant point or event in a project." So, the correct answer is C.
10. B	Mandatory dependencies are those that are legally or contractually required or inherent like the work. External dependencies involve a relationship between project activities and non-project activities. These dependencies are usually outside the project team's control.
11. C	Velocity is the measure of team productivity in an iteration. Since agile uses story points for estimations, Option C is the most accurate.
12. A	You need to find the incorrect statement. Using elimination technique: A. Leads are used in limited circumstances to delay a successor activity with respect to the predecessor activity. FALSE – Lead is to accelerate (doing it before time)

	B. Lags are used in limited circumstances to delay a successor activity with respect to the predecessor activity. TRUE
13. C	Let's see all the options. Choice A needs people to work overtime which is denied. So, option A is not feasible. Option B – Put more resources into the project is also denied. Choice C - We need to analyze the schedule to see what can be possible and achievable, and then changing the plan accordingly seems the only valid choice. Choice D – Reduce the scope and be one valid choice, but the decision cannot be taken until the reduction in scope is discussed with the customer. Out of all the choices given, Choice C is the correct option at this time.
14. C	Understand that two activities are in discussion - Setting up the booth and toll charge. The toll charge is external mandatory but setting up the booth is internal (part of the contract), so you can set up the booth and let the toll charge decision happen in parallel.
15. C	This is a good question :) Crashing requires money. You can crash only when the CPI is > 1, i.e., and when the project has financial reserves.
16. C	Activity A has a duration of 2 weeks with a 10% probability of exceeding the timelines means that it is 80% probable that activity A will finish within 2 weeks.
17. D	Use the TRUE/FALSE technique:

A.   Leads are employed in limited circumstances to advance a successor activity on the predecessor activity. TRUE

B.   Lags are used in limited circumstances to delay a successor activity on the predecessor activity. TRUE

C.   Crashing shortens the schedule duration for the least incremental cost by adding resources. TRUE

D.   Fast tracking is a technique used to shorten the schedule duration for the least incremental cost by adding resources. FALSE, In fast-tracking, the activities are performed in parallel.

Out of all the choices, Choice D is incorrect and is hence the correct option.

7. COST MANAGEMENT

TOPICS WE COVER IN THIS CHAPTER

→ Estimation Techniques	→ Cost Of Quality
→ Funding Limit Reconciliation	→ EVM: CPI, SPI, SV, CV, ETC, EAC, PV, EV, TCPI, EAC,
→ Reserve Analysis	→ Definitive Estimates
→ Product Analysis	→ ROM Estimates
→ Reserve Types	→ Agile Project Costs

PROJECT: MOVIE

My daughter was planning to watch a movie with her friends. They discussed how much money each of them was supposed to put in to make it work, who would handle the money and how it would be spent. After all these discussions with her friends, she came over and asked me for the money.

I asked her – how much money do you need for this little project of yours to go out, watch a movie, and come back(Can you notice the WBS items?).

She told me:

→ Traveling = $20

→ Movie cost = $40

→ Snacks = $40

Hence, she needs a total of $100.

I asked her a few more questions, like who all coming along. Return timings etc.

And gave her $150. Why extra? Anything to cover for risks like cab prices etc.

So you can notice that estimates are from the team, but the final budget is arrived in consultation with the senior management.

Why should we be concerned with cost planning and monitoring?

One of the major focus is cost, specifically for fixed-scope projects. We need to complete the project within the approved budget.

7.1 COST MANAGEMENT OVERVIEW

Objective: Project Cost Management is concerned with the estimation and completion of the project within the baselined budget to complete the project.

Process Name	Process Group	Why
Plan Cost Management	Planning	Defining how what, when etc
Estimate Costs	Planning	Working with SMEs to estimate project costs
Determine Budget	Planning	Getting approval from management for the approved budget
Control Costs	Monitoring & Controlling	Planned Vs. Actual and Action

PROCESS FLOW

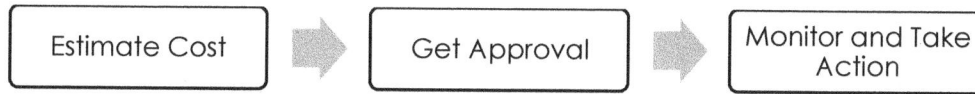

7.2 PLAN COST MANAGEMENT

The focus is on how costs will be estimated and controlled. Many times, the project cost estimation may be in $, but sometimes it could be in person-hours. Many IT projects are given resources, and budgets are based on the person-hour formula. Similarly, many other industries can use their own method to measure costs.

The Cost Management Plan describes how costs will be estimated and controlled. For a few industries, the cost can be person-hours like IT. Roadways project may calculate the cost in kilometers. What is the level of accuracy of estimates and other details?

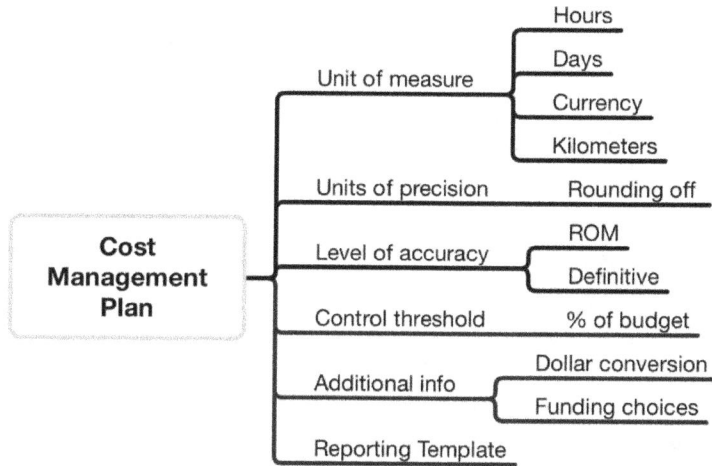

7.3 ESTIMATE COSTS

We estimate how much financial resources are required to complete project deliverables/activities.

Later, these estimates are used to get authorization from senior management to arrive at an approved budget. So, we need all the homework sorted to validate the estimates.

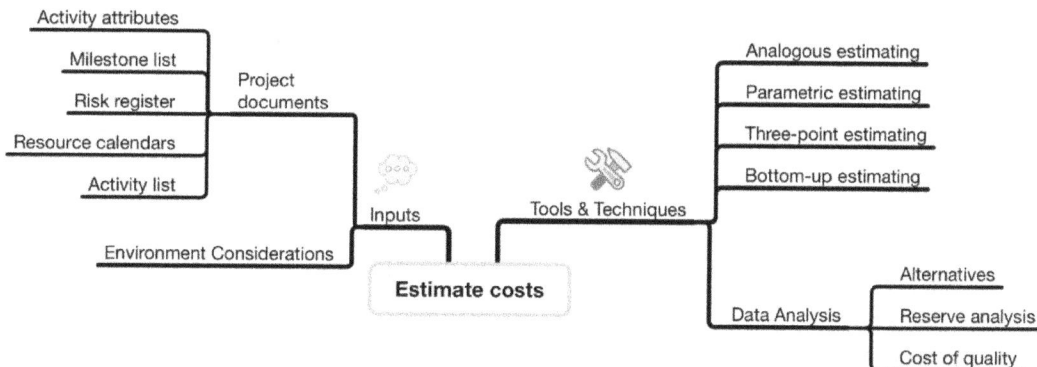

Also, note that all the estimates are an approximation. The approximation can deviate from actual costs. We need to remember the estimate ranges, which are:

ROUGH ORDER OF MAGNITUDE (ROM)
The Rough Order of Magnitude or Order of Magnitude is broad level estimations. They can deviate by -25% to +75%.

DEFINITIVE ESTIMATE
The more you move in execution, the better you will be able to estimate. These estimates are called Definitive Estimates and can be as accurate as -5% to +10%

To estimate cost, we use the same estimation techniques which we used earlier. **Let's recap:**

Estimation Technique	Also Called	Keyword	Description	Accuracy	When to use
ANALOGOUS	Top-down, quick and dirty estimates	**Similar**	Quick & easy estimate at the initial phases of the project	Less accurate than other methods	In the initial project phase, when details are not available
PARAMETRIC		**Calculations**	Calculation using some formulas, with the historical data as the basis	The estimates can go wrong if the base data is incorrect	When much historical data is present to calculate the unit cost
BOTTOM-UP	Detailed	**Adding estimates**	Breaking down to activity level and allocating cost, and then adding cost together is bottom-up	Most expensive (resource consuming) but very accurate	When the most accurate results are required, they can be used only in later stages of the project
THREE-POINT	PERT/ Average estimates	**Optimistic, pessimistic, and most likely parameters**	The estimates on expected duration can be arrived at using PERT or Average estimate formulas	Tends to provide a better estimate	When the risks are higher, the project needs to forecast with a confidence

7.3.1 LET'S PLAY: ESTIMATION TECHNIQUES

Select the estimation technique used in the scenarios:

1. The director of the business unit asked you to prepare estimates for a new project that your team will be undertaking. You gathered information from all possible sources of PMO/Peers/Historical data and used a calculation sheet to derive the estimate for the project.

    A. Bottom-up estimations

    B. Three-Point estimations

    C. Analogous estimations

    D. Parametric estimations

2. The senior management wanted to have quick and dirty estimates for a new RFP response. You consulted an architect and the pre-sales division and prepared a response based on a similar RFP that was bid last time.

    A. Bottom-up estimations

    B. Three-Point estimations

    C. Analogous estimations

    D. Parametric estimations

3. To come up with estimates for outsourcing a piece of work, you consulted the team leads on the probable pricing of the work. The risks were huge, so you derived the cost using optimistic, pessimistic, and most likely estimates

    A. Bottom-up estimations

    B. Three-Point estimations

    C. Analogous estimations

    D. Parametric estimations

4. To arrive at the final estimates, your new boss divided the work package among the team leaders and asked them to come up with detailed estimates by breaking down all the activities. He planned to add them together to come up with an overall estimate for the program.

    A. Bottom-up estimations

    B. Three-Point estimations

    C. Analogous estimations

    D. Parametric estimations

7.4 RESERVE ANALYSIS

Remember how, in the case study, I gave my daughter an extra budget than the cost estimates – why?

It was given to her to cover any risks that the project may encounter. Let's talk about risks and reserves.

CONTINGENCY RESERVES

To handle any risk in the project, the Project Manager sets aside some funds, also called contingency reserves.

The contingency reserves, once allocated, are part of the project budget, and the Project Manager controls them. Contingency reserves can be – additional money, extra time, extra resources, etc. You get the picture, right?

MANAGEMENT RESERVES

The senior management, which includes the program manager and portfolio manager, puts some funds aside to handle any risk that might arise in their portfolio or program.

Contingency Reserves	Management Reserves
The reserves which are kept in the project to work with any risk events	The sponsor keeps some money aside for all the projects/operations/programs.
The Project Team plans for it and use it. You can identify them as - Schedule buffer, Resource Buffer, Cost buffer etc	The Team does not own the funds and it is not considered as part of the budget
The PM has full control on it.	PM gets approval for this budget when the team asks from the sponsor (Think RED color Status Report)

These reserves are not in the project budget. The Project Manager has no control over these funds but may ask for them if and when any big, unforeseen risk emerges. The senior management may allocate a few funds from the management reserves to the Project Manager. Think of a dashboard that you prepare that shows a RED color status. The RED color signifies that you are asking for either more funds, more time, or more human resources. The senior management may then allocate more resources from the management funds.

7.4.1 LET'S PLAY: RESERVE TYPES
Select the correct reserves.

1. You are a Project Manager. You kept some reserve to address risks in your project while estimating costs. Project Cost Baseline consists of this reserve.

    A.   Management Reserve

    B.   Contingency Reserve

2. You have encountered a procurement risk that you did not plan for during Planning. So, you do not have adequate funds to manage it. You approach your senior management for funds.

    A.   Management Reserve

    B.   Contingency Reserve

3. You, the Project Manager, manage and control this reserve.

    A.   Management Reserve

    B.   Contingency Reserve

4. You, the Project Manager, do not administer and control this reserve.

    A.   Management Reserve

    B.   Contingency Reserve

COST OF QUALITY
While planning for costs, you need to calculate the overall cost of quality. Some examples of quality costs are testing costs, failure costs, etc. How many testers do we use? All the costs should be counted and estimated.

7.5 DETERMINE BUDGET
The process of aggregating the estimated costs of activities and work packages is to arrive at a Budget, also called Cost Baseline, in consultation with the funding authority.

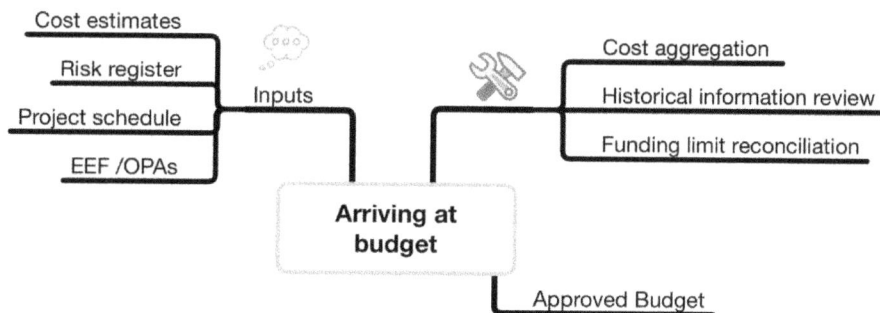

The next step is to get the budget approved and funds allocated to the project. This is done along with senior management to arrive at the funding schedule and get the budget baseline (do you remember the definition of baseline??).

To understand the funding pattern and overall cost baseline, let's understand how a large project like a highway of 100 miles is constructed.

Are you given the funds for the entire construction? No - rather, you are allocated funds for the next 10 miles only (or one phase). This means that as per planned milestones, the project would be getting the agreed-upon funds. It is also agreed that your project will get a total of 1 million as funds. This is called Cost Baseline, or Budget in other words.

COST AGGREGATION

Your management takes all costs estimated by you and your team and may add overhead costs to arrive at the overall spending required on the project.

RESERVE ANALYSIS

The management might also inspect the risks and may consider revising both contingency reserves as well as management reserves. Understand that the management reserves are not in a Project Manager's control and are not within the project budget.

EXPERT JUDGMENT

Discussion with SMEs can lead to an overall consensus on a baseline budget.

HISTORICAL INFORMATION REVIEW

The senior management will consider another project of similar nature and historical information to see the pattern before arriving at the overall budget.

FUNDING LIMIT RECONCILIATION

Funding Limit Reconciliation is checking whether the project has enough money or person-hours to carry out planned activities as per the plan.

Reserve Analysis is to be done to see if the project has enough contingencies (cost buffers, resource buffers, Schedule buffers, etc.)

A funding Limit analysis is done for each phase to see if the project has enough funds to complete all the tasks and complete planned activities.

COST CALCULATIONS FOR AGILE PROJECTS?

For agile projects, the iteration is fixed, and the resources are fixed. Do we estimate the cost of agile projects?

Not actively.

We may calculate the total cost for iterations and the overall cost of the releases/product.

7.6 EARNED VALUE MANAGEMENT

Video Available (YouTube)

SEARCH THIS TOPIC AT THE CHANNEL

Earned Value Management (EVM) is a methodology that uses certain variables to assess project performance on Cost and Schedule.

EVM defines project progress objectively in the context of project Schedule and project cost. EVM uses some terms. If you understand them, then you should have no issues in dealing with the EVM questions in the PMP exam.

Term	Name	Formula	What Is It?
BAC	Budget at Completion	No formula	Approved Budget
PV	Planned Value	PV = BAC* Planned % Complete	What your schedule says you should have spent
EV	Earned Value	EV = BAC * Actual % Complete	How much work is completed, and the value is earned
AC	Actual Cost	No Formula	How much you've spent so far
SPI	Schedule Performance Index	SPI = EV/PV	Whether you're behind or ahead of schedule
SV	Schedule Variance	SV = EV-PV	How much ahead or behind schedule you are
CPI	Cost Performance Index	CPI = EV/ AC	Whether you're within your budget or not
CV	Cost Variance	CV = EV – AC	How much above or below your budget you are

BAC: BUDGET AT COMPLETION.
It is the overall budget or Cost Baseline that is approved for your project.
There is no formula. This is what is allocated to you.

PV: PLANNED VALUE
This is the amount of WORK, which should have been completed as per the project plan.

Formula: PV = BAC * Planned % Complete

EV: EARNED VALUE

This is the amount of WORK that is completed.

Can it happen on your project that you are supposed to complete a module in four days, and you have completed only 75% by the end of the fourth day? That's a normal scenario – right? So EV can be more or less than PV. We, as Project Managers, would be very happy if EV = PV, i.e., We did what we planned for.

Formula: EV = BAC * Actual % complete

AC: ACTUAL COST

This is the overall money that has been spent on the project while getting the project done.

This would be calculated by using Work Information Data (WPD)

To remember the formulas, just remember that EV always comes first. To calculate SPI or schedule variance, the other term to use is PV. To calculate CPI and cost variance, use AC.

	Name	Formula
BAC	Budget at Completion	No formula
PV	Planned Value	PV = BAC* Planned % Complete
EV	Earned Value	EV = BAC * Actual % Complete
AC	Actual Cost	No Formula

SPI (SCHEDULE PERFORMANCE INDEX)

How is your project doing with regards to schedule (behind/ahead or at par)?

CPI (COST PERFORMANCE INDEX)

How is your project doing with regards to Cost (Spending More/Less or at par)?

SV (SCHEDULE VARIANCE)

How much more or less is your project behind or ahead.

CV (COST VARIANCE)

How much more or less is your project spending.

TO-COMPLETE PERFORMANCE INDEX (TCPI)

To-Complete Performance Index (TCPI) is the required spending rate to complete the project work within the approved budget, i.e., Budget at Completion. In case of Budget at Completion (BAC) is no longer viable, you as a Project Manager must consider Estimate at Completion (EAC).

LET'S TAKE AN EXAMPLE

In a cricket match, the first team plays and sets the Total Target Runs required to win (BAC – Budget at Completion). The team going afterward chases the target to win the match. You must have often seen these two indices on the screen during the match:

→ Current Run Rate: the rate at which the team is making runs = CPI

→ Required Run Rate: the rate at which the team should make runs to win = TCPI

SUMMARIZING

→ Target/Total Runs to make = Budget at Completion (BAC)

→ Current Run Rate = Cost Performance Index (CPI)

→ Required Run Rate = To-Complete Performance Index (TCPI)

7.6.1 QUESTION EVM

A Project Manager is preparing the weekly status report. She was allocated 200 hours to complete the project. She spent 80 hours and had completed 40% of the work so far. As per the plan, she should have completed 50% of the work. Calculate SPI, SV, CPI, and CV of the project?

BAC = 200 Hours, AC = 80 Hours

PV = BAC * Planned % complete = 200 * 50% = 100

EV = BAC * Actual % complete = 200 * 40% = 80

SPI = EV/PV = 80/100 = .8, SV = EV- PV = 80 -100 = -20

CPI = EV/AC = 80/80 = .8

CV = EV – AC = 80 – 80 = 0

So what is the status of this project?

CPI is 1, which means that the project is **ON Budget**

SPI is less than 1, which means that the project is **Behind Schedule**.

If you are the PM of this project, what action will you take to control the project?

SUMMARIZING ONCE AGAIN

CPI < 1	CPI = 1	CPI > 1
Over Budget	On Budget	Under Budget
SPI < 1	SPI = 1	SPI > 1
Behind Schedule	On Schedule	Ahead of Schedule

7.6.2 EARNED VALUE MANAGEMENT FORMULAS

	Name	Formula	What is it?
BAC	Budget at Completion	No formula	Approved Budget
PV	Planned Value	PV = BAC* Planned % Complete	What your schedule says you should have spent
EV	Earned Value	EV = BAC * Actual% Complete	How much of the project's value you've really earned
AC	Actual Cost	No Formula	Actual spending on the projects
SPI	Schedule Performance Index	SPI = EV/PV	Whether you're behind or ahead of schedule
SV	Schedule Variance	SV = EV-PV	How much ahead or behind schedule you are
CPI	Cost Performance Index	CPI = EV/ AC	Whether you're within your budget or not
CV	Cost Variance	CV = EV – AC	How much above or below your budget you are
EAC	Estimate at Completion	EAC = BAC/CPI Mostly Used	The expected total cost of completing all work.
EAC	Estimate at Completion	EAC=AC+BAC–EV	If future work will be accomplished at the planned rate
ETC	Estimate To Complete	ETC = EAC - AC	The expected cost to finish the remaining work

7.6.3 LET'S PLAY: EVM SCENARIO1

You are working on a construction project for which you have a total budget of $30 Million. You check your records and find that you've spent $14 Million so far. The team has completed 40 percent of the project work, but when you check the schedule, it says that they should have completed 50 percent of the work. Calculate the SPI and CPI along with CV and SV.

7.6.4 LET'S PLAY: EVM SCENARIO2

A new Project Manager in your company has been asked to prepare a report for a project where the work is being performed at the budgeted rate. He asks for your help and provides these values to you.

BAC = $50,000,

Earned value (EV) = $25,000,

Planned value (PV) = $24,000 and

Actual cost (AC) = $28,000.

What is the value of Estimate At Completion (EAC)?

7.6.5 LET'S PLAY: EVM SCENARIO3

A project is estimated to cost $10,000 with a timeline of 60 days.

The manager, while preparing the dashboard, fills in the following information.

Days consumed = 50%

Project completion status = 40%

The actual costs spent so far are $3,000.

Calculate the Cost Performance Index, Schedule Performance Index, Schedule Variance, and Cost Variance.

7.7 MODULE END QUESTIONS - PMP STYLE

1. You are preparing the estimates for the project SPARTA. You discuss the data with a fellow Project Manager and get relevant information from the Project Management Office. Once you have the base data, you work out the estimate using function point analysis (A function point is a unit of measurement to express the amount of business functionality an information system, as a product, provides to a user. The cost, in dollars or hours, of a single unit is calculated from past projects). Which estimation technique did you use?

   A. Bottom-up

   B. Analogous

   C. Three Point

   D. Parametric

2. You're managing a highway construction project. Your total budget is $65,000, and there is a total of 7,500 hours of work scheduled on the project. You calculated further and found that your project has an SPI of 1.6 and a CPI of 0.9. What is the BEST thing to do?

   A. Reduce resources

   B. Put more resources

   C. Ask for more funds from management

   D. Trigger contingency reserves

3. EVM develops and monitors three key dimensions for each work package and control account: Planned Value (PV), Earned Value (EV), and Actual Cost (AC). What does EV-PV denote?

   A. Cost Difference

   B. Cost Variance

   C. Schedule Difference

   D. Schedule Variance

4. You are working on the transformation of a trading hub platform from one technology stack to a web-based. Your task is to provide integration points between various seller systems. You have 4 team members. There are 8 integration points to be completed. The project's total duration is 20 days. As per the plan, you should have completed at least 50% of the work by today, which is the end of day 10. You are worried that your team is already doing overtime, has spent 55% of the allocated hours, and was only able to complete 40% of the work. What is the CPI of your project?

   A. 0.8

   B. -64

   C. 0.73

   D. -96

5. Your team is working on the project KYC. The project duration is 20 days. As per the plan, you should have completed at least 50% of the work by the 10th day. You are worried that your team is already doing overtime and has spent 60% of the allocated hours and was only able to complete 45% of the work. What is the SPI of the project?

   A. 0.8
   B. 0.9
   C. 0.73
   D. 0.75

6. You are working on an SAP automation project named STS, for which you have a total budget of 3,000,000. STS spend recorded in the PMIS is 1,750,000. Currently, the STS team has completed 40% of the work. However, they should have completed 50% of the work as per the schedule. Calculate the CPI and CV.

   A. CPI is 0.69, CV is -550000
   B. CPI is 0.80, CV is 300000
   C. CPI is 1.69, CV is -550000
   D. CPI is 0.80, CV is -300000

7. You're managing a construction project named XPRESS. The total budget for project XPRESS is 65 million with a duration constraint of 6-months. The status report of project XPRESS shows the CPI of 1.2 and SPI of 0.7. What is the health of project XPRESS?

   A. Project XPRESS is ahead of schedule, and the cost is overspent.
   B. Project XPRESS is behind schedule, and the cost is under control
   C. Project XPRESS is ahead of schedule, and the cost is under control.
   D. Project XPRESS is behind schedule, and the cost is overspent

8. A project report shows CPI of 0.5, SPI of 1.2, and EAC of $1.5 million. What was the original budget assuming CPI is constant throughout the project?

   A. 750,000
   B. 3,000,000
   C. 7,500,000
   D. 300,000

9. A project shows CPI as 0.9 and SPI as 0.8. What does this information convey?

   A. The project is delayed
   B. The project is ahead of schedule
   C. The project work is per the plan
   D. Not adequate information provided

10. You are invited to a steering team meeting where you need to present the project's status to the audience. You are also asked to forecast the total estimated cost for the current cost performance in view. Which of the following EVM terms would be helpful to describe the information sought?

    A.   Budget at Completion

    B.   Actual Costs

    C.   Estimate at Completion

    D.   Estimate to Complete

11. The project NEIL has a CPI of .98 and SPI of .7. How is the project doing?

    A.   The project is ahead of schedule and is overspent

    B.   The project is ahead of schedule and is under budget

    C.   The project is behind schedule and is under budget

    D.   The project is behind schedule and is overspent

12. For any ongoing project, what does a negative Cost Variance indicate?

    A.   The Earned Value currently exceeds the Planned Value.

    B.   The Planned Value currently exceeds the Earned Value.

    C.   The Earned Value currently exceeds the Actual Cost.

    D.   The Actual Cost currently exceeds the Earned Value.

13. Rough Order of Magnitude Estimation has tolerances of

    A.   -50% to +50%

    B.   −25% to +75%

    C.   -15% to + 25%,

    D.   -5% to +10%

14. Which of the following statement is FALSE regarding Project Funding Requirements?

    A.   Funding requirements are derived from Cost Baselines

    B.   The total funds required are the Cost Baseline plus the contingency reserve amount

    C.   Funding usually occurs in incremental amounts that are continuous and hence appear as S-shaped curves

    D.   Management reserves are not part of the project Cost Baseline but are included in the budget for the project.

15. **Definitive Estimate tolerance is?**

     A.   -50% to +50%

     B.   −25% to +75%

     C.   -15% to + 25%

     D.   -5% to +10%

7.8 ALL ANSWERS

ANSWERS: 7.3.1 LET'S PLAY: ESTIMATION TECHNIQUES

Scenario	Estimation Type	Keyword
1.	Parametric	Calculations
2.	Analogous	Quick, Similar
3.	Three-Point	Optimistic, pessimistic, and most likely estimates
4.	Bottom-up	Detailed estimates by breaking down activities

ANSWERS: 7.4.1 LET'S PLAY: RESERVE TYPES

1. You are a Project Manager. You kept some reserve to address risks in your project while estimating costs. Project Cost Baseline consists of this reserve.	Contingency Reserve
2. You have encountered a procurement risk that you did not plan for during Planning. So, you do not have adequate funds to manage it. You approach your senior management for funds.	Management Reserve
3. You, the Project Manager, manage and control this reserve.	Contingency Reserve
4. You, the Project Manager, do not administer and control this reserve.	Management Reserve

ANSWERS: 7.6.3 EVM SCENARIO 1

TERM	DATA	VALUE
BAC		30,000,000
PV	50%	15,000,000
EV	40%	12,000,000
AC		14,000,000
CPI	EV/AC	0.86
SPI	EV/PV	0.8
CV	EV - AC	-2000000
SV	EV - PV	-3000000

ANSWERS: 7.6.4 EVM SCENARIO2

TERM	DATA	VALUE
BAC		50,000
PV	50%	24,000
EV	40%	25,000
AC		28,000
EAC	BAC/CPI	56,000
CPI	EV/AC	0.89
SPI	EV/PV	1.04
CV	EV - AC	-3,000
SV	EV - PV	1000

ANSWERS: 7.6.5 EVM SCENARIO3

TERM	DATA	VALUE
BAC		10,000
PV	50%	5,000
EV	40%	4,000
AC		3,000
EAC	BAC/ CPI	7,500
CPI	EV/AC	1.33
SPI	EV/PV	0.80
CV	EV - AC	1,000
SV	EV - PV	-1000

ANSWERS 7.7 MODULE END QUESTIONS

1. D	Parametric estimating is an estimating technique in which an algorithm is used to calculate cost or duration based on historical data and project parameters.
2. A	Since you are ahead of schedule, SPI >1, and performing slightly low on costs, CPI <1, the best thing to do would be to control the spending by reducing resources which is choice A.

3. D	Schedule Variance = EV – PV

4. C	TERM	DATA	VALUE
	BAC	Total Days	20
	PV	50%	10
	EV	40%	8
	AC	55%	11
	CPI	EV/AC	0.73

5. B	TERM	DATA	VALUE
	BAC	Total Days	20
	PV	50%	10
	EV	45%	9
	AC	60%	12
	SPI	EV/PV	0.9
	CPI	EV/AC	0.75

6. A	TERM	DATA	VALUE
	BAC	Total Days	30,00,000
	PV	50%	1,500,000
	EV	40%	1,200,000
	AC		17,50,000
	CPI	EV/AC	0.69
	SPI	EV/PV	0.8
	CV	EV - AC	-550,000
	SV	EV - PV	-300,000

7. B	SPI <1 conveys schedule delay and CPI >1 conveys cost under control.
8. A	EAC = BAC /CPI BAC = EAC * CPI BAC = 750,000
9. A	The project is behind schedule as SPI <1
10. C	Total cost at the end of the project is referred to as Estimate at Completion, and hence Choice C is most correct. Choice D, ETC is how much more money is required to complete.
11. D	Your project is behind schedule, and the budget is overspent. PMBOK does not use the words "under budget or over budget."
12. D	The formula for cost variance is EV- AC. That means that the actual cost spent on the project is more than the earned value of the project.
13. B	Rough Order of Magnitude Estimation has a range of -25% to + 75%

14. C	Funding requirements are an incremental ladder and not a continuous S curve. Funds are released periodically during a period post-reconciliation of activity resource requirements and funding limits for that period.
15. D	As more information is known, Definitive Estimates could narrow the range of accuracy to -5% to +10%.

8. DELIVERABLE QUALITY

TOPICS WE COVER IN THIS CHAPTER

→ Quality Planning	→ Quality Tools
→ Prevention vs. Correction	→ Deliverable Journey
→ Control Charts	→ Grade and quality
→ Inspection	→ Sampling
→ Matrix diagrams	→ Mind mapping
→ Affinity diagrams	→ Problem-solving
→ Scatter diagrams	→ Design for X
→ Check-sheet	→ Checklist

BHOPAL GAS TRAGEDY

The Bhopal disaster, also referred to as the Bhopal Gas Tragedy, was a gas leak incident in India. It is considered the world's worst industrial disaster resulting in 3,787 deaths and 558,125 injuries.

This was the cost of not maintaining quality.

This is the worst example, but I just wanted you to think about how drastically things can go wrong if the quality is not adhered to.

Bhopal gas tragedy was an extreme example where several checks and balances were ignored, causing this tragedy to occur.

Could we have avoided it? Wouldn't prevent this catastrophic event have been better than dealing with it when it happened? Yes – Any day.

8.1 QUALITY MANAGEMENT OVERVIEW

Objective: Quality Management's focus is to determine quality policies, objectives, and responsibilities so that the project will satisfy the needs for which it was undertaken and produce the desired deliverables by preventing errors.

Process Name	Process Group	Why
Plan Quality Management	Planning	Defining standards, checklists, Audits cycle, test approach, and matrices
Manage Quality	Executing	Performing audits
Control Quality	Monitoring and Controlling	Internal Testing of the completed deliverables

Quality Management is to plan the quality activities that allow for both prevention (ensuring that error does not crop up in the product) as well as a correction (ensuring that you find out the bug/issue and correct it before the customer discovers it).

8.2 QUALITY AND GRADE

Before we move further, we need to understand the difference between Quality and Grade. Is there any difference? Most of us link grade with quality (the better the grade – the better the quality) or if more expensive -> better grade -> better quality.

This is INCORRECT. Why?

QUALITY
As per PMBOK: "Conformance to requirements" and "fit for use." Low quality is always a problem in a project.

GRADE
A category or rank is given to entities having the same functional use but different technical characteristics. A low grade may not be the problem. **Let us understand quality and grade with an example:**

My daughter uses a pen from Reynolds - it writes well, and she is happy with the results.

My husband, on the other hand, uses a Cross pen - it is shiny, writes well, and he is happy with the pen. Is there a problem with the quality of either of the pens?

No – Both pens conform to requirements and are fit for use. The quality of both pens is fine. What is the difference? Only the grades – The technical specifications for both the products are different.

8.2.1 LET'S PLAY: QUALITY VS. GRADE
Monika needs a laptop for home office usage. She wants a laptop with at least a two-year warranty period as she plans to upgrade the laptop after two years and has no intentions of spending any money on the machine other than at the time of purchase. She has heard that the laptop may heat up and is specifically looking for one that does not heat up during at least 5 hours of continuous use. She wants a nice-looking laptop, preferably white. She finally bought a laptop. Associate each situation with quality or Grade:

1. **The laptop heats after one hour of usage.**

    A.   Quality
    B.   Grade

2. **The laptop has come with a one-year warranty.**

    A.   Quality
    B.   Grade

3.   The laptop has a glossy surface made of steel.

    A.   Quality
    B.   Grade

4.   The laptop has self-illuminating keys, a useful feature when working at nighttime.

    A.   Quality
    B.   Grade

5.   Monika placed her order for a white laptop but received a black one.

    A.   Quality
    B.   Grade

8.3 PLAN QUALITY

The process of identifying quality requirements & standards for the project and its deliverables and documenting how the project will demonstrate compliance with it.

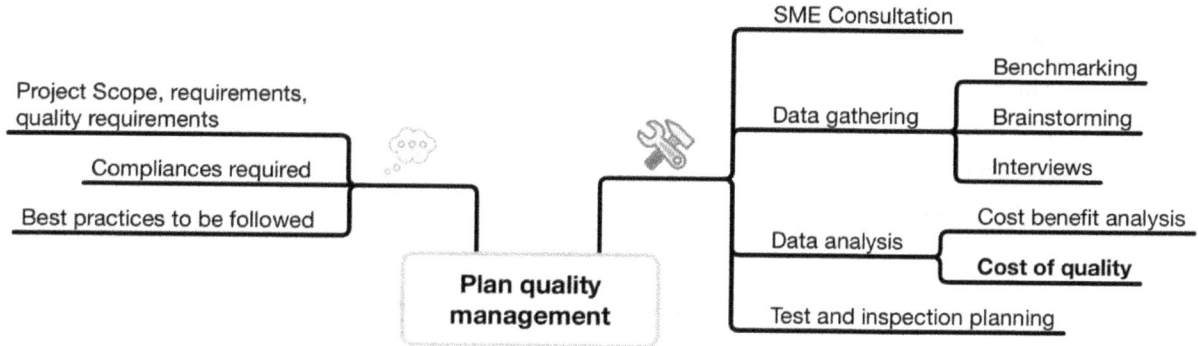

COST-BENEFIT ANALYSIS

ABC firm put a 1:1 ratio of programmer vs. tester whereas XYZ firm has a ratio of 4:1. Both are delivering quality products. However, it shows how much each organization or project put in to achieve the required quality as well as the required gain from investing in quality.

COST OF QUALITY (COQ)

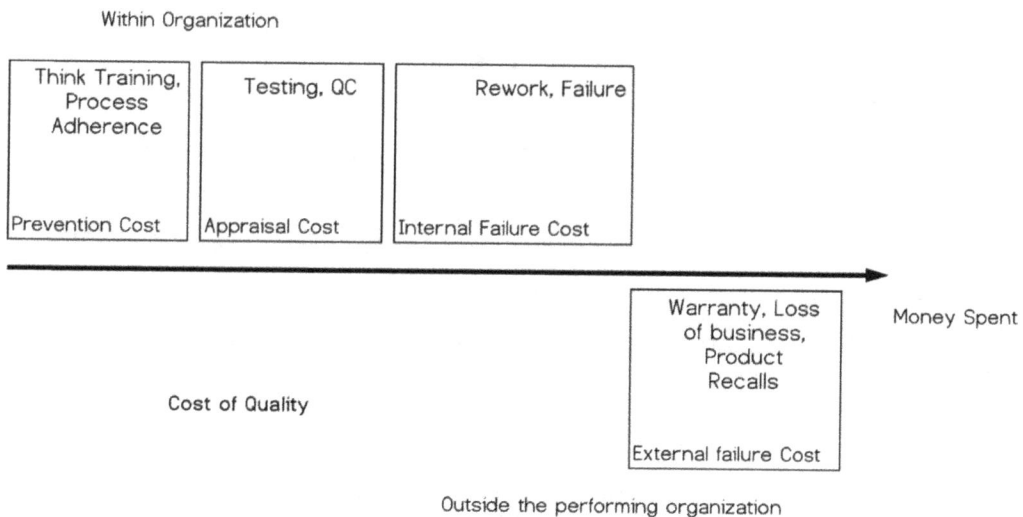

Cost of quality includes all costs incurred over the life of the product, which can be categorized as:

→ Investment in preventing non-conformance to requirements (Quality Assurance)

→ Appraising the product or service for conformance to requirements (Quality Control)

→ Failing to meet requirements (Rework)

→ Customer finding the problem is a huge cost and should be kept in mind while planning for quality management

TEST AND INSPECTION PLANNING:

As a project team, you will ensure the number of test cycles and testing methodologies so that the product which is handed over to the customer is usable and defect-free.

8.4 MANAGE QUALITY

Manage Quality focus on implementing the standards and auditing them to prevent defects.

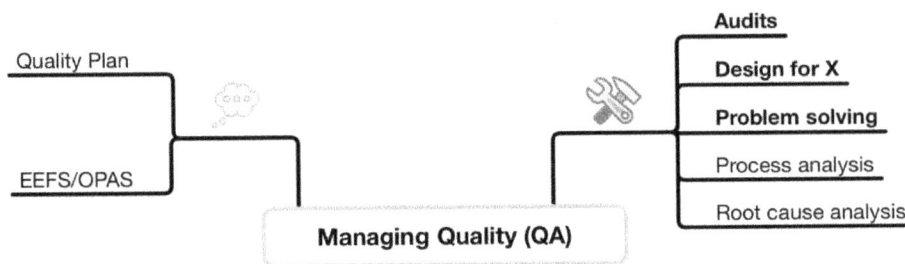

AUDITS

A quality audit is a structured, independent process to determine if project activities comply with organizational and project policies, processes, and procedures. The objectives of a quality audit may include:

→ To identify all good and best practices being implemented;

→ To identify all nonconformity, gaps, and shortcomings;

→ To share good practices introduced or implemented in similar projects in the organization and industry;

→ To proactively offer assistance in a positive manner to improve implementation of processes to help the team raise productivity; and

→ To highlight contributions of each audit in the lessons learned repository of the organization.

DESIGN FOR X

Also referred to as DfX, these are technical guidelines to design for a particular attribute. For example, a few products will be designed for safety, and a few may be inclined towards usability.

DESIGN FOR SUPPLY CHAIN

A product can be developed from the beginning to be supply chain efficient. The idea is to design the new product and its supply chain in a simultaneous manner. Traditionally, the supply chain was an afterthought (created after the product design phase was complete), which would result in a longer cycle time and fewer profits.

QUALITY IMPROVEMENT METHODS
Quality improvements can be achieved using tools like 6 Sigma or PDCA methodologies.

8.5 CONTROL QUALITY
Control Quality is focused on checking the deliverables to ensure that the deliverables conform to the requirement/specifications.

After the deliverables are made by the team, what happens next? Do you hand it over to the customer for acceptance testing? No, you don't. Your team tests the finished deliverables for any defect.

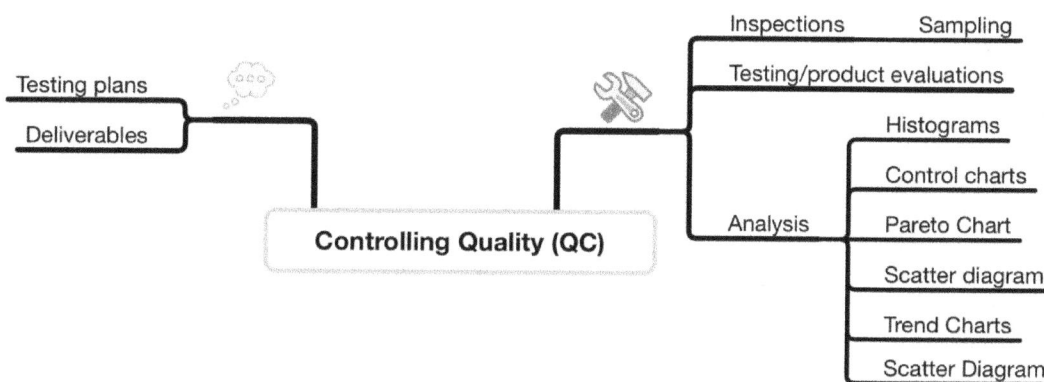

CORRECTIVE ACTION
Suppose the deliverables need to be corrected. You correct it once and send it again for the testing(QC).

PREVENTIVE ACTION
Determine if the process needs to be changed in order to get better quality of deliverables.
Summarizing

STATISTICAL SAMPLING
Statistical sampling involves choosing part of a population of interest for inspection.
An example can be: Selecting ten engineering drawings at random from a list of seventy-five.
Why should you use sampling? Sampling reduces the time and costs.

ATTRIBUTE SAMPLING (BOOLEAN)
The result either conforms or does not conform. Results in a Yes or NO. It can be captured using a checklist.

VARIABLE SAMPLING

Data is in the "variable" form, and the result is rated on a continuous scale that measures the degree of conformity

E.g., 80% of people know configuration management.

INSPECTION

Referred to as reviews, peer reviews, audits, or walkthroughs. Examining the deliverable and checking whether it conforms to the specification or not.

TESTING/PRODUCT EVALUATIONS

Organized and structured investigation to find defects in the produced deliverables. Different domains may need specific testing. For example, a software application may need unit testing, integration testing, and system testing.

8.6 TOOLS FOR QUALITY

CAUSE AND EFFECT DIAGRAM

Also known as fish-bone diagrams or as Ishikawa diagrams. The problem is the Head of the Fish, and all the probable causes are listed. The fishbone diagram could be industry-specific or could be standardized, showcasing primary and secondary causes.

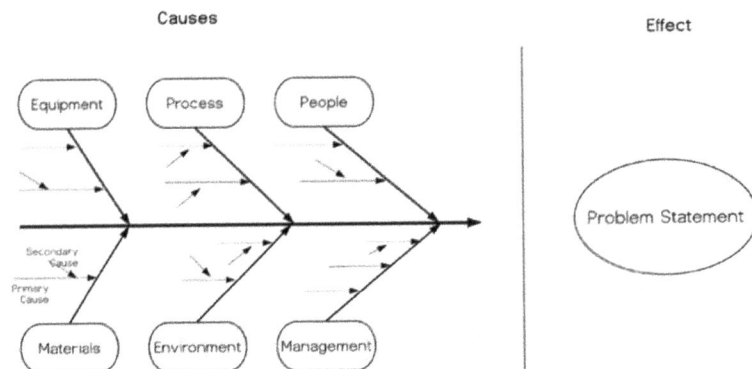

HISTOGRAM

You have a problem in real life or in operations that is reoccurring. What would you do?

Hmm, you would do Root Cause Analysis (RCA). But what after RCA??

You might want to visually compare all the root causes to eliminate the top few. You do it by plotting a histogram.

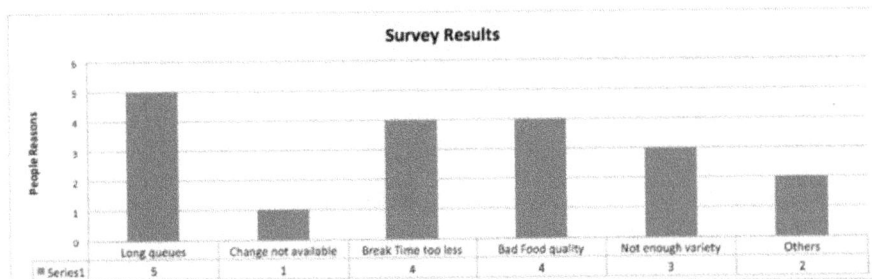

Matrix Diagram

Data is represented using various representations. The relationship can be represented using matrix charts. There are various representations available using L, T, Y, C, X, and roof-shaped matrix.

You can learn more about matrix charts here:

http://asq.org/learn-about-quality/new-management-planning-tools/overview/matrix-diagram.html

Mind Mapping

Visual representation of related ideas.

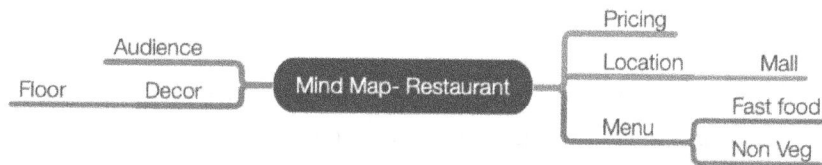

FLOWCHARTS

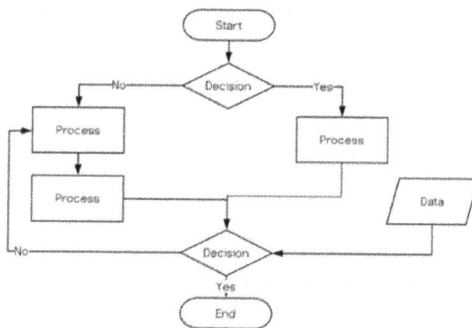

Flowcharts are used to analyze the process to find out unnecessary waiting time or non-usable process components and hence are also referred to as process maps.

Trend Charts

Single variable plotted over a period of time.

Gold prices

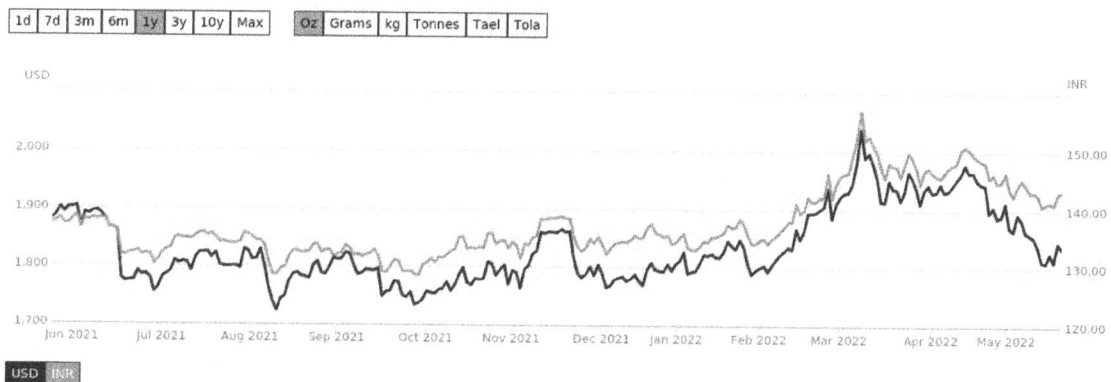

SCATTER DIAGRAMS

Scatter diagrams are also called correlation charts. It shows a relationship between 2 variables.

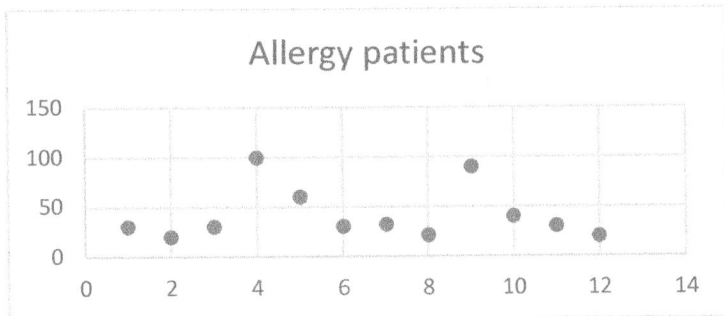

CHECKLISTS

A checklist is an easy way to implement a standard. The corresponding standard requirements are listed in a usable manner, and the concerned user will conform to the listed items.

CHECK-SHEETS

Also known as tally sheets.

Do not confuse them with the checklist. Checklists are data points/checking points with Yes and No tick marks. The check sheets have columns for data.

Checklist Vs Checksheet

CONTROL CHARTS

Control Charts are used to determine whether or not a process is stable or has predictable performance.

Upper and lower specification limits are based on the requirements of the agreement. They reflect the maximum and minimum values allowed. There may be penalties associated with exceeding the specification limits.

For repetitive processes, the control limits are set at ±3 sigma around a process mean.

A process is considered out of control when:

- A data point exceeds a control limit
- Seven consecutive plot points are above the mean
- Seven consecutive plot points are below the mean

OBSERVATIONS:

Sample Data Points

MEAN/CENTERLINE

A centerline is drawn at the value of the mean of the statistic

UPPER AND LOWER CONTROL LIMITS

- Indicate the threshold at which the process output is considered statistically 'unlikely.'
- 3+- standard errors from the centerline
- **If the process goes above this limit, corrective action must be taken.**

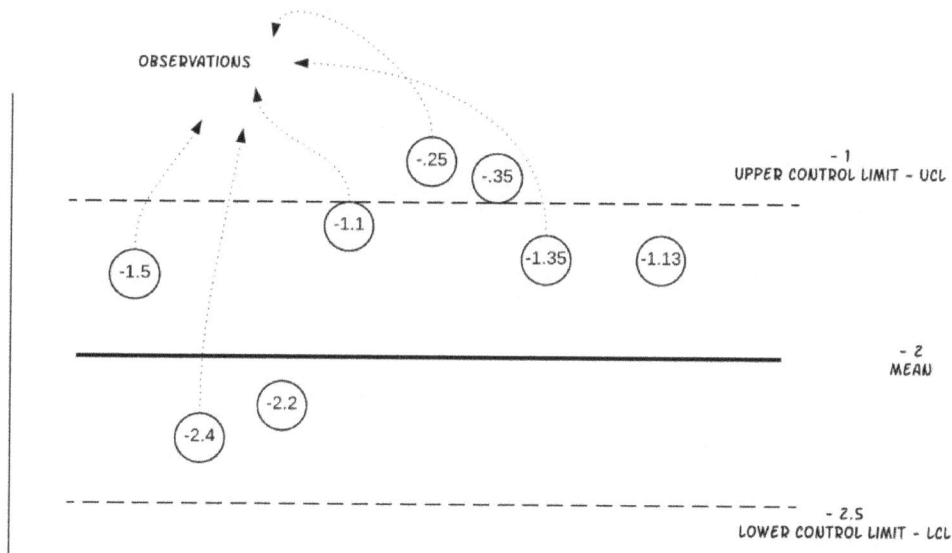

UPPER AND LOWER SPECIFICATION LIMITS

- Provided in the contract, and you cannot cross them.

WHAT IS THE RULE OF SEVEN?

- It is a rule of thumb or heuristic.
- It refers to non-random data points grouped together in a series that total seven on one side of the mean.
- The rule of seven tells you that although none of these points are outside of the control limits, they are not random, and the process may be out of control.
- This type of situation needs investigation, and a cause should be found.

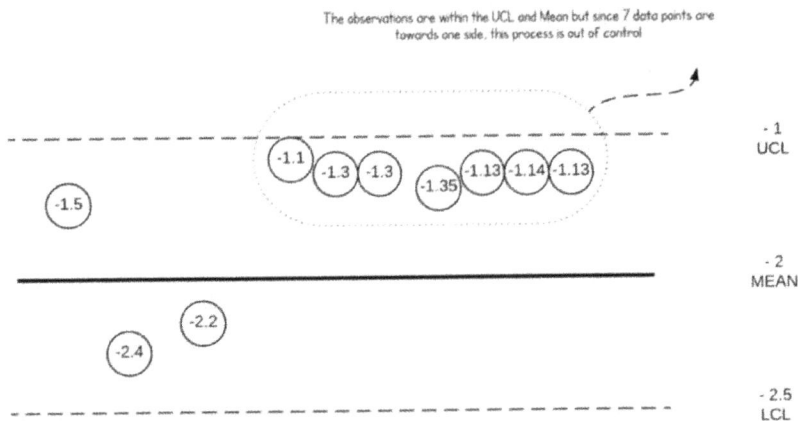

The observations are within the UCL and Mean but since 7 data points are towards one side, this process is out of control

8.6.1 LET'S PLAY: CONTROL CHART

Please refer to the observations below for a control variable X:

-1.5, -2.4. -2.2, -1.1, - .25, -.35, -.1.35, -1.13

The UCL is -1 and LCL is – 2.5 and the mean is -2.

Please select the correct statement.

A. The process is IN control

B. The process is OUT of control as one of the observations lies beyond the control limit

C. The process is OUT of control as Rule of Seven applies

D. Not enough information available

8.6.2 LET'S PLAY: QUALITY TOOLS

Match the quality tools used in the scenarios:

Scenario	Quality Tool
1. Costs incurred over the life of the product by investment in preventing nonconformance to requirements, appraising the product or service for conformance to requirements, and failing to meet requirements	Flow Charts
2. Also referred to as process maps because they display the sequence of steps and the branching possibilities that exist for a process that transforms one or more inputs into one or more outputs.	Cost of Quality (COQ)
3. The problem statement placed at the head of the fish-bone is used as a starting point to trace the problem's source back to its actionable root cause	Histogram
4. Vertical bar chart is used to identify the vital few sources that are responsible for causing most of a problem's effects.	Control Charts
5. _____ are used to determine whether or not a process is stable or has predictable performance. Upper and lower specification limits are based on the requirements of the agreement.	Fish Bone Diagram

8.6.3 LET'S PLAY: QA VS. QC

Scenarios depict some actions. These actions are taken to ensure the quality of the product.

Select the process where the actions are taken:

1. The applications developed by your team had many errors, and it was reoccurring. Things like using a variable without context, etc. To control, you defined coding standards.

    A.   Manage Quality (QA)

    B.   Control Quality (QC)

2. You work in a cheese factory as a cheese taster. Some of the cheese you tasted was rejected because it did not conform to the quality standard.

    A.   Manage Quality (QA)

    B.   Control Quality (QC)

3. You work as a magazine editor for a leading fashion brand. You have created a Quality Task Force that is responsible for proofreading and reviewing the content before anything is published.

    A.   Manage Quality (QA)

    B.   Control Quality (QC)

4. Your team is working on a website development project for one of your clients. Before starting the project, you organized training to share the best practices of website development with your team. You also shared with them the lessons learned from previous similar projects.

    A.   Manage Quality (QA)

    B.   Control Quality (QC)

5. You work as a marketing manager. You have bought a subscription for an application that checks your marketing collateral for errors and formatting before it is released.

    A.   Manage Quality (QA)

    B.   Control Quality (QC)

8.7 PROBLEM SOLVING

Problem-solving would be required in various project stages and is vital for managing project issues. Listed are typical steps to solve a problem:

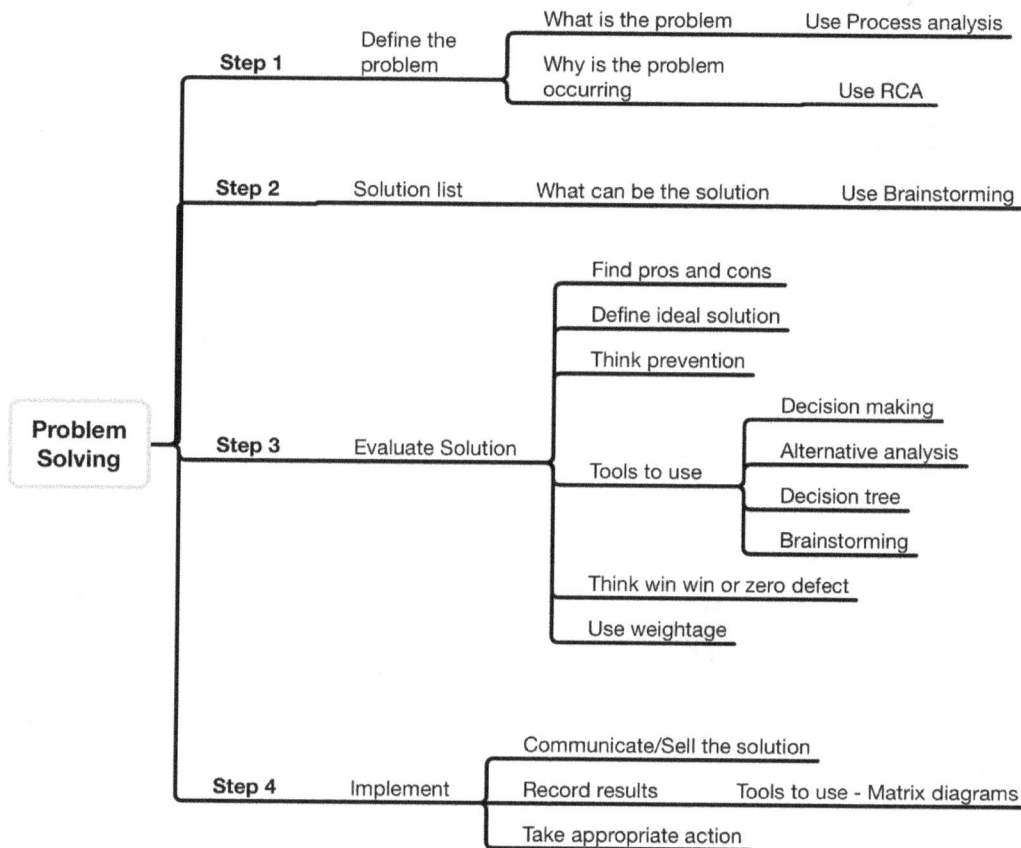

8.8 PERFORM QUANTITATIVE RISK ANALYSIS

Quantitative Risk Analysis is performed on more significant risks to establish the quantifiable threat. It requires a large quantity of data and analysis and is an optional process.

This process requires a lot of data to be gathered before analyzing the risk can happen. For example: is there a risk of rain today?

The meteorological department will gather an abundance of information on the past trends, and then this information is simulated to check the chances of rain in XYZ location.

A TYPICAL OUTPUT OF THE PROCESS IS:

-   With a confidence level of 50%, the project would finish in 100 days
-   With a confidence level of 90%, the project may finish in 150 days.

STEP 1: GATHER DATA

To do quantitative analysis, you need a lot of data, as was mentioned earlier.

What are your sources of data?

For specific projects – it could be sensors—for example, weather forecasts, power plant sensors, and controller readings.

For some projects, this could be collected using surveys, questionnaires, interviews, etc.

We may get data from overall customer behavior or website traffic for some projects.

STEP 2 : REPRESENT DATA

With huge data, the representation need more complex tools. Few tools are

- Graphs
- Trend charts
- Tornado diagrams

STEP 3: ANALYZE DATA

Uses techniques like Modeling and Simulation, EMV. Lets Understand them:

MODELING AND SIMULATION

Once you have Optimistic, Pessimistic, and Most Likely Estimates, tools like Microsoft Project Server can be used for the simulation that can provide you with the simulated results. You can use modeling to simulate the project costs or project schedule.

The given diagram shows the Monte Carlo Simulation for total project costs:

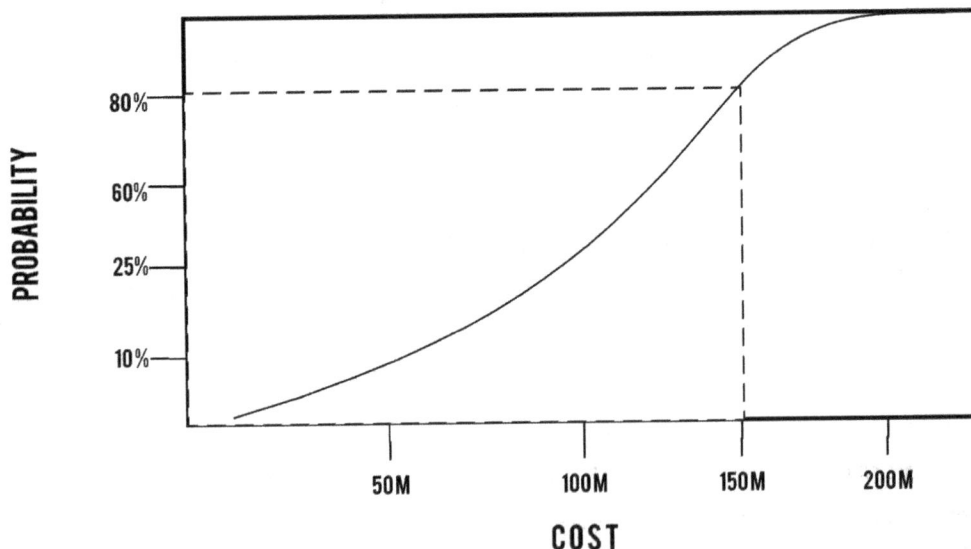

THE DIAGRAM SHOWS THAT THE SOFTWARE PREDICTS WITH A 75% CONFIDENCE LEVEL THAT THE PROJECT WILL COMPLETE WITH A SPEND OF $140 MILLION.

SENSITIVITY ANALYSIS
TORNADO DIAGRAM

Sensitivity analysis helps decide the risks that have the most potential impact on the project.

For example, if I'm the owner of the Umbrella manufacturing organization, I need to find out all the factors that can influence the sale and revenue of the product for:

- Rain or no rain
- Price competitiveness
- Availability of the product
- Marketing effectiveness

These can be shown using a tornado diagram to showcase the sensitivity of each effect on the total sale of the umbrella.

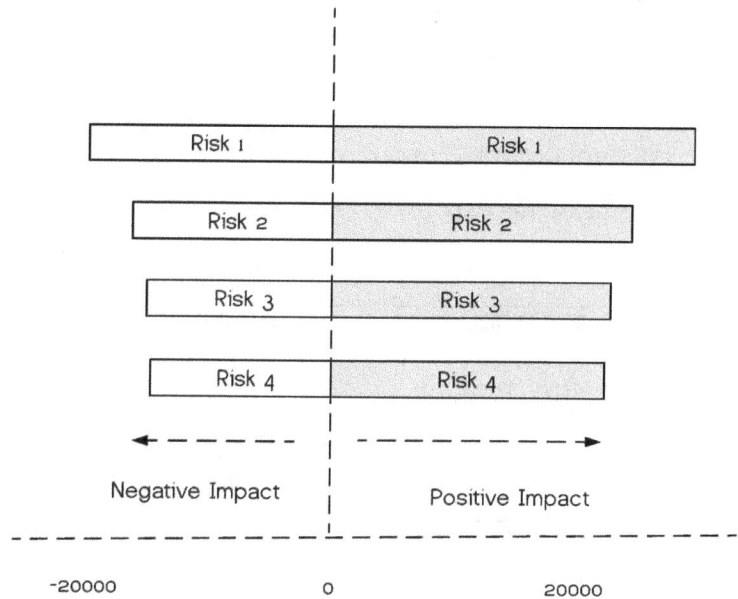

A tornado diagram looks like this: (a tornado, right.)

We see from the tornado diagram that Risk1 carries the most effect on the entire project objectives and should be treated well.

EXPECTED MONETARY VALUE (EMV)

Expected Monetary Value (EMV) analysis is a mathematical concept that calculates the average outcome when the future includes scenarios with probabilities of possibilities.

The EMV of opportunities will usually be expressed as positive values, while those of threats will be negative.

LET'S LEARN EMV USING AN EXAMPLE:

You have the following data:

You are on an expedition for wildlife photography. You are taking costly equipment with you. There is a risk of high winds of high probability and high impact. You decided to buy tents for the risk response. Please select which tent to buy. You have the following information:

Cost

- Heavy tent: $350/-
- Lighter Tent: $130

Chance Of High Winds: 35%

Loss expected if you buy the Heavy Tent:

- High Winds: $48
- Low Winds: $10

Loss expected if you buy the Light Tent:

- High Winds: $953
- Low Winds: $15

By analyzing this data, you can infer that you need to buy a specific tent but think about the scenarios that may be more complex and will contain complex scenarios and paths with different probabilities and values.

LET'S DRAW THE DATA USING EMV:

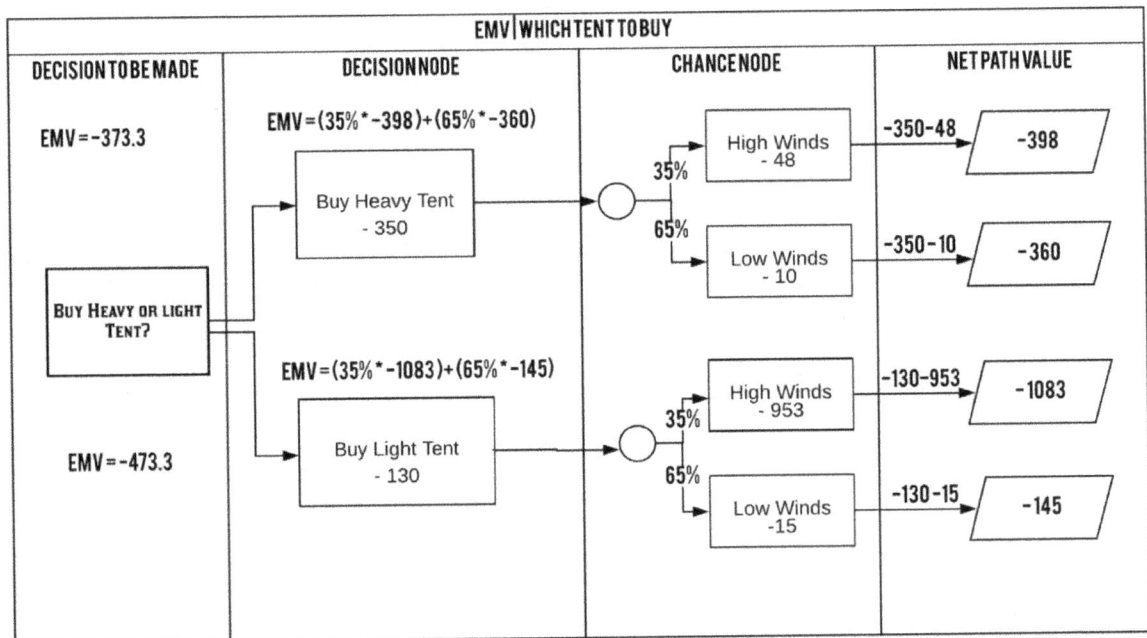

EMV | WHICH TENT TO BUY			
DECISION TO BE MADE	**DECISION NODE**	**CHANCE NODE**	**NET PATH VALUE**

EMV = -373.3

EMV = (35% * -398) + (65% * -360)

Buy Heavy Tent - 350

35% High Winds - 48 → -350-48 → -398

65% Low Winds - 10 → -350-10 → -360

BUY HEAVY OR LIGHT TENT?

EMV = -473.3

EMV = (35% * -1083) + (65% * -145)

Buy Light Tent - 130

35% High Winds - 953 → -130-953 → -1083

65% Low Winds -15 → -130-15 → -145

Don't get scared by the picture. It's straightforward.

first of all, we need to represent the data.

→ The first node is the DECISION NODE. In this node, just write the decisions.

→ The second part is the decisions node, draw rectangles and write the alternate decisions, one node for one decision.

→ The third node is Probability or Chance. In the current case, the winds have a probability associated. Write the probability for the High Winds and Low Winds.

Now, we write all the values that are provided to us. For example, how much money is spent if we buy a heavy tent? Write that value. In case of high winds, there are losses. Write the value provided here.

→ We draw the NET PATH VALUE as the last nodes.

At any point in time, only one path can be true. So, let's calculate what one of the paths will say if we buy the light tent:

If we buy a light tent, then we spend $130. Since money is out, it should be shown as negative.

If there are LOW WINDS on that day, then losses are -$15.

If this path becomes TRUE, the total money out from the project is: (-130) +(-15) = -145.

Now calculate all the other paths individually.

Arriving at the total cost of the decision:

IF YOU SELECT A DECISION, LET'S SAY, BUYING A HEAVY TENT.

Then the TOTAL COST OF THE DECISION is the addition of all path values with their probability distribution.

What does it mean?

→ Net path value for HIGH winds for heavy tent is -398.

→ Net path values for LOW windsfor heavy tent is -360.

The probability of high winds is 35%, and low winds is 65%.

→ TOTAL EMV = probability1 * net path value + …. + PraboabilytyN* Net path value

→ EMV for HEAVY tent = (35% * -398) + (65% * -360) = - 373.3

Similarly

EMV FOR LIGHT TENT = (35% * -1083) + (65% * -145) = - 473.3

Which decision would you select?

THE ONE WHERE EMV IS MOST POSITIVE OR THE ONE WHERE EMV IS LEAST NEGATIVE

So which decision will we take?

BUYING THE HEAVY TENT IS A BETTER DECISION, GIVEN THE DATA (LEAST NEGATIVE)

8.9 MODULE END QUESTIONS - PMP STYLE

1. _____ is an analytical technique used to determine the basic underlying reason that causes a variance, defect, or risk. (Fill in the blanks)

    A.   Process analysis

    B.   Alternative analysis

    C.   Root cause analysis

    D.   Document analysis

2. James is the newly appointed Project Manager of a security-related application development project. James wants to proactively make sure that each deliverable is up to the project's standards. Which of the following tools can help James?

    A.   Quality Management Plan

    B.   Process Improvement Plan

    C.   Quality Matrix Charts

    D.   Quality Checklists

3. Rachel has been assigned to look into the defects of all testing cycles. She is finding more and more defects per inspection cycle. She created a Quality Task Force to identify the cause of these defects. What action is taken by Rachel by forming the quality task force to identify the root cause so that they can be eliminated in future testing cycles?

    A.   Improve quality

    B.   Defect repair

    C.   Preventive action

    D.   Corrective action

4. Which diagramming technique can be used to show the relationship between two variables?

    A.   Matrix diagrams

    B.   Histogram

    C.   Flowcharts

    D.   Scatter diagram

5. Jane is using flowcharts to improvise the process followed by the team. She is using the PDCA approach to implement the changes. PDCA is also referred to as:

    A.   Juran circle

    B.   Philip Crosby circle

    C.   Deming circle

    D.   Ishikawa circle

6. Lisa is a Project Manager for a laptop manufacturing company. In one of the recent lines of new laptops introduced, a problem of overheating has been identified. Lisa decided to check the finished laptop at random to check for heating. Which process is performed by Lisa?

   A.   Audit
   B.   Control Quality
   C.   Manage Quality
   D.   Sampling

7. To capture the quality measurement data, one can use:

   A.   Performance reviews
   B.   Root cause analysis
   C.   Quality matrix
   D.   Control charts

8. You use a Pareto chart for the purpose of quality control. Which of the following statements is TRUE about Pareto charts?

   A.   50-50 principle (50 percent of all problems are due to 50 percent of the causes)
   B.   20-80 principle (20 percent of all problems are due to 80 percent of the causes)
   C.   80-20 principle (80 percent of all problems are due to 20 percent of the causes)
   D.   90-10 principle (90 percent of all problems are due to 10 percent of the causes)

9. Performing document reviews for the completed artifacts would be part of:

   A.   Inspection
   B.   Correction
   C.   Defect Repair process
   D.   Prevention

10. Kevin wants to compare the test results of the current cycle with the past cycles and find out the trends. Suggest the appropriate tool which he can use.

   A.   Histograms
   B.   Control chart
   C.   Scatter diagram
   D.   Cause and effect diagram

11. You are engaged in a book publishing project. Your team is checking the book contents for any grammatical mistakes (proofreading). This is achieved by using automated software. Which quality activity is performed by using the automated software?

    A.   Using automated software reduces the grammar mistakes by identifying the defects and hence should be classified as a corrective action.

    B.   Using automated software reduces the grammar mistakes by identifying the defects and hence should be classified as inspection.

12. As a result of similar defects in many deliverables, the team checked for the root cause and implemented an additional step in the process. This action of adding an additional check decreased the defects by a significant percentage. Changing the process to include the additional step is:

    A.   A preventive action

    B.   A corrective action

    C.   Defect repair

    D.   Process audit

13. Many deliverables were found with defects. The testing team sent the deliverables back to the developers so that they could correct the deliverable, and then the fixed deliverable could be resubmitted for the next testing cycle. How would you classify this scenario?

    A.   Preventive Action

    B.   Corrective Action

14. Correlation charts are also called:

    A.   Control Charts

    B.   Histograms

    C.   Scatter diagrams

    D.   Pareto diagrams

15. Your team is checking the book content for any grammatical errors using automated software. The result sheets are then sent to the author so that the author can correct them. Which activity is performed by the author?

    A.   Prevention

    B.   Correction

16. You work in aerospace, designing the aviation control panel. The emphasis is to simplify the control panel so that it is easier for the pilots to understand the indicators. The most useful tool to achieve the desired results would be:

    A.   Design for X

B.   User interface design

C.   Histograms

D.   Pie charts

17. Please help Ana to invest in preventive costs spent so that she can reduce the overall cost of quality in her project. What would these costs be considered?

A.   Training costs

B.   Inspections costs

C.   Reviews costs

D.   Warranty period costs

18. Which tool will help you to arrive at the root cause of any issue?

A.   The SIPOC Model

B.   Scatter diagrams

C.   Design of Experiments

D.   Ishikawa diagrams

19. Which of these is not an example of a tree diagram?

A.   Work breakdown structure

B.   Team structure

C.   Decision tree

D.   Control charts

20. Select the INCORRECT statement.

A.   Prevention is keeping errors out of the process.

B.   Prevention is keeping errors out of the deliverables.

C.   Correction is keeping errors out of the hands of the customer.

D.   Inspection is to keep errors out of the hands of the customer and is a preventive activity.

21. You have the following information: UCL 3, LCL -3. The mean is 0. The following observations are found. What can you deduce from the process results?

Observation no	1	2	3	4	5	6	7	8
Data	-2	-2.5	0.25	2	1.5	1	2.2	2.1

A.   The process is IN control.

B.   The process is OUT of Control because of Rule of Seven.

C.   The process is OUT of Control because one observation lies on the UCL.

D.   The process is OUT of Control because one observation lies on the LCL.

22. You have the following information: UCL 3, LCL -3. The mean is 0. The following observations are found are given. You found that the next observation is 2.2. How is the process state?

Observation no	1	2	3	4	5	6	7	8
Data	-2	-2.5	0.25	2	1.5	1	2.2	2.1

    A.   The process is IN control.

    B.   The process is OUT of Control because of the Rule of Seven.

    C.   The process is OUT of Control because one observation lies on the UCL.

    D.   The process is OUT of Control because one observation lies on the LCL.

8.10 ALL ANSWERS

ANSWERS: 8.2.1 LET'S PLAY – QUALITY VS. GRADE

1.	The laptop heats after one hour of usage.	Quality	Customer Requirement
2.	The laptop has come with a one-year warranty.	Quality	Customer Requirement
3.	The laptop has a glossy surface made of steel.	Grade	Technical specification
4.	The laptop has self-illuminating keys, a useful feature when working at nighttime.	Grade	Technical specification
5.	She placed her order for a white laptop but received a black one.	Quality	Customer Requirement

ANSWERS: 8.6.1 LET'S PLAY: CONTROL CHART

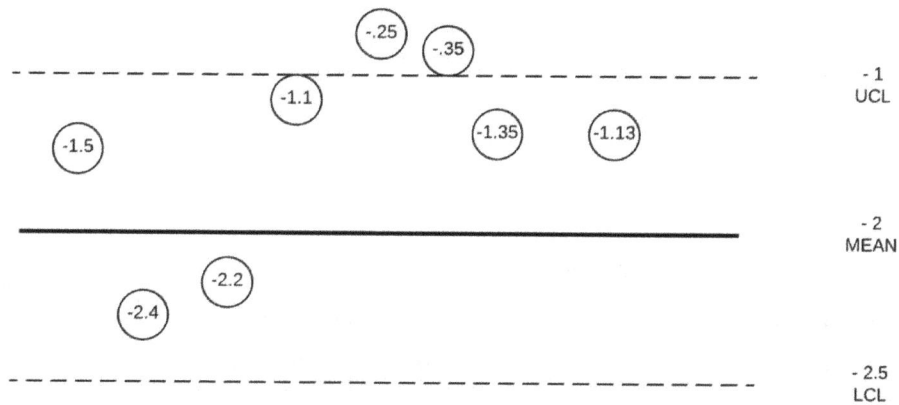

To find this, we need to draw a control chart with UCL and LCL, and then you can arrive at the correct answer.

You can infer that observation #5 is out of UCL, and hence the process is out of control.

Choice B would be the most appropriate answer.

ANSWERS: 8.6.2 LET'S PLAY: QUALITY TOOLS

Scenario	Quality Tool
1. Costs incurred over the life of the product by investment in preventing nonconformance to requirements, appraising the product or service for conformance to requirements, and failing to meet requirements	Cost of Quality (COQ)
2. Also referred to as process maps because they display the sequence of steps and the branching possibilities that exist for a process that transforms one or more inputs into one or more outputs.	Flow Charts
3. The problem statement placed at the head of the fish-bone is used as a starting point to trace the problem's source back to its actionable root cause	Fish Bone Diagram
4. Vertical bar chart is used to identify the vital few sources that are responsible for causing most of a problem's effects.	Histogram
5. _____ are used to determine whether or not a process is stable or has predictable performance. Upper and lower specification limits are based on the requirements of the agreement.	Control Charts

ANSWERS: 8.6.3 LET'S PLAY: QA VS. QC

Scenario	Answer	Why
1. The applications developed by your team had many errors, and it was reoccurring. Things like using a variable without context etc. To control, you defined coding standards.	Manage Quality	Defining coding standards will prevent errors from happening. Preventive actions are performed in Manage Quality processes.
2. You work in a cheese factory as a cheese taster. Some of the cheese you tasted was rejected because it did not conform to the quality standard.	Control Quality	Cheese is the end product if you test the product for faults that comes under Quality Control. The activity results in finding defects. You find defects in Control Quality Process.

3. You work as a magazine editor for a leading fashion brand. You have created a Quality Task Force that is responsible for proofreading and reviewing the content before anything is published.	Control Quality	Don't get fooled here by the word "Quality Task Force." Check what the work of the quality task force is. They are proofreading and reviewing the end deliverables. The activity results in finding defects. You find defects in Control Quality Process. The activity results in finding defects. You find defects in Control Quality Process.
4. Your team is working on a website development project for one of your clients. Before starting the project, you organized training to share the best practices of website development with your team. You also shared with them the lessons learned from previous similar projects.	Manage Quality	Training will eliminate the source of the defects and hence would be classified as preventive action. Preventive actions are part of the Manage Quality process.
5. You work as a marketing manager. You have bought a subscription for an application that checks your marketing collateral for errors and formatting before it is released.	Control Quality	Checking the deliverable can be automated, but this is again performed on the finished product to check for errors. QC, my friends. The activity results in finding defects. You find defects in Control Quality Process.

ANSWERS: 8.9 MODULE END QUESTIONS - PMP STYLE

1. C	Root cause analysis (RCA). Root cause analysis is an analytical technique used to determine the basic underlying reason that causes a variance, defect, or risk. A root cause may underlie more than one variance, defect, or risk. It may also be used as a technique for identifying the root causes of a problem and solving them. When all root causes for a problem are removed, the problem does not recur.
2. D	Quality checklists help to make sure that each repetitive deliverable is up to the project's standards.
3. C	RCA is a preventive measure to ensure that future deliverables are defect-free.
4. D	The Scatter diagram shows a relationship between the 2 variables.
5. C	PDCA (plan–do–check–act or plan–do–check–adjust) is an iterative four-step management method used in business for the control and continuous improvement of processes and products. It is also known as the Deming circle/cycle/wheel.
6. B	Checking the finished laptop for defects at random is sampling.
7. C	A quality matrix can be used to capture the quality data. Matrix diagrams help find the strength of relationships among different factors, causes, and objectives that exist between the rows and columns that form the matrix. Depending on how many factors may be compared, the Project Manager can use different shapes of matrix diagrams; for example, L, T, Y, X, C, and roof-shaped. They facilitate identifying the key quality metrics that are important for the success of the project.
8. C	The Pareto principle states that for many outcomes, roughly 80% of consequences come from 20% of the causes (the "vital few"). Other names for this principle are the 80/20 rule, the law of the vital few, or the principle of factor sparsity.
9. A	One can think of it as a preventive process, but it is not. If a deliverable is made and submitted for the next stage, any review on that deliverable is inspection. The result of a review process is defects/bugs/errors in the deliverables. The team then corrects the defects. A preventive process should have eliminated the defect in the first place, e.g., having a code review checklist.

10. A	Histograms are used to do a comparative analysis and can show a trend line with all the comparative data. Hence, Option A is the best answer.	
11. D	Using automated software reduces the grammar mistakes by identifying the defects and hence should be classified as a corrective action: FALSE Using automated software reduces grammar mistakes by identifying the defects and hence should be classified as inspection.: TRUE.	
12. A	Reducing future defects by changing the process is a preventive action.	
13. A	To update the deliverable so that the defects are eliminated from the deliverable is considered a defect repair activity.	
14. C	Correlation charts are also called scatter diagrams.	
15. D	Closing the defects is corrective action and takes place in the Control Quality process.	
16. A	Design for X, also referred to as DfX, means designing the products with some focus. Designing for usability would be the focus while designing the aviation control panel.	
17. A	Out of all the activities, the only preventive activity is training. Ana should spend more on training so that the team delivers a better, error-free product. Thus, reducing the overall cost of quality.	
18. D	The best tool to perform RCA is the Fish-Bone diagram, also called the Ishikawa diagram.	
19. D	Control charts are not hierarchical in nature and is the correct answer.	
20. D	Using TRUE/FALSE technique: A. Prevention is keeping errors out of the process: TRUE B. Prevention is keeping errors out of the deliverables: TRUE C. Inspection is keeping errors out of the hands of the customer: TRUE D. Inspection is to keep errors out of the hands of the customer and is a preventive activity: FALSE	
21. A	The process is in control because the observations have not exceeded the UCL/ LCL	
22. B	If you plot the graph, you will notice that 7 observations are above the mean	

9. PROCUREMENTS

IMPORTANT TOPICS FOR THE PMP EXAM

→ Project Manager's role in Procurements	→ Procurement SOW
→ Contract types	→ Make or Buy
→ Steps for buying	→ Selection criteria scenario
→ Control Procurements	→ Claim administrations
→ Inspection vs. Audit	→ Seller selection

CORE CONCEPT - PROCUREMENT

In all the other knowledge areas, you are working as a Project Manager, and you work for the performing organization. In the procurement knowledge area, that changes, and you act as a customer.

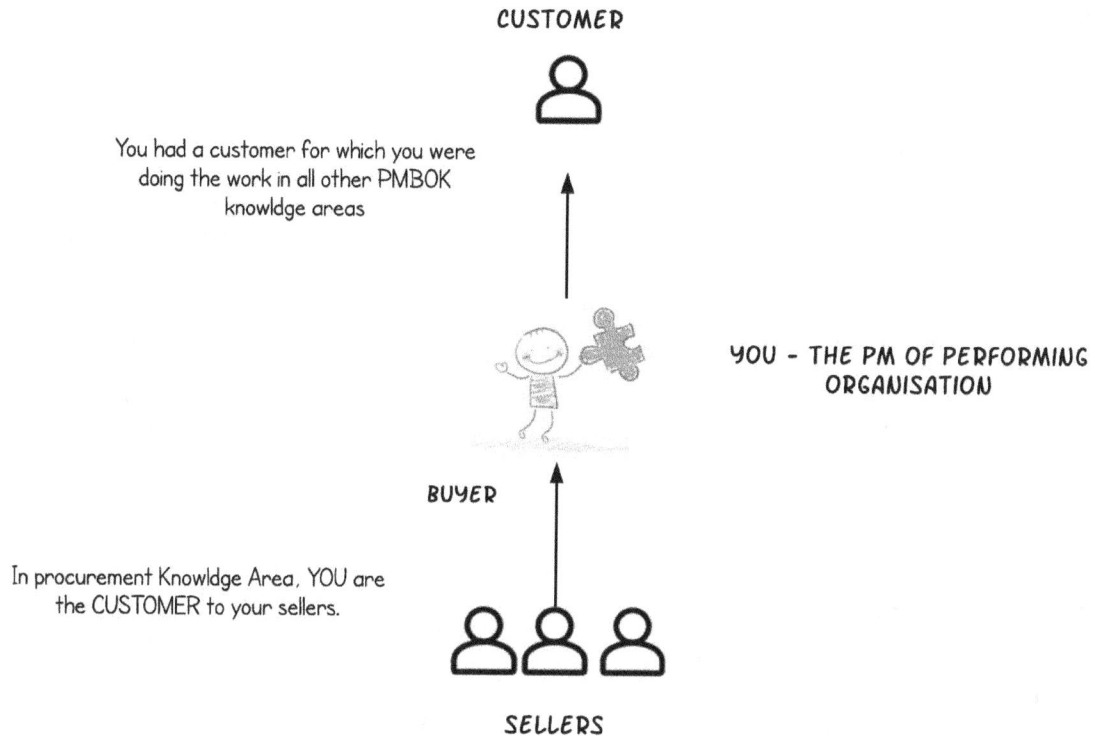

CUSTOMER

You had a customer for which you were doing the work in all other PMBOK knowldge areas

YOU - THE PM OF PERFORMING ORGANISATION

BUYER

In procurement Knowldge Area, YOU are the CUSTOMER to your sellers.

SELLERS

Since you are procuring from the outside, someone else would be doing the work for you. You become the CUSTOMER, and the SELLER would be the performing organization.

AN EXAMPLE

You are managing a software website for a customer. You need to host the software and need five SUN machines to host it at different locations (The hardware box). You cannot manufacture it and need to buy from a vendor. Now let's find out what actions are performed in which process of procurement management:

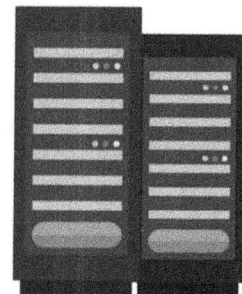

Activities	Process
Plan for when to buy, who is responsible for purchasing, and what type of machine/specification to get the product or shortlist seller	Plan Procurement Management

Advertise to the world/sellers asking for the quotes.

The seller may ask questions and respond, and once the

responses are collected, compare as per the qualifying **Conduct Procurements**

criteria and negotiate the final contract with the supplier.

Contracts are in place.

The supplier starts preparing the deliverables. Here, in this

case, it is a hardware box.

The box is shipped to the buyer (In this case you)

Once the deliverables arrive, check the box for all the

specifications and possible defects. Once satisfied, you will

receive the box and sign off on the receipt. **Control Procurements**

This may trigger some payment milestones as well.

The next set of machines will also go through the

acceptance cycle.

After the seller delivers everything, you initiate closure of

procurement.

9.1 PROCUREMENT MANAGEMENT OVERVIEW

Objectives: Procurement Management is about buying or acquiring products, services, or results from outside the project team.

Process Name	Process Group	Why
Plan Procurement Management	Planning	Planning what to buy, when to buy, how to buy
Conduct Procurements	Executing	Advertising and evaluating proposals and selecting the supplier
Control Procurements	Monitoring & Controlling	Managing results/services from suppliers, payments, and closing

One thing to note is that the deliverables from suppliers are received in Control Procurement. If you do not have products or services available, you buy from an outside organization or outside the department. The procurement could be as simple as Windows licenses, hardware boxes, or contractors (resources). Anything you acquire from outside the organization/group/department is managed in the Procurement Management knowledge area.

You, as Project Manager, do not deal in procurements but help the procurement team guide them as to what products/services are needed. The procurement team executes the negotiations and contracts

9.2 PLAN PROCUREMENTS

Plan procurements document what, how, and when a buying for the project will take place. Plan Procurement Management is part of the planning process group and results in documenting the analysis of make or buy, along with:

- What to buy (statement of work)
- When to buy
- What would be the contract terms?
- How to select the seller
- Do we need independent consultants?
- How to check for the quality of the deliverables
- When to release payments

Most of the Project Management Planning activities are carried out simultaneously and will constitute the integrated Project Management Plan.

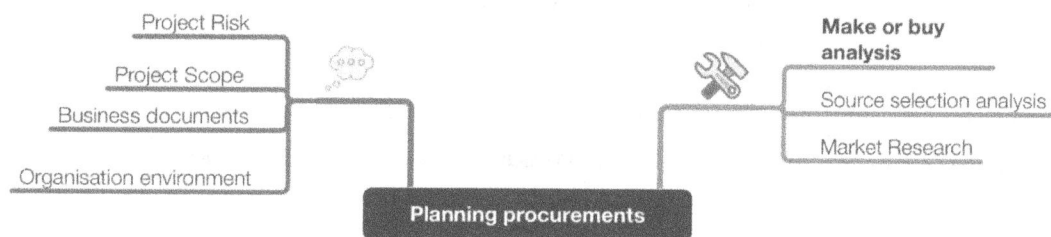

MARKET RESEARCH

You, or the procurement team, do the market research to see if the product or services are available in the market. If it is, then you will also research the price range and probable sellers.

MAKE-OR-BUY ANALYSIS

A make-or-buy analysis is a general management technique used to determine whether a particular work can best be accomplished by the project team or should be purchased from outside sources.

Various factors can influence the make or buy, such as:

- Is it cheaper to buy from outside?
- Is the workforce adequate within the current organization?
- Do we have enough ramp-up time?
- Is it too risky to be executed (Remember transfer as risk response)?

9.3 TYPES OF CONTRACTS

SCENARIO 1:

I want to get a custom-made dinner table and chair set. The dinner table's design is documented in detail and taken from one of the home furnishing magazines.

I called the carpenter and showed him the design. He had a few questions, and I had all the answers at that time, not requiring any research. After all the detailing on design, wood type, and color, I asked him the primary question:

"What is the price, and how much time for this?"

He responds that $500 is the amount with a 30-day turnaround.

I agreed.

The carpenter has the final price after considering all the raw material and service costs. What if the wood price changes tomorrow?

Do I (the buyer) pay him more than the contract (USD500)?

No. Why? Simply because of the contract which we signed. We signed on a fixed price for the whole unit. As a buyer, I'm safeguarded by this type of contract.

SCENARIO 2:

After a few days, I realize that I need a good set of Almira cupboards covering one of the walls of my bedroom. I had no clue about the design or the type of wood, but I knew that I needed an Almira. So, I called my carpenter again.

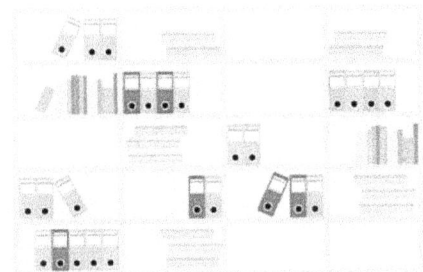

He gave me options:

→ Option 1: Wood type teak, USD 30.00 per square foot
→ Option 2: Wood type Hardwood - USD 25.00 per square foot. I said OK for option 1, and he started work.

Whenever we use words such as; PER PERSON, PER HOUR, or RATE, these contacts are Time and material contracts.

SCENARIO 3:

After a few days, my Society Residence Association (RWA) called me and asked me to get a memento for the prize distribution event.

I asked them about what design, material, or any other specifications. They said, "We trust you, get whatever you like."

So, I called my carpenter again.

I had no answers to any of his questions. I told him that I didn't know what I wanted but let's try and create something beautiful for RWA.

He mentioned that since the specifications are not clear, he would not be able to quote any amount. To which I said, "Don't worry about that part. I would reimburse you for all legitimate costs and your service fee." The guy went back home happy.

If the wood price changes tomorrow, who would bear the increased cost? I do, as the buyer. This type of contract is called the COST PLUS contract.

FIXED-PRICE CONTRACTS

Buyers must precisely specify the product or services being procured.

FIRM FIXED-PRICE CONTRACTS (FFP)

→ The cost for goods is set at the outset and does not increase unless the scope of work changes.

→ Any price rise due to an unfavorable environment is the responsibility of the seller, who is obligated to complete the effort.

FIXED-PRICE INCENTIVE FEE CONTRACTS (FPIF)

→ Business incentives are tied to achieving agreed metrics.

FIXED PRICE WITH ECONOMIC PRICE ADJUSTMENT CONTRACTS (FP-EPA)

→ The administration period spans a considerable period of years, as is desired with many long-term relationships.

→ E.g., inflation changes or cost increases

COST PLUS CONTRACTS

When the extent of work cannot be accurately defined at the start and needs to be adjusted, or when high risks may exist in the effort.

Seller is compensated - all actual costs, plus a fee.

COST-PLUS FIXED-FEE CONTRACTS (CPFF)

→ The fee is paid only for concluded work and does not change due to seller performance.

COST-PLUS INCENTIVE FEE CONTRACTS (CPIF)

→ Predetermined incentive fee based upon attaining certain performance

→ Both the buyer and seller share costs based upon a pre-negotiated cost-sharing formula, e.g., an 80/20

COST PLUS AWARD FEE CONTRACTS (CPAF)

→ A Predefined FIXED AWARD is set based on SLAs

TIME AND MATERIAL CONTRACTS

Hybrid Type Of Contractual Arrangement, Aspects of BOTH Cost-reimbursable And Fixed-price Contracts. The full value of the transaction and the specific quantity of items to be delivered may not be specified by the buyer at the time of the contract award.

Conversely, T&M contracts also resemble fixed unit price arrangements when certain parameters are specified in the contract.

T&M contracts are often used for:

→ Staff Augmentation

→ Acquisition of Experts

→ Any outside support

Buyer pays a rate for resources/services/products.

The Keywords to identify this type of contract is:

→ Per Hour

→ Per Unit

RELATIONSHIP BETWEEN CONTRACT AND RISKS

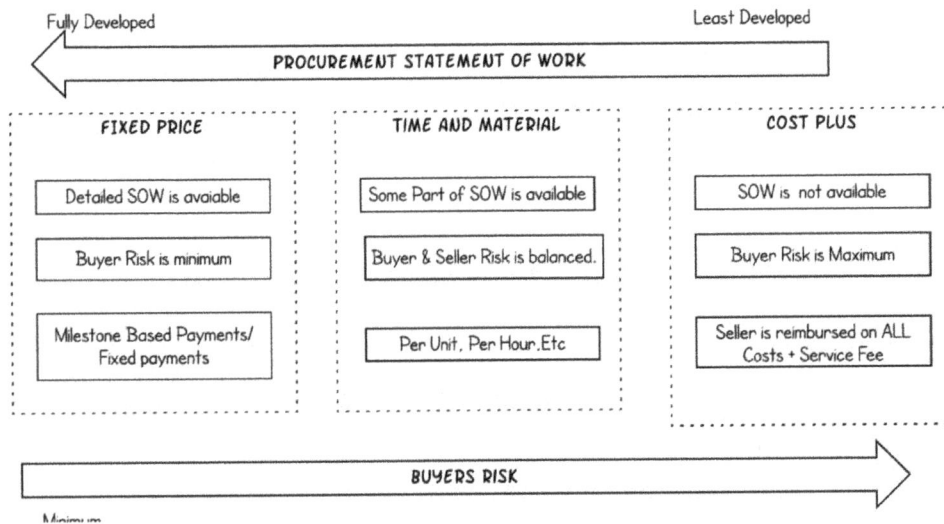

Fully Developed   Least Developed

← PROCUREMENT STATEMENT OF WORK

FIXED PRICE	TIME AND MATERIAL	COST PLUS
Detailed SOW is avaiable	Some Part of SOW is available	SOW is not available
Buyer Risk is minimum	Buyer & Seller Risk is balanced.	Buyer Risk is Maximum
Milestone Based Payments/ Fixed payments	Per Unit, Per Hour, Etc	Seller is reimbursed on ALL Costs + Service Fee

BUYERS RISK →

Minimum

9.3.1 LET'S PLAY: CONTRACT TYPES
Map the right contract with the definition:

Description	Contract Type Used
1. A contract having special provisions allowing for predefined final adjustments to the contract price due to changed conditions, such as inflation or cost increases (or decreases) for specific commodities. Otherwise, the cost does not change	Cost Plus Incentive Fee
2. The seller is reimbursed for all allowable costs for performing the contract work and receives a percentage based upon achieving certain performance objectives as set forth in the contract. The seller also shares losses as per the contract agreement.	Fixed Price with EPA
3. Contracts that specify rates per hour or categories of materials at specified rates per unit.	Fixed Price
4. In this contract, the buyer should precisely specify the product or services to be procured. Any changes to the procurement specification can increase the costs to the buyer.	Time and Material

9.4 CONDUCT PROCUREMENTS

The process of obtaining seller responses, selecting a seller, and awarding a contract.

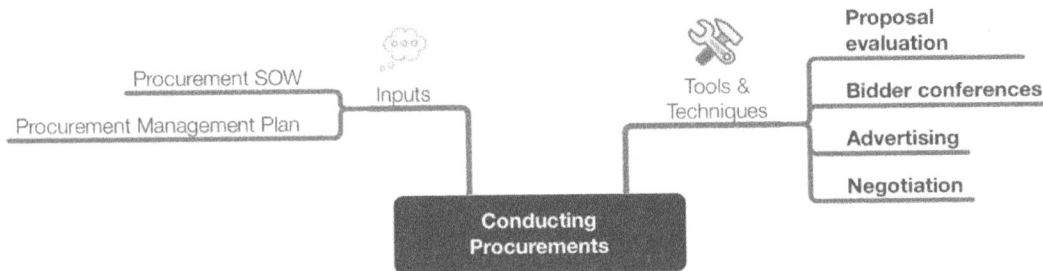

The process steps:

1. Advertising – in newspapers, websites, RFP, etc.
2. The seller may have a few questions on the RFP, so you get into bidder conferences to provide any clarification.
3. Based on the RFP, Sellers would submit their proposals.
4. You, along with the procurement team, evaluate the proposal using Proposal Evaluation techniques as defined in the Procurement Plan.
5. You might utilize independent estimates by the independent consultant to arrive at a suitable price range and technical specifications.
6. Based on the selection criteria and analytical techniques, you shortlist the possible vendors.
7. The next thing is to negotiate and arrive at a win-win contract and award the contract to the most deserving seller.
8. The seller, based on the contract, would update you on the estimated plan and schedule (A resource calendar from the seller would be available).

Sometimes the specification may change at the time of awarding the contract with respect to the planned RFP. This would lead to a change request in the plan.

ADVERTISING

To get a response on the SOW, you need to advertise with various media. This could include print (newspaper), online and company website, or TV advertisement.

BIDDER CONFERENCES

Bidder conferences (contractor conferences, vendor conferences, and pre-bid conferences) are meetings between the buyer and all prospective sellers prior to the bid submission event. Bidder conferences ensure that all potential sellers have a clear and shared understanding of the procurement requirements and that no bidders receive preferential treatment.

PROPOSAL EVALUATION TECHNIQUES

This could be a technical evaluation, a price bid evaluation, or a combination of both using weighted criteria.

NEGOTIATIONS

Procurement negotiations clarify the structure, requirements, and other terms of the buyer so that a shared agreement can be reached prior to signing the agreement. The final contract language reflects all agreements reached. Subjects covered should include responsibilities, authority to make modifications, applicable terms and governing law, technical and business management approaches, proprietary rights, contract financing, technical solutions, the overall program, payments, and price. Negotiations conclude with a contract document that can be executed by both buyer and seller.

The Project Manager may not lead negotiations but may be present during meetings to provide assistance and clarification of the project's technical, quality, and management requirements.

SOURCE SELECTION CRITERIA

A source selection criteria will be used to evaluate the sellers as per the plan. The selection criteria can be any of the choices given.

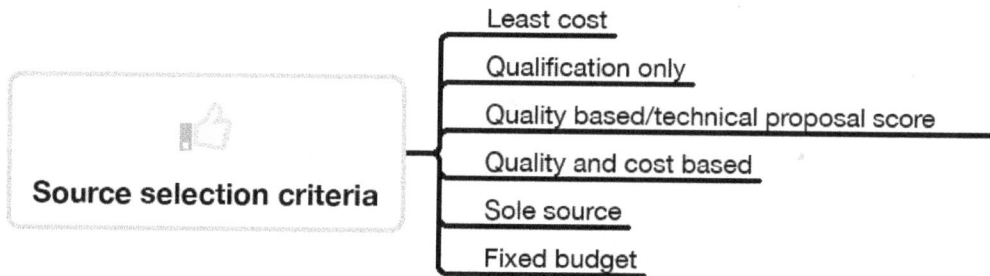

```
                                   Least cost
                                   Qualification only
                                   Quality based/technical proposal score
  Source selection criteria        Quality and cost based
                                   Sole source
                                   Fixed budget
```

9.5 CONTROL PROCUREMENTS

In Control Procurements, the emphasis is on managing procurement relationships, monitoring contract performance, and closing the contract.

Control procurement is working with the seller, verifying the deliverable, and ensuring it meets the contract terms and specifications while keeping a healthy relationship between the seller and yourself as the buyer.

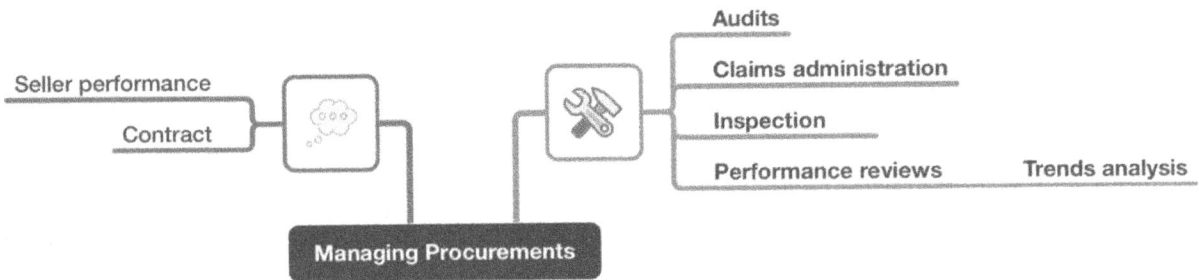

Change requests can be raised by the seller at this point. You need to have a change control system in place as a buyer organization.

You also need to monitor and control the seller's progress and the quality of submitted deliverables.

CLAIMS ADMINISTRATION

There could be non-agreement on some of the change requests or claims made by the seller. These contested changes are also called claims, disputes, or appeals.

Claims should be documented, processed, monitored, and managed throughout the contract life cycle. If the claim cannot be resolved between buyer and seller, then it may have to be handled by alternative dispute resolution (ADR). Another department in the buyer's organization generally manages ADR.

PERFORMANCE REVIEWS

A procurement performance review is a structured evaluation of the seller's progress to achieve project scope and quality, within cost and on schedule, as compared to the agreement. It can also include

A synopsis of audit and inspection results. The objective of a seller performance review is to identify performance successes or failures. This also focuses on seller work progress and contract non-compliance. This allows the buyer to quantify the seller's demonstrated ability or inability to perform work. Such reviews may take place as a part of project status reviews.

INSPECTION AND AUDITS

Inspections are performed on finished deliverables, and audits are performed to check for process adherence. Both inspection and audits are performed by the buyer.

9.6 MODULE END QUESTIONS - PMP STYLE

1. Mike is managing project NEXT-PI. Mike identifies a few skills gaps within the team. He released an RFP (Request for Proposal) for skill training. Many learning institutes responded. Mike evaluated the responses on the organization's capability and instructor's profile. He finally arrived at 2 shortlisted institutes. Which selection criteria did he use?

    A.   Sole source

    B.   Least cost

    C.   Qualification only

    D.   Technical Proposal score

2. Noah is meeting with all the sellers and responding to the queries raised by them. The sellers wanted answers on the RFP released by Noah. These answers will help sellers to decide the scope of work. This meeting can best be described as:

    A.   Bidder conferences

    B.   Vendor negotiations

    C.   A Meeting

    D.   Focus groups

3. Bidder conferences are conducted to achieve the objective of:

    A.   To make sure that all questions from potential sellers are answered privately

    B.   To make sure that all potential sellers are treated equally and have access to the same information

    C.   To make sure that potential sellers are treated equally based on the type of questions asked

    D.   To make sure that all potential sellers have access to the information they asked for

4. In which document can you find the procurement phase exit criteria?

    A.   Project schedule

    B.   Procurement management plan

    C.   Procurement strategy

    D.   Statement of work

5. Nina is working as a Project Manager for the project LANKA. She decided to procure specialists as contractors and discussed a $30 per hour, per resource pricing with the seller. What type of agreement did she use?

    A.   Fixed Price

    B.   Time and Material

C. Cost Reimbursable

D. Cost Plus Award Fee

6. **Which agreement carries the maximum risk for the seller?**

  A. Fixed Price

  B. Time and Material

  C. Cost Reimbursable

  D. Cost Plus Award Fee

7. **You recently joined as a Project Manager of an ongoing project. You want to know about the full specification of the work that is outsourced or planned to be outsourced. These details can be found in:**

  A. Procurement Management Plan

  B. Project Charter

  C. Requirement document

  D. Organizational Process Assets

8. **Bob, the seller, performed all the work as specified in the agreement and obtained appropriate sign-offs. However, Jack, the buyer, is not happy with the results. In this case, the contract would be considered as:**

  A. Null and void

  B. Incomplete

  C. Complete

  D. Waived

9. **What advantages does a buyer derive from a Fixed Price Contract?**

  A. Lower cost risk

  B. Higher cost risk

  C. No risk at all

  D. The risk is equal for both seller and buyer

10. **What is the full form of BOOT in the context of procurement?**

  A. Build, Own, Operate, Transfer

  B. Bid, Own, Operate, Transfer

  C. Build, Own, Oversee, Transfer

  D. Bid, Own, Oversee, Transfer

11. Identify the odd one out:

    A.   Sole source

    B.   Least cost

    C.   Cost plus

    D.   Quality based

12. In order to select the right seller, you form an independent committee to evaluate the proposals. The proposals will be evaluated using the predefined criteria as per the procurement plan. Which technique is being used?

    A.   Proposal evaluation technique

    B.   Independent estimates

    C.   Make or buy decision

    D.   Procurement Negotiation

13. In which document can one find the source selection criteria?

    A.   Project plan

    B.   Procurement Management Plan

    C.   Statement of work

    D.   Agreements

14. You are the buyer and want to select the contract which is LEAST risky for you. However, you do not have a handle on the requirements as they have been changing and will continue to be like that. You are using the agile methodology to deal with the ongoing requested changes. Which type of contact would be most optimal:

    A.   Fixed-price

    B.   Cost Plus Incentive Fee

    C.   Cost Plus Fixed Fee

    D.   Time and Material

15. In which document would you define source selection criteria?

    A.   Conduct Procurement

    B.   Plan Procurement Management

    C.   Plan Procurements

    D.   Control procurement

16. Procurement negotiations while selecting the seller have the objective of:

    A.   Buyer to get a fair price

    B.   Buyer to get the Lowest price

C.   To clarify the terms, roles, and structure of the contract

D.   To establish superiority

17. The contract terms are per month payouts provided the seller shows the time-sheets as evidence. The buyer will have the right to deduct the seller's payment in case the seller does not keep up with SLAs as per the agreement. What type of contract is this?

A.   Cost Plus Incentive Fee Contracts

B.   Cost Plus Award Fee Contracts

C.   Fixed Price Incentive Fee Contracts

D.   Time and Material Contracts

18. You are developing the total IT solution stack for business analysis for an online e-commerce firm. The solution is an integrated stack of software and hardware. Your company is focused on software services. What is the next step to initiate the procurement process for the hardware components?

A.   Advertise the RFP

B.   Evaluate seller proposals

C.   Make a procurement statement of work

D.   Award contract

19. What is the objective of having an incentive clause in the agreement?

A.   Reducing the fixed cost component.

B.   Motivating seller's team.

C.   Reducing production costs.

D.   Aligning seller's and buyer's objectives.

20. In which document can you find the legal jurisdiction and payment terms for project procurements?

A.   Procurement management plan

B.   Procurement strategy

C.   Project management plan

D.   Statement of work

9.7 ALL ANSWERS

ANSWERS: 9.3.1 LET'S PLAY: CONTRACT TYPES

Description	Contract Type Used
1. A contract having special provisions allowing for predefined final adjustments to the contract price due to changed conditions, such as inflation or cost increases (or decreases) for specific commodities.	Fixed Price with Economic Price Adjustment Contracts
2. The seller is reimbursed for all allowable costs for performing the contract work and receives a predetermined incentive fee based upon achieving certain performance objectives as set forth in the contract.	Cost Plus Incentive Fee Contracts
3. Contracts that specify rates per hour or categories of materials at specified rates per unit.	Time and Material Contracts
4. In this contract, the buyer should precisely specify the product or services to be procured, and any changes to the procurement specification can increase the costs to the buyer.	Firm Fixed Price Contracts

ANSWERS: 9.6 MODULE END QUESTIONS - PMP STYLE

1. D	Evaluating proposals and giving a score is the method of selecting and shortlisting sellers based on the quality of the proposal. Also referred to as Quality based or Technical proposal score-based evaluation.
2. A	A bidder conference is a meeting between the buyer and all prospective sellers before the submittal of a bid or proposal.
3. B	Bidder Conferences are conducted to make sure that all potential sellers are treated equally and have access to the same information. Option D is a tricky choice. However, a bidder conference's objective is not to respond only to selected vendors' questions but rather to assure that all of the information is available to all the vendors.
4. C	Procurement phases, entry, and exit criteria are part of the procurement strategy document.
5. B	This is a Time and Material (rate) contract where the seller is paid per hour or per unit.
6. A	In a Fixed Price Contract, the seller carries the most risk.
7. A	The Procurement Management Plan determines how to select a contractor for a contract.

8. C	Since the seller has completed all the work as specified in the agreement, the contract is complete.
9. A	Always keep in mind that such questions are asked from the buyer's point of view unless otherwise specified. In a Fixed Price (FP) contract, the cost risk of the buyer is less because of the nature of FP contracts. In FP contracts, if the scope does not change, the buyer pays the amount agreed to in the contract. Any adverse situations like attrition, rising material costs, and natural disasters have to be borne by the seller.
10. A	BOOT stands for Build Own Operate Transfer. These are procurement delivery methods.
11. C	Sole Source, Least Cost, and Quality-Based are all techniques for seller selection. However, Cost Plus is a type of contract.
12. A	The process of evaluating a seller proposal by using predefined criteria is an example of a proposal evaluation technique.
13. B	The Source Selection Criteria are defined at the time of planning and can be found in the procurement management plan.
14. D	Time and material contracts can be the next best contract after fixed-price contracts if you do not have firm requirements.
15. B	Source selection criteria are defined at the time of planning and can be found in the procurement management plan
16. C	Procurement negotiations clarify the structure, requirements, and other terms of the purchases so that agreement can be reached before signing the contract. The final contract language reflects all agreements reached.
17. D	Per month payments for the per-unit price is Time and Material contracts. Every contract type can have SLAs.
18. C	The first step is to evaluate if you can make the product/service. Once you decide to buy, then the next step is to create the SOW so that you can get the seller's estimations of the work.
19. D	An incentive clause in the agreement helps in aligning the buyer's and seller's goals.
20. A	A procurement management plan contains procurement integration with other project processes, a timetable for procurement activities, procurement phases and entry and exit criteria, jurisdiction and payout currency, role and responsibility, etc.

10. RISK MANAGEMENT

IMPORTANT TOPICS FOR THE PMP EXAM

→ Positive and negative risk	→ Contingent response strategy
→ Risk acceptance	→ Probability and Impact
→ Issues and Risks	→ Implement risk response
→ Overall project risk	→ Risk assessment parameters
→ Bubble chart	→ SWOT
→ Prompt Lists	→ Risk parameters

The reason projects are treated differently from operations is because you are doing it for the first time, and the chances of failing are huge. That's the reason why so much planning and emphasis on monitoring and controlling is needed

10.1 RISK MANAGEMENT OVERVIEW

Objective: Risk Management is about reducing threats and leveraging opportunities as and when they arise.

Process Name	Process Group	Why
Plan Risk Management	Planning	Defining thresholds, scales, who, and when for risks
Identify Risks	Planning	Identifying what can go wrong
Perform Qualitative Risk Analysis	Planning	Identifying the risk priorities
Plan Risk Responses	Planning	Planning the alternates to reduce risks
Implement Risk Responses	Executing	Implementing the response when a risk event occurs
Monitor Risks	Monitoring & Controlling	Check if new risks are present

Project risk management knowledge area deals with identifying the risks and planning for response in advance, i.e., during the planning phase, to ensure that the team is ready to handle any unknowns (risks). The risks should be actively monitored and controlled to ensure that risk management is effective.

10.2 PLAN RISK MANAGEMENT

Defining the approach to identify and respond to risks.

Plan Risk Management is part of the planning process group and results in documenting who, when, and how the Risk Management activities would be carried out in the project.

There are crucial aspects that are defined at this time:

Risk management plan
- Stakeholder risk appetite
- Risk management guidelines
- Reporting formats
- Tracking
- Probability and impact definition
- Risk strategy
- Methodology
- Role and responsibilities
- Funding
- Risk categories
- Timing

→ What is the risk appetite of my organization/department?

→ The overall risk rating criteria and scales.

→ Risk owners and tracking periodicity.

→ Risk impact and probability scales. Etc.

Most of the risk management activities are carried out simultaneously and will constitute the integrated Project Management Plan.

Stakeholder analysis can be used to assess the stakeholder appetite for risk management of the project.

10.3 IDENTIFY RISKS

The objective of identifying risks is to determine and list as many risks as possible. Participate in facilitation meetings with the customer. They can tell you the business risks. Ask an SME, and scan through all the earlier projects, historical data, and contracts; all of these can give you leads on what can possibly go wrong.

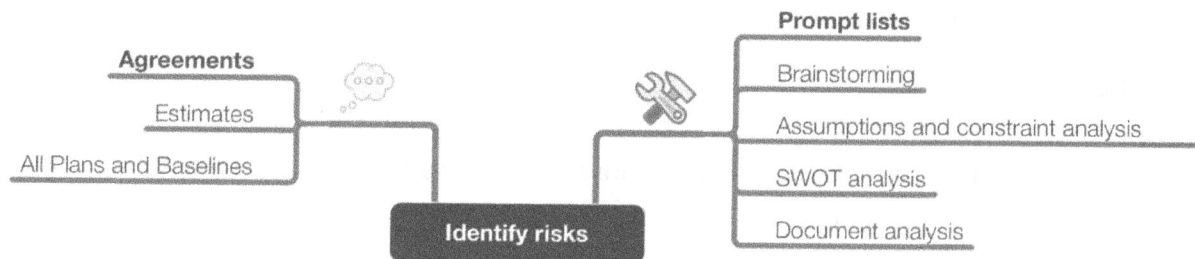

If you check all plans, baselines, and all the older projects, these can help you identify the project risks.

BRAINSTORMING

Brainstorming with project teams and customers can help you unearth many risks. Many mature organizations have risk checklists so that the team can simply find out the risk applicable to their project. Interviews with domain experts can help identify the risks with projects, especially complex domain-specific risks.

ASSUMPTION ANALYSIS

Assumptions can go wrong, and this may lead to risks. Check all of the assumptions from the documented requirements n and other plans. Check if they have any ambiguity or any chances to be untrue. Mark them as risks. Constraints, if not met, are a risk to project success. Identify and check all the constraints.

SWOT ANALYSIS

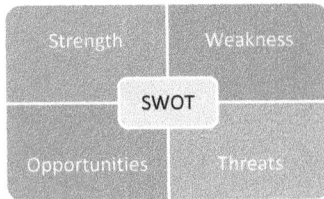

This technique considers the project against each of the strengths, weaknesses, opportunities, threats (SWOT), and views to increase the extent of identified risks by including internal risks. The technique starts with the identification of the strengths and weaknesses of the organization, focusing on the project, team, or the business area in general. SWOT analysis also is used to identify opportunities for the project that can arise from organizational strengths and any threats resulting from organizational weaknesses.

DOCUMENTATION ANALYSIS

You should always review all available documents for risk. It could be SLAs in contracts, milestones, or a baselined scope. All of these could have risk elements in them.

PROMPT LISTS

A prompt list is a predefined category of risks. An organization can develop its own prompt list for projects, or some of the domains also have a predefined prompt list. A few of the standard examples of prompt lists are:

PESTLE:
Political, Economic, Social, Technological, Legal, Environmental

TECOP:
Technical, Environmental, Commercial, Operational, Political

VUCA:
Volatility, Uncertainty, Complexity, Ambiguity

Using a prompt list ensures that the team checks the risks against each factor and identifies the risks in a structured manner. This ensures risk identification across all types of risks, unlike brainstorming, which is quick and responsive but may be skewed towards some specific risks.

10.3.1 LET'S PLAY: RISKS IDENTIFICATION TECHNIQUES

Match the following

Risk Scenario	Technique Used
1. You wanted to identify as many of the risks as possible in your project, so you called a joint meeting with the customer, PMO, your senior management, and the architect.	Interviews
2. You've sent a questionnaire to all the functional heads to find any risks to the success of the project. You did not want any biases, so these inputs were sought anonymously.	Documentation Reviews
3. You looked at the assumption log to ensure that the project success criterion may not get hampered by anything unexpected.	Brainstorming
4. You use the Fish Bone diagram technique to gain insight into the behavior of a risk.	Delphi
5. You meet personally with many different stakeholders: the sponsor, customer, team members, and experts. You seek answers to questions about what they think could go wrong on the project.	Assumption Analysis
6. You look through all the project documents, including contracts, to see any risk possibilities.	Root Cause Analysis

10.4 PERFORM QUALITATIVE RISK ANALYSIS

The goal of the qualitative analysis is to prioritize risks by assessing and combining their probability of occurrence and impact.

Once the risks are listed, then the next logical step is to find the risk priority. Some of us do it by instinct, but the most efficient method is to define and allocate probability and assess the impact of the risks and then arrive at the risk rating. In some projects, you can add the dimension of urgency to get overall risk ratings of the risks.

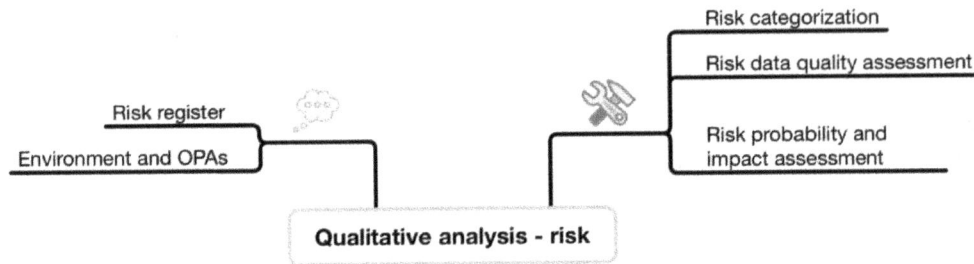

A risk register will be updated for risk priority and risk impact after this process.

RISK PROBABILITY AND IMPACT ASSESSMENT

While planning for risks, you should have agreed with your team on an impact and probability scale. Why?

In your mind, the impact could be high, or the probability of the event happening is high, but for others, it might not be. It is a good idea to discuss and decide on the definition of High/Medium/Low on both probability and impact scales.

Let's discuss this to give you some idea:

A TYPICAL IMPACT SCALE:

Project Risk Impact Scale	Low	Medium	High
Value	1	2	3
Cost	Cost increase < 10%	Cost Increase 10 - 30%	> 30%
Time	<5%	5 - 25% of time increase	>25% increase in schedule

THE ABOVE IS A 3-POINT SCALE.

Let's look at only the time aspect if a risk occurs on the project:

Here, the team has decided that if a risk happens and the impact is <5% on the Project Schedule, then the risk impact would be considered Low.

If the risk occurs on the project and it results in less than a 10% increase in the schedule, then the risk would be classified as Medium impact.

If the risk occurs on the project and it results in less than a 25% increase in the schedule, then the risk would be classified as High impact.

You get the picture.

Now you can decide the probability scale for your project yourself.

Project Risk Probability Scale	Low	Medium	High
Value	1	2	3

PROBABILITY AND IMPACT MATRIX

A probability and impact matrix is a framework for mapping the likelihood of each risk event and its impact on project objectives if that risk occurs. Risks are prioritized as per the grid. The probability and impact matrix shows how risk should be treated. For example, if the risk probability is low and impact is also low, then accept the risk.

PROBABILITY -- >>>>>			
PROBABILITY & IMPACT MATRIX	LOW	MEDIUM	HIGH
LOW	ACCEPT	MAY ACCEPT	MUST MANAGE
MEDIUM	MAY ACCEPT	MUST MANAGE	MUST MANAGE
HIGH	MUST MANAGE	MUST MANAGE	EXTENSIVE MANAGEMENT

IMPACT

If the risk probability is high and the impact is high, then put extensive management to control the risk.

BUBBLE CHART

Data is plotted and shown in many aspects. A bubble chart shows data on 3 aspects as given:

Bubble size = Impact value

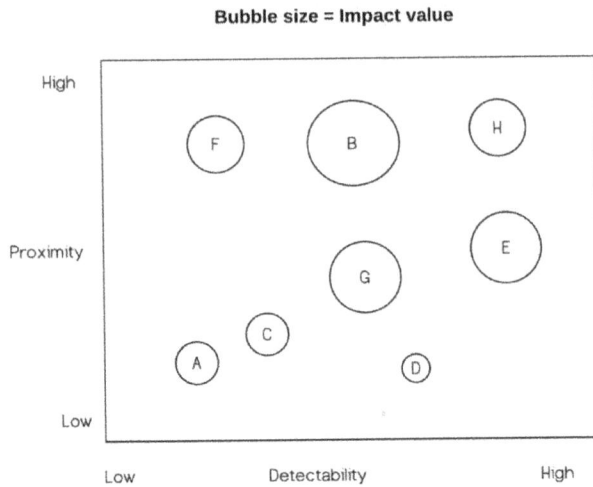

RISK CATEGORIZATION OR PROMPT LISTS

Using a category to define the risk in a structured way to identify the risk.

You might want to use an RBS (Risk Breakdown Structure) to ensure that you are not ignoring a certain type of risk and are adequately covered on all risks.

A mature organization might give you a risk template with the risk categories pre-populated – based on historical data. If your organization does not have one, then you might want to create a template and send it to them.

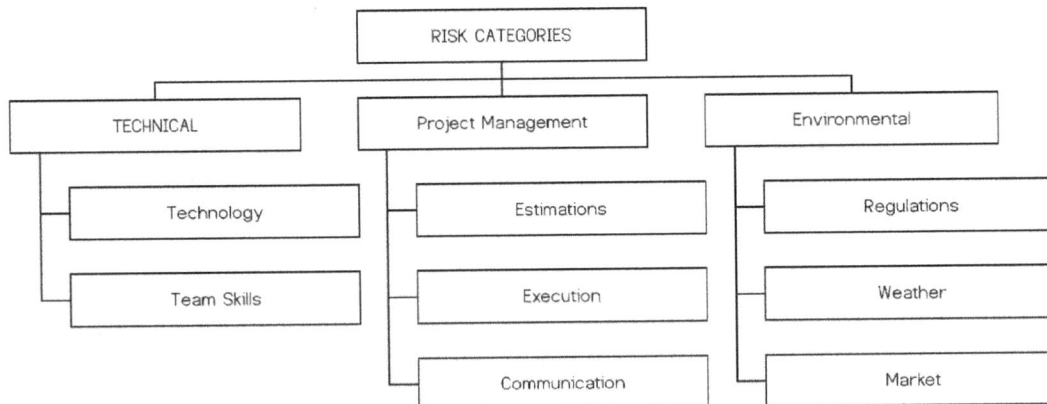

10.5 RISK PARAMETERS

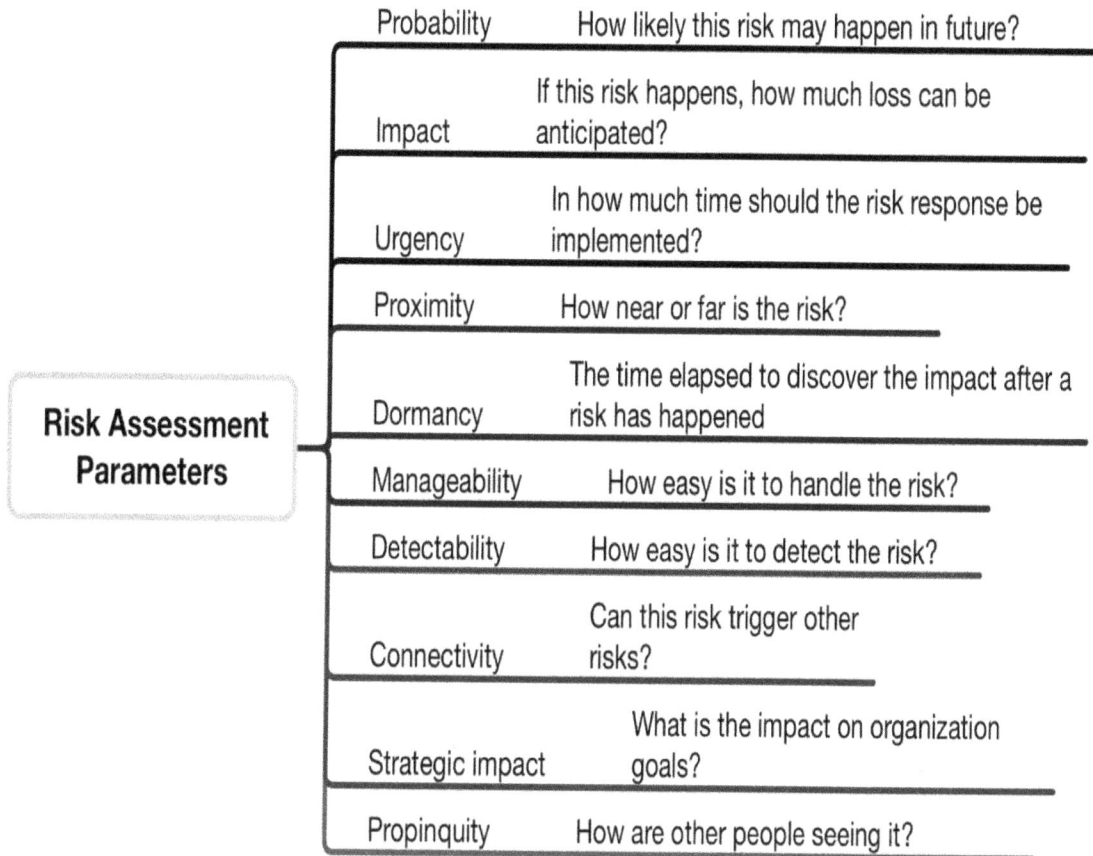

Probability	How likely this risk may happen in future?	

Risk Assessment Parameters

- Probability — How likely this risk may happen in future?
- Impact — If this risk happens, how much loss can be anticipated?
- Urgency — In how much time should the risk response be implemented?
- Proximity — How near or far is the risk?
- Dormancy — The time elapsed to discover the impact after a risk has happened
- Manageability — How easy is it to handle the risk?
- Detectability — How easy is it to detect the risk?
- Connectivity — Can this risk trigger other risks?
- Strategic impact — What is the impact on organization goals?
- Propinquity — How are other people seeing it?

10.5.1 LET'S PLAY: KNOW RISK TERMS

Select the correct term used for the risk assessment parameter:

#	Term	Description
1.	Probability	Can this risk trigger other risks?
2.	Impact	How are other people seeing it?
3.	Urgency	How easy is it to detect the risk?
4.	Proximity	How easy is it to handle the risk?
5.	Dormancy	How likely is this risk may happen in the future?
6.	Manageability	How much time should the risk response take to be implemented?
7.	Detectability	How near is the risk?
8.	Connectivity	If this risk happens, how much loss can be anticipated?
9.	Strategic Impact	What is the impact on the organization's goals?
10.	Propinquity	The time elapsed to discover the impact after a risk has happened.

10.6 PLAN RISK RESPONSES

The process of developing options and actions to enhance opportunities and reduce threats to project objectives.

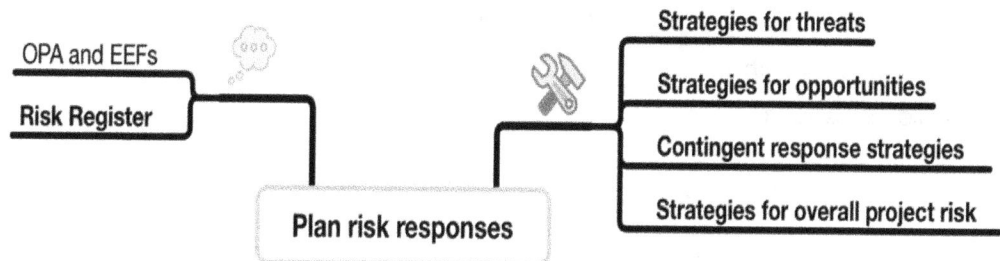

Once all the risks are identified, and ranking is done, then you need to plan the responses for all the risks on the project. Now, some people use a term called to mitigate, that's a popular expression but does not justify the overall response planning for risks.

You might have a few risks, but if planned/responded to with the right strategy, you can save money on the project.

→ A risk can result in more costs, also called THREAT.

→ Risk can lead to gaining money or saving money, also called OPPORTUNITY.

You know threats – schedule slippage due to attrition, and so on.

But what is an opportunity – e.g., Airtel outsourcing all OSS work to IBM to save on costs as well as focusing on their customer because they had the risk of workforce attrition and technical competency. Did outsourcing save money for Airtel – yes, you bet!

So, in the Plan Risk Responses, we plan for all the threats as well as opportunities.

STRATEGIES FOR NEGATIVE RISKS OR THREATS

ESCALATE

- The risks which are out of control of the project team are escalated
- The escalation level can be program/portfolio level
- Senior management decides on the risk response

AVOID

- This involves actually changing the project plan so that a particular risk can't happen
- Changing the project plan may inadvertently introduce new risks, called "Secondary risks."
- Risk probability becomes ZERO.

MITIGATE

- Steps are taken to reduce the likelihood and/or the impact of an identified risk.
- The risk which remains is called "Residual Risk."

- For example: keeping a buffer
- Risk probability or impact reduces but does NOT reach ZERO

TRANSFER

- Transfer to 3rd party.
- The risk probability and impact DOES NOT change
- Only the ownership changes
- For example - outsourcing

ACCEPT

Do Nothing

Let's summarize the risk response technique for threats:

Threat Strategy	Description	Changes in Probability	Changes in Impact	Extra Information
AVOID	Change the current course of action	Reduced to ZERO	No impact. Probability is zero	The alternate path/steps may introduce risks, also called secondary risks. They should also be assessed while planning for risk responses.
MITIGATE	Steps are taken to reduce the expected loss if a risky event happens	Reduced to an acceptable level	Reduced to an acceptable level	The overall risk does not become zero. Risk is reduced to an acceptable level The remaining risk is called residual risk and is monitored and controlled throughout the project life cycle.
TRANSFER	Risk is transferred to the third party	No Change	The impact is transferred to another entity.	The overall risk management ownership is given to another entity. Examples can be outsourcing, insurance, and Annual maintenance (AMC).
ACCEPT	Do nothing	No Change	No Change	There may be some contingency reserves that are kept. No steps are taken to

				reduce the risk impact or probability.
ESCALATE	Escalate to senior management	No Change	No Change	Ownership changes

STRATEGIES FOR POSITIVE RISKS OR OPPORTUNITIES

ESCALATE

- The risks, which are out of control of the project team, are escalated
- The escalation level can be program/portfolio level
- Senior management decides on the risk response

EXPLOIT

- Increasing the probability to 100%
- Opposite of AVOID
- Assigning an organization's most talented resources to the project to reduce the time to completion or to provide lower costs than originally planned.

SHARE

- Sharing the ownership
- Opposite of TRANSFER
- Forming risk-sharing partnerships, teams, special-purpose companies, or joint ventures

ENHANCE

- Increase the probability and/or the impacts
- Opposite of MITIGATE
- Adding more resources to an activity to finish early.

ACCEPT

- Do nothing

Let's summarize the risk response technique for opportunities:

Strategy	Description	Changes in Probability	Changes in Impact	Any Extra Information
EXPLOIT	Change the current course of action to realize the opportunity	Increased to 100%		Steps are taken for the opportunity to be realized, and benefits are reaped.

ENHANCE	Steps are taken to increase the expected gains and/or increase the probability	Increased	Increased	
SHARE	The benefits are shared with the third party	Shared	Shared	Joint Ventures (JV) are assigned to handle the risks together and gain benefits together.
ACCEPT	Do nothing	No Change	No Change	This is a common response to handle a threat and opportunity.
ESCALATE	Escalate to senior management	No Change	No Change	Ownership changes

The parallel between threat and opportunity responses:

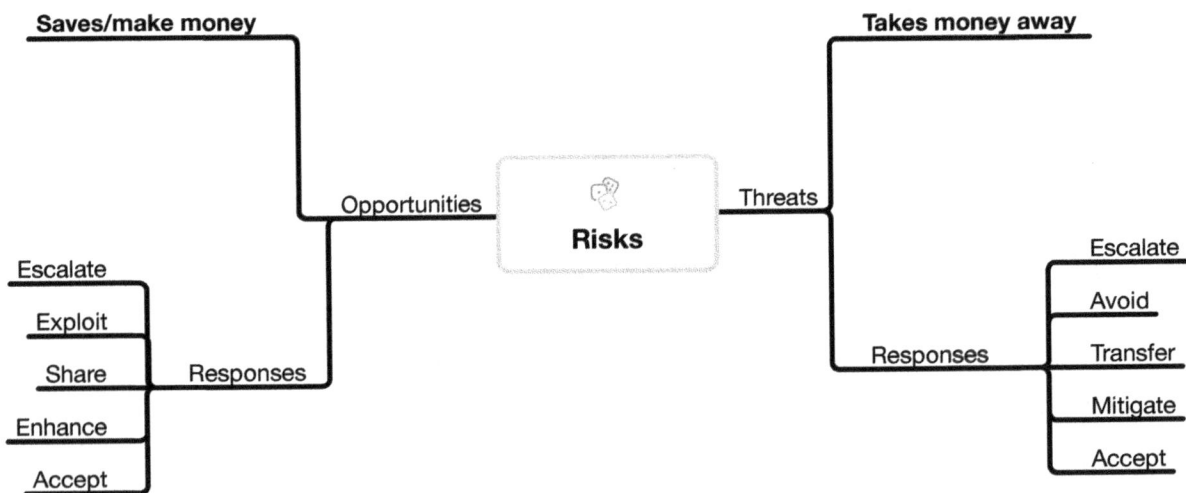

CONTINGENT RESPONSE STRATEGIES

These are predefined responses to certain events which have known triggers and can induce a big impact. Think disaster recovery drill, file and data backups, etc

Some responses are designed for use only if specified events occur. For some risks, it is appropriate for the project team to make a response plan that will only be executed under certain predefined conditions if it is believed that there will be sufficient warning to implement the plan. Events that trigger the contingency response, such as missing intermediate milestones or gaining higher priority with a supplier, should be defined and tracked. Risk responses identified using this technique are also called contingency plans or fallback plans and include unique triggering events that set the plans in effect.

RISK AUDITS

A third party checks to verify that your project is adequately covered for risks. The audits check to see if the project has identified typical risks, the risk plan adherence, and coverage of the risks.

STRATEGIES FOR OVERALL PROJECT RISKS

Risks are applicable to a project as a whole. Think dynamic technology or working in a non-friendly climate. The overall project risks can be handled by the techniques shown in the mind map.

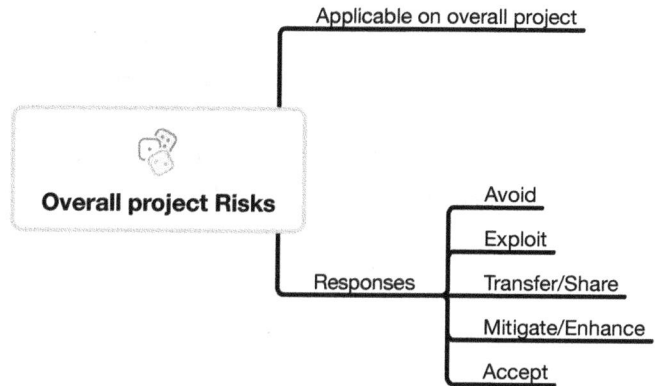

Strategy	Description
Avoid	Reducing the probability to zero.
Exploit	Increasing the probability to 100%
Transfer/SHARE	Work with sellers to share the benefits or losses.
Mitigate /ENHANCE	Depending on the risk/opportunity, take steps to increase or decrease the probability or the impact or both.
Accept	Do nothing,

AGILE CONSIDERATIONS

Agile iteration length is small, resulting in minimizing the risk associated with the deliverables. Risk management as an approach applies to the overall project for both agile and predictive projects. Agile emphasizes the usage of spikes to eliminate risk (Risk due to unproven skills or products or technology)

10.6.1 LET'S PLAY: RISK RESPONSES

You planned to go out for an outing with your friends for a few days. To ensure that everything is nice and smooth, you anticipated a few risks and implemented a strategy to handle them. Identify the strategy/response selected for each scenario:

1. A chance of heavy rain could lead to car skids. You purchased new tires to avoid an accident due to rain.

   A. Avoid
   B. Mitigate
   C. Transfer
   D. Accept

2. You canceled the rappelling activity as the weather forecast was not favorable.

   A. Avoid
   B. Mitigate
   C. Transfer
   D. Accept

3. The weather forecast has a 99% probability of rain, but the team decided to go on a river rafting activity. Everyone said, "we will stop if the weather conditions turn bad."

   A. Avoid
   B. Mitigate
   C. Transfer
   D. Accept

4. Driving a car in rainy weather can lead to accidents, but at the same time, it's a beautiful view. So, you hired a cab to take you out for mountain scenery. You had to pay for the cab, but it was worth the money.

   A. Avoid
   B. Mitigate
   C. Transfer
   D. Accept

5. Before traveling, you noticed that the main route had a traffic jam, so you took a longer route to avoid the jam. The new route has a toll and goes through a national park. This was the best time spent watching the scenery.

   A. Avoid
   B. Mitigate
   C. Transfer
   D. Accept

10.7 ISSUES AND RISKS

ISSUE:

A current condition or situation that may have an impact on the project objectives. In other words, it is an action item that the project team must address. An Issue is:

→ A present event

→ Has happened on the project

→ You have to work on it NOW

→ The response is adhoc to an issue and is called WORKAROUND

→ They are documented in the Issue log till closure

RISK:

A future event that may happen or not, and if that event does happen, will have an impact on the product objectives. A risk is:

→ A future event

→ Have some probability (it may happen)

→ You can respond to the risk (even elimination can be on the response)

→ They are documented in the Risk Register for further assessment and planning

10.7.1 LET'S PLAY: IDENTIFY A RISK OR AN ISSUE:

The Visconti Country project is nearing completion (your new home), and you should take possession of the new home in about a month. You have been working to manage and control the schedule and cost as per the initial estimates. However, the project came with particular challenges.

Select if these are issues or risks.

Scenario	Risk/Issue
1. **You received a letter from the bank stating that the mortgage rate has increased by 1%. This will increase the project spending by at least 10%**	A. Risk B. Issue
2. **Heavy rains are forecasted in the next week. This has the potential to delay the project completion by a few days.**	A. Risk B. Issue
3. **Few of the workers went on a strike.**	A. Risk B. Issue
4. **Some of the windows you bought were of the wrong size and should now be returned. This is a lot of rework.**	A. Risk B. Issue
5. **A new shopping mall is planned near your house. If that comes up in the next two years, It will significantly increase property valuation.**	A. Risk B. Issue

10.8 MODULE END QUESTIONS - PMP STYLE

1. Which of the following lists the ways in which adverse risks can be handled? Select the best Answer.

    A.   Escalate, Avoid, Mitigate, Share, Do Nothing

    B.   Escalate, Avoid, Mitigate, Transfer, Do Nothing

    C.   Escalate, Avoid, Mitigate, Transfer, Accept

    D.   Escalate, Avoid, Mitigate, Share, Accept

2. Which of the following statements is TRUE regarding a probability and impact matrix?

    A.   Probability and impact matrix multiplies the risk's probability by the cost of the impact so that the expected value of the risk can be identified.

    B.   The probability and impact matrix is predetermined thresholds that use the risk's probability multiplied by the impact of the risk event to determine an overall risk score.

3. Mike is a Project Manager working on a construction project. Mike identified a few risks that might affect the outcome of a few project activities. He decided to reduce the impact of these events if they did take place. In which of the following ways has he chosen to handle these risks?

    A.   Avoid

    B.   Mitigate

    C.   Transfer

    D.   Accept

4. Adding a buffer to the end of the schedule project segment is called the critical chain method. If a risk of delay in the schedule is identified and a buffer is added as a result, what type of response is this?

    A.   Accept

    B.   Mitigate

    C.   Transfer

    D.   Avoid

5. Jack, the Project Manager, is currently involved in risk identification for his project. He got all his team members in a room to generate ideas. Which of the following information-gathering techniques is he using?

    A.   Brainstorming

    B.   Delphi technique

    C.   Root-cause identification

    D.   Interviews

6. You are the Project Manager for the high-profile project NANCY. During risk planning, you documented your results in the risk register, including both negative and positive risks. Which techniques can be used to handle both positive and negative risks?

   A. Escalate and Mitigate

   B. Escalate and Accept

   C. Escalate and Exploit

   D. Escalate and Enhance

7. The project VINA underwent many challenges. Few of them were handled successfully by the Project Manager Kim. A new risk event seems to be triggering again and looks like it is beyond the project's control to handle. What would be your advice to Kim?

   A. Add the risk to the risk register

   B. Add the risk event to the risk register and implement the response

   C. Add the risk event in the risk register and escalate

   D. Add the risk even in the risk register and brainstorm with the team

8. What is the meaning of a low dormancy risk?

   A. A risk that is easier to predict

   B. A risk that is perceived as high impact

   C. A risk that is difficult to trace

   D. A risk that is easier to trace

9. What is the primary objective of identifying risk tolerances?

   A. To identify the risk appetite of the organization

   B. To assist the Project Manager in estimating the project

   C. To assist the project team in scheduling the project

   D. To assist management in knowing what other managers have to say about the project

10. Identification of new risks, reassessment of old risks, and closing of outdated risks are made as part of the Monitor Risks Process. How frequently should project uncertainty reassessment be scheduled?

    A. Throughout the project life cycle

    B. It is left to the wisdom of the Project Manager

    C. Reassessment must be done at the 25 percent, 50 percent, and 75 percent stages of project completion

    D. Reassessment must be done at the 20 percent, 40 percent, 60 percent, and 80 percent stages of project completion

11. One of the controllers started showing a gradual increase in temperature. This can lead to the total failure of the equipment. This is an example of:

    A.   Trigger

    B.   Risk

    C.   Check sheet

    D.   Technical performance indicator

12. Typical risk register contents items are:

    A.   Identified risks, risk owners, risk responses, and triggers

    B.   Identified risks, risk owners, risk responses, and probability and impact matrix

    C.   Identified risks, risk owners, risk responses, and risk approach

    D.   Identified risks, risk owners, risk responses, and risk reassessment duration

13. The project AXAA is an expensive initiative to launch a new device in the market. The success of project AXAA will hugely impact the product portfolio of your firm. This device will compete with other companies operating in this space, and these are big giants like Amazon and Google. Speed to market is the only aspect that can help you in winning this product battle. How would you, as a Project Manager, consider the risk of delay for the project AXAA?

    A.   The risk of delay is a threat and should be considered and planned

    B.   The risk of delay is a project-level risk and should be planned accordingly

    C.   The risk of delay is a portfolio level risk and should be planned at the portfolio level

    D.   The risk of delay should be planned at the project and portfolio level- both

14. A _____ is a risk response strategy developed in advance before risks occur; it is meant to be used when identified risks become a reality.

    A.   Management plan

    B.   Contingency plan

15. A _____ risk is one that is inherent in a business endeavor, such as when a company assumes that it will spend money and make money and that any project undertaken carries with it the potential for success or failure, profit, or loss. _____ risk is a risk that has only the potential for loss and no potential for profit or gain.

    A.   Insurable, Business

    B.   Threat, Opportunity

    C.   Business, Insurable

    D.   Opportunity, Threat

16. **When should the risk register be updated?**

    A.   At the time of risk planning, only

    B.   At the time of risk incidents

    C.   As and when an issue arises

    D.   Throughout the project life cycle

17. **You planned for a holiday trip to one of the hills. At the beginning of the trip, you received news that one of the roads had been jammed for the past few hours, so you opted to travel by helicopter. What response did you choose?**

    A.   Avoid

    B.   Mitigate

    C.   Transfer

    D.   Accept

18. **You are in a workshop. At the end of the seminar, you asked people to give views about what could go wrong if action A is implemented. People used yellow sticky notes, and then you categorized them on a functional aspect. After some discussion, people voted for the top 3 Risks of the project. Which tool did you use?**

    A.   Affinity diagram

    B.   Brainstorming

    C.   Idea/mind mapping

    D.   Nominal Group Technique

19. **Tremors were felt in the office building, and the floor manager helped everyone to vacate the building. This resulted in 100% success because the team usually practices the drill every month. The evacuation is:**

    A.   Ad-hoc response to a risk

    B.   Contingent risk response

    C.   Planned response

    D.   Implement risk response

20. Jacob, the Project Manager, while working on the plan, put extra resources as buffers. This was the response to the risk of increasing the percentage of employee attrition. Which risk response strategy was selected by Jacob?

    A.   Avoid

    B.   Mitigate

    C.   Transfer

    D.   Accept

21. A risk that can likely trigger the other risks on the project can be categorized as:

    A.   Having a high impact

    B.   Having high connectivity

    C.   Having high propinquity

    D.   Having high proximity

22. Refer to the diagram and select the risk name which has high proximity and the highest impact value.

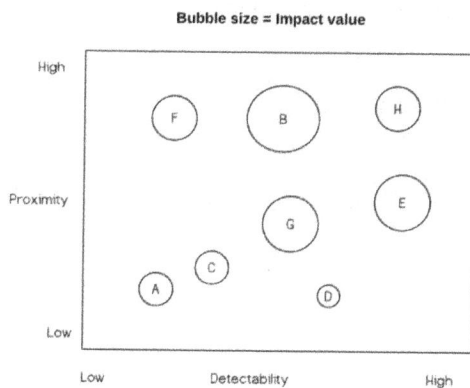

Bubble size = Impact value

    A.   Risk H

    B.   Risk B

    C.   Risk F

    D.   Risk G

10.9 ALL ANSWERS

ANSWERS: 10.3.1 LET'S PLAY: RISKS IDENTIFICATION TECHNIQUES

Risk Scenario	Technique Used
1. You wanted to identify as many of the risks as possible in your project, so you called a joint meeting with the customer, PMO, your senior management, and the architect.	Brainstorming
2. You've sent a questionnaire to all the functional heads to find any risks to the success of the project. You did not want any biases, so these inputs were sought anonymously.	Delphi
3. You looked at the assumption log to ensure that the project success criterion may not get hampered by anything unexpected.	Assumption Analysis
4. You use the Fish Bone diagram technique to gain insight into the behavior of a risk.	Root cause analysis
5. You meet personally with many different stakeholders: the sponsor, customer, team members, and experts. You seek answers to questions about what they think could go wrong on the project.	Interviews
6. You look through all the project documents, including contracts, to see any risk possibilities.	Documentation Reviews

ANSWERS: 10.5.1 LET'S PLAY: KNOW RISK TERMS

Probability	How likely is this risk may happen in the future?
Impact	If this risk happens, how much loss can be anticipated?
Urgency	How much time should the risk response take to be implemented?
Proximity	How near is the risk?
Dormancy	The time elapsed to discover the impact after a risk has happened.
Manageability	How easy is it to handle the risk?
Detectability	How easy is it to detect the risk?
Connectivity	Can this risk trigger other risks?
Strategic impact	What is the impact on the organization's goals?
Propinquity	How are other people seeing it?

ANSWERS: 10.6.1 LET'S PLAY: RISK RESPONSES

Scenario	Response Strategy	Why?
1	Mitigate	Probability is reduced to some extent.
2	Avoid	The risk probability is reduced to zero.
3	Accept	Do nothing.
4	Share	You gained (not money), and you shared with a
5	Exploit	Opportunity increased to 100%.

ANSWERS: 10.7.1 LET'S PLAY: IDENTIFY A RISK OR AN ISSUE:

Scenario	Risk/Issue	Why
1. You received a letter from the bank stating that the mortgage rate has increased by 1%. This will increase the project spending by at least 10%	Issue	11% Increase is already applicable as of now.
2. Heavy rains are forecasted in the next week. This has the potential to delay the project completion by a few days.	Risk	A future event having probability and impact
3. Few of the workers went on a strike.	Issue	Present event – the team is facing it currently
4. Some of the windows you bought were of the wrong size and should now be returned. This is a lot of rework.	Issue	Present event – the team is facing it currently
5. A new shopping mall is planned near your house. If that comes up in the next two years, It will significantly increase property valuation.	Risk	Future event having probability and a positive impact. Opportunity.

ANSWERS: 10.8 MODULE END QUESTIONS - PMP STYLE

1. C	Check the question. Does it ask how you would handle a threat? Escalate, avoid, mitigate, transfer, accept – all are ways to handle threats. Hence, Option C is the correct answer.
2. B	The probability and impact matrix multiply the probability of occurrence of the risk and its impact on project objectives to determine a risk score. Using this score and a predetermined matrix, you determine if the score is high, medium, or low.
3. B	The mitigate risk response strategy is used to take action to ensure that the events cause as little damage as possible to the project activities.
4. B	The Project Manager reduced the impact of unplanned leaves. Adding buffer does not avoid the delay of project activities and cannot classify as avoid. Mitigate is the best fit.
5. A	Check the keyword ideas. Brainstorming is a type of information-gathering technique that is used to generate ideas.
6. B	Only the escalate and accept response is used to handle both positive as well as negative risks. Hence, B is the correct answer.
7. C	Check that the risk is already identified as it occurred earlier. Option A is not the right option to select. Since the risk event seems to be out of project control, the best thing would be to escalate the event and take support from the management. Option C is the correct option.
8. D	Dormancy is the risk parameter to assess the time elapsed to discover the impact after a risk has happened. Low dormancy risk means that the risk is easier to trace.
9. A	Identifying risk tolerances helps in understanding how much appetite the organization has for absorbing risks.
10. A	Identification of new risks, reassessment of old risks, and closing of outdated risks should be made throughout the project.
11. A	Triggers are symptoms of the risk.
12. A	The probability and impact matrix, risk approach, and risk reassessment duration are part of the risk plan. Option A is the best option.
13. D	The risk of delay can have a major impact on the portfolio and is a crucial aspect to project success. This risk should be identified and treated at both the project and portfolio levels.

14. D		A contingency plan is a risk response strategy developed in advance before risks occur; it is meant to be used if and when identified risks become a reality. An effective contingency plan allows a Project Manager to react quickly and appropriately to the risk event, mitigating its negative impact or increasing its potential benefits. A contingency plan may include a fallback plan for risks with high impact
15. A		Business risk is one that is inherent in a business endeavor, such as when a company assumes that it will spend money and make money and that any project undertaken carries with it the potential for success or failure, profit or loss. An insurable risk is a risk that has only the potential for loss and no potential for profit or gain. An insurable risk is one for which insurance may be purchased to reduce or offset the possible loss.
16. D		The risk register should be updated continuously throughout the project.
17. A		Reducing the probability to ZERO is avoid strategy as the risk response.
18. D		Nominal Group Technique. A technique that enhances brainstorming with a voting process is used to rank the most useful ideas for further brainstorming or privatization.
19. B		A contingent risk response is a step-by-step response to identified risks. These are also called fallback plans.
20. B		Mitigate is to reduce the probability or the impact, or both.
21. B		A risk having high connectivity means that the risk can trigger other risks in the project.
22. B		High proximity and high impact. You need to check the big bubble at the high proximity parameter. This is risk B.

PEOPLE

11. STAKEHOLDERS

IMPORTANT TOPICS FOR THE PMP EXAM STAKEHOLDER ANALYSIS

Stakeholder Management	Stakeholder Identification
Data Gathering	Surveys/Questionnaires
Brain-Writing	Direction Of Influence
Representation	Stakeholder Dimensions
Stakeholder Plan And Engagement Level	Decision-Making Techniques
Communication Methods	Stakeholder types

Introduction: Project Volta

Project Volta

An organization, BIGB, decided to transform the shared services operations. They called this project VOLTA. BIGB had around 15 offices across the globe. Each location had its own support services like marketing, human resources, payroll, benefits, and finance team, making up to 30% - 40% of the overall task force. Moving most of the shared services to a global shared service hub made a huge difference in the overall margins. It was decided that most of the roles could be transferred to India. The processes were to be streamlined along with SLAs (Service Level Agreements) so that business goes on as usual.

Now, who will be impacted by this change?

- Everyone within the organization.
- Everyone within the organization is a stakeholder of project VOLTA.
- Would there be people who oppose the change?
- Would there be people who accept the change?

The Project Manager of VOLTA had a huge task ahead of him to categorize each stakeholder and engage with them to be successful.

11.1 STAKEHOLDER MANAGEMENT OVERVIEW

Objective: Stakeholder management focuses on identifying stakeholders, understanding their expectations, and effectively engaging them through project execution.

Process Name	Process Group	Why
Identify Stakeholders	Initiating	Identifying who all can impact/influence the project
Plan Stakeholder Engagement	Planning	The current level of engagement and how to effectively engage
Manage Stakeholder Engagement	Executing	Managing stakeholders as per the plan
Monitor Stakeholder Engagement	Monitoring & Controlling	Planned Vs. Actual and taking action

Communication and stakeholder engagement go hand in hand, and both drive the way in which you would manage and engage people as you move toward successful project completion.

11.2 IDENTIFY STAKEHOLDERS

Identify Stakeholders is to identify entities who may affect or get affected by the activities or outcome of a project. We, as the project team, gather information regarding their interests, influence, and impact so that they can be engaged better in the project to ensure project success.

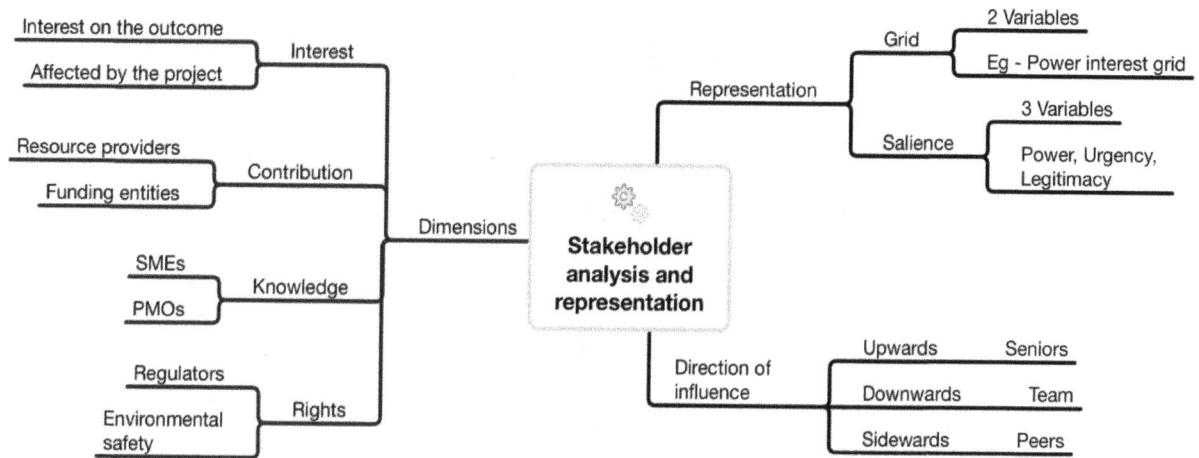

A stakeholder is an entity that gets impacted by the project outcome. An entity/person who can influence your project towards success or failure is also considered a stakeholder.

Try and obtain a list of all influencers and all those impacted by the project outcome. Do not leave anyone out. The rule of thumb is to write down everyone you can think of and add them to the project stakeholder register.

Here is a sample stakeholder register. Check the column: Interest and authority.

No	Type	Name	Designation	Contact Details	Email	Interest	Authority
1	Internal	ZZZ				High	High
2	Customer	VVV				Low	High
3	Seller	VVV				High	Low

STAKEHOLDER ANALYSIS

You either start meeting the stakeholders, conduct workshops, or send a survey to assess their interest in your project. Once you have the data, you may want to analyze the stakeholders in context. There are many dimensions available, as shown in the stakeholder dimension mind-map.

DATA REPRESENTATION

Data can be represented using grids (2 dimensions), cubes (3 dimensional), or using a salience model (3 dimensional with specific dimensions/aspects).

POWER AND INTEREST GRID

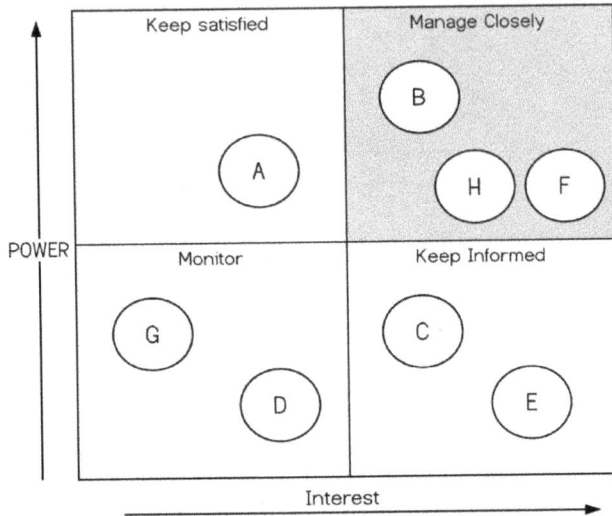

One of the categorizations which most people work with is the Power Interest grid, as shown in the picture power Interest Grid.

A, B, C, etc., All are the identified stakeholders in a project. They have been plotted on the grid according to their interest and authority.

PERSON A:

This person is high in power and has a low interest.

How do you manage people like these? Send them correct and adequate information as and when they want it. Not before, not after, not too much, and not too little. Keep them satisfied with the information they need.

These are the people whom you should not be CCing. If they are CCed, you may receive a shouting email – take me out of this communication thread. Never a good thing.

PERSON G AND D:

These people fall under low power and have low interest.

They cannot help in the project activities or affect you in a negative way. Also, they are not interested in knowing about the project.

How should you deal with them?

Do not do any extra work. Do not produce reports to send them as they are not interested in following the project progress or any other information. However, keep track of them and see if they get promoted or if their interest level changes. If that happens, you need to change their mapping and manage them accordingly.

PERSON C AND E:

These people are low in power and have high interests.

These are the people who are quite interested in the project but have low authority. Examples of these stakeholders can be sellers or team members.

Keep them informed on relevant project information. They are interested.

PERSON B, H, AND F:

These people are high in power and have high interests.

They can help the project when needed as they are powerful. Keep them engaged with the project.

But how?

Develop trust, engage in conversations and keep them posted on project successes and setbacks.

SALIENCE MODEL:

The salience model is used to describe the stakeholders using three dimensions which are given below:

POWER: LEVEL OF AUTHORITY OR INFLUENCE.
URGENCY: NEED ATTENTION ON A CRITICAL BASIS.
LEGITIMACY: IS THE INVOLVEMENT REASONABLE?

How would you identify all the stakeholders? Start with the charter. Meet the person who signed the charter and get to know his /her expectations from the project. A good question to ask in this meeting would be:

How interested would you be in the project updates? Daily, Weekly, or Monthly. This question would help you assess his/her interest level in the project.

Another assessment which you might want to do is finding out their authority level. How do you assess the authority? Network, ask people, check organization chart, etc.

It could happen that the sponsor may direct you to two or more people under him and say – these are your day-to-day contacts. That's good news. Have meetings with them and try to understand their authority and interest level by assessments, networking, and asking the right questions.

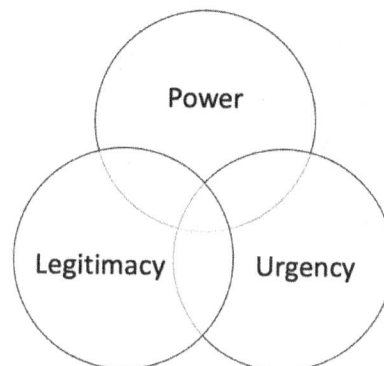

11.2.1 LET'S PLAY: STAKEHOLDER ANALYSIS

Match how would you plan to handle given type of stakeholders:

Power	Interest		Strategy
1. High	High		A. No Extra Work-Monitor
2. High	Low		B. Manage Closely
3. Low	High		C. Keep Satisfied
4. Low	Low		D. Keep Informed

11.3 PLAN STAKEHOLDER ENGAGEMENT

Once we understand the stakeholder's communication needs and interest in the project, we plan for better engagements.

For a project to be successful, a good stakeholder engagement plan will lead to better stakeholder management.

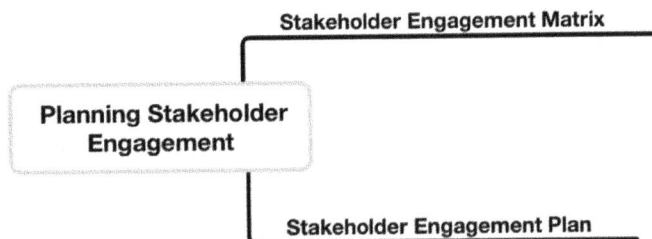

Stakeholder Engagement Assessment Matrix

You can create the current engagement level and plan for future engagements and actions so that the stakeholders are involved. This requires one to understand the current engagement level. A few ways the engagement level can be mapped or represented in the stakeholder register are given below:

Stakeholder Type	Color	Description
Supportive	Green	Aware of the project and potential impact and supportive of changes.
Leading	Dark Green	Aware of the project and potential impact and actively engaged in ensuring the project is a success.
Resistant	Red	Aware of the project and potential impact and resistance to change.
Unaware	No color	Unaware of the project and potential impact.
Neutral	White	Aware of the project yet neither supportive nor resistant.

Let's think of project VOLTA. Stakeholders will have various attitudes towards project VOLTA based on their roles.

- A few people, like senior management, will be pro-project – it will help them save money.
- There will be some who are losing jobs because of the change brought by VOLTA: these people will oppose the project.
- Some may not care.

The Project Manager of VOLTA needs to consider the current state and desired future state of all the stakeholders.

How can you influence stakeholders to change their attitude towards the project? Activities that can enhance the engagement with stakeholders should be planned. These are:

- Building trust by communicating
- Showcasing the value/benefit of the project
- Develop Interpersonal relationships
- Show what's in it for them
- Find acceptable solutions

11.3.1 LET'S PLAY: STAKEHOLDER ENGAGEMENT GRID

Match how would you plan to handle the type of stakeholders:

ENGAGEMENT LEVEL	DESCRIPTION
1. Unaware	Aware of the project and potential impacts and supportive of changes.
2. Resistant	Aware of the project and potential impacts and actively engaged in ensuring the project is a success.
3. Neutral	Aware of the project and potential impacts and resistance to change.
4. Supportive	Unaware of the project and potential impacts.
5. Leading	Aware of the project yet neither supportive nor resistant.

11.4 MANAGE STAKEHOLDER ENGAGEMENT

Manage Stakeholder Engagement is executing the engagements as per the plan. Meeting people, handling issues, and exchanging information using interpersonal and management skills. This may lead to assessing the overall engagement and can lead to change in the approach.

Whenever there is any escalation/issue, get into a meeting (interactive communication) rather than email or anything else.

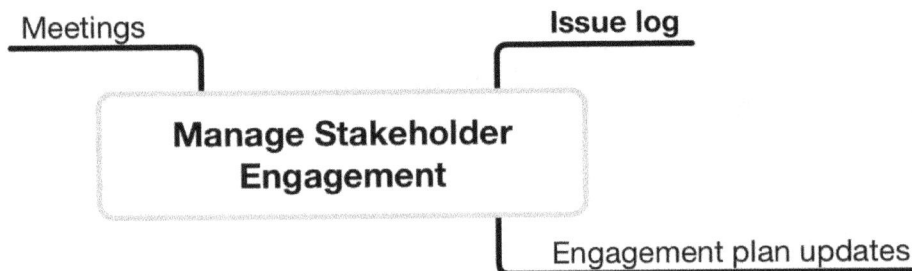

Meetings

Issue log

Manage Stakeholder Engagement

Engagement plan updates

11.4.1 LET'S PLAY: DECISION-MAKING TECHNIQUES

1. A team wanted to go out for dinner on Friday. However, not everyone was on board for Friday, so the dinner was canceled and shifted to Monday, which was agreed on by everyone.

    A.   Plurality

    B.   Majority

    C.   Autocratic decision making

    D.   Unanimity

2. The Project Manager told all the developers to work on weekends until a milestone is met, as there have been unexpected delays in the schedule.

    A.   Plurality

    B.   Majority

    C.   Autocratic decision making

    D.   Unanimity

3. The marketing team wanted to choose a perfect icon for the summer campaign. Everyone had their favorites, so the team decided to vote. The icon that was selected had the most votes. The selected icon was not liked by 55% of the people.

    A.   Plurality

    B.   Majority

    C.   Autocratic decision making

    D.   Unanimity

4. The marketing team wanted to choose a perfect icon for the summer campaign. Everyone had his or her favorites, so the team decided to vote. The icon that was selected had the most votes. The selected icon was liked by 55% of the people.

    A.   Plurality

    B.   Majority

    C.   Autocratic decision making

    D.   Unanimity

11.5 MODULE END QUESTIONS - PMP STYLE

1. You just received a communication from your client in which the client, Nancy, expressed her displeasure with the way the project is progressing so far. In your view, the project is progressing well. What is the best thing to do?

    A. Reach out to your supervisor and ask her to call the client.

    B. Ignore her. The client does not have any facts.

    C. Send the progress report to the customer showcasing the fact that the project is on track.

    D. Arrange a meeting with the client to understand the issues and then plan accordingly

2. Who is a Resistant stakeholder?

    A. the stakeholder who talks bad about your personality

    B. The stakeholder who does not like you

    C. The stakeholder who has a negative mindset

    D. A stakeholder who does not want to change as per project change

3. Michael is categorizing the project stakeholders using the direction of influence. Kate is highly influential with senior management of the customer organization. Help Michael to place her in the appropriate category.

    A. Upward influence

    B. Downward influence

    C. Outward influence

    D. Side-ward influence

4. You are currently working as a Project Manager at SUPPL. You are given responsibility for moving the office infrastructure to the newly procured office. You are currently identifying project stakeholders and placing them in the appropriate power/interest quadrant. Which of the following stakeholder expectations should be closely managed?

    A. High Power - Low Interest
    B. High Power - High Interest
    C. Low Power - Low Interest
    D. Low Power - High Interest

5. Harry is performing stakeholder analysis for the first time. Which process group is Harry in?

    A. Initiating
    B. Planning
    C. Executing
    D. Monitoring and Controlling

6. Stakeholders' analysis results in stakeholder identification. Stakeholders' stakes can be a combination of the following dimensions except:

   A.   Interest, influence, ownership

   B.   Right, interest, will

   C.   Interest, influence, rights

   D.   Interest, influence, knowledge

7. When is the right time to perform stakeholder analysis in a project?

   A.   Initiating

   B.   Planning

   C.   Executing

   D.   Throughout the project life cycle

8. How would you recommend handling a senior stakeholder who has no interest in your project?

   A.   Ignore him. He does not have any interest in my project

   B.   Identify areas of interest and try and meet often (virtually or physically)

   C.   Understand his information needs and work towards fulfilling them efficiently

   D.   Always copy him in the emails

9. You are assigned to manage the project WISHTOWN. The scope of the project WISHTOWN is to construct a township on the outskirts of a city. The planned end date is two years from now. Due to unexpected climatic and weather conditions, you are far behind schedule. To whom should you inform the status and issues?

   A.   Project Sponsor

   B.   According to the Communication Plan

   C.   Project Team Members

   D.   Client

10. Kevin needs your help to achieve better stakeholder involvement in his project. Help Kevin to get the right approach.

   A.   Invite the stakeholders to attend project status meetings

   B.   Send status reports to the stakeholders

   C.   Have the stakeholders touch base periodically, leading to stakeholder analysis and planning

   D.   Constantly update the stakeholders on the status of all project changes

11. In the daily status meeting, you asked your team how the morale is. They answered using Thumbs up or Thumbs down. You are using:

    A.   Roman voting to understand team morale

    B.   Fist of Thumb to understand team morale

    C.   Polling to understand team morale

    D.   Dot voting of thumb to understand team morale

12. Julia wants to represent the project stakeholders in a format that can showcase the stakeholder's power, knowledge, and rights in a context. Which representation technique would be most helpful?

    A.   Power/ knowledge and Power/ rights grid

    B.   Power, knowledge, and rights cube

    C.   Power/ knowledge grid

    D.   Salience Model

13. Salience model is describing classes of stakeholders based on their _____, _____ and _____. Fill in the blanks.

    A.   Influence, Impact, Power

    B.   Power, urgency, legitimacy

    C.   Influence, rights, legitimacy

    D.   Impact, rights, legitimacy

14. Ray is the project sponsor of the project VANNA. Ray diligently participated in the steering team meetings to ensure the smooth functioning of the project. He also reached out to Jia, the Project Manager, if she needed any help with resource mobilization for the project. How would you categorize Ray as a stakeholder?

    A.   Ray is a supportive stakeholder

    B.   Ray is a leading stakeholder

    C.   Ray is a negative stakeholder

    D.   Ray is a positive stakeholder

15. You are working on the stakeholder analysis and writing plans to influence the behavior of a few stakeholders towards a more positive outcome. Which process are you engaged in?

    A.   Monitoring and Controlling

    B.   Closing

    C.   Executing

    D.   Planning

16. When you meet the stakeholders - what is the most likely outcome?

    A. Issues

    B. Applause

    C. Rewards

    D. Support

17. The ability to understand and relate to others' emotions is _____, a core skill of emotional intelligence. Fill in the blank.

    A. Social skill

    B. Empathy

    C. Motivation

    D. Engagement

18. Ria feels that her boss Steve is unfair towards her. He asks for various types of ad-hoc reports on where she spends unplanned time. If she lags in any other activity due to these requests by Steve, then she needs to cover them by putting in extra hours. This is not a single episode. Now she is getting such reporting requirements from the customers as well. What would be your advice to Ria to solve this problem:

    A. Confront Steve

    B. Manage Steve's expectations

    C. Send project reports more often to Steve and the customer

    D. Analyze stakeholders and their information needs again

19. You asked the team to write their ideas in a notebook before the team met in person. This will help you save time in the stakeholder meeting. Which technique did you use?

    A. Brainstorming

    B. Brainwriting

    C. Brainstorming with brainwriting

    D. Data analysis

20. Identify Stakeholders should focus on:

    A. Making relevant information available to stakeholders as planned.

    B. Understanding project stakeholder information needs and defining a communication approach.

    C. Identifying all people or organizations impacted by the project and documenting relevant information regarding their interest, involvement, and impact on project success.

    D. Communicating and working with stakeholders to meet their needs and address issues as they occur.

11.6 ALL ANSWERS

ANSWERS: 11.2.1 LET'S PLAY: STAKEHOLDER ANALYSIS

Power	Interest	Strategy
1. High	High	Manage Closely
2. High	Low	Keep Satisfied
3. Low	High	Keep Informed
4. Low	Low	No Extra Work-Monitor

ANSWERS: 11.3.1 LET'S PLAY: STAKEHOLDER ENGAGEMENT GRID

ENGAGEMENT LEVEL	DESCRIPTION
1. Unaware	Unaware of the project and potential impacts.
2. Resistant	Aware of the project and potential impacts and resistance to change.
3. Neutral	Aware of the project yet neither supportive nor resistant.
4. Supportive	Aware of the project and potential impacts and supportive of changes.
5. Leading	Aware of the project and potential impacts and actively engaged in ensuring the project is a success.

ANSWERS: 11.4.1 LET'S PLAY: DECISION-MAKING TECHNIQUES

Question	Correct Answer	Why?
1. A team wanted to go out for dinner on Friday. However, not everyone was on board for Friday, so the dinner was canceled and shifted to Monday, which was agreed to by everyone.	Unanimity	100% agreement
2. The Project Manager told all the developers to work on weekends until the milestone is met as there were delays in the schedule.	Autocratic decision making	One person took the decision
3. The marketing team wanted to choose a perfect icon for the summer campaign. Everyone had their favorites, so the team	Plurality	The decision was liked by less than 50%

decided to vote. The icon that was selected had the most votes. The selected icon was not liked by 55% of the people.		
4. The marketing team wanted to choose a perfect icon for the summer campaign. Everyone had his or her favorites, so the team decided to vote. The icon that was selected had the most votes. The selected icon was liked by 55% of the people.	Majority	The decision was liked by more than 50%

ANSWERS: 11.5 MODULE END QUESTIONS - PMP STYLE

1. D	In the case of any conflicts/perceptions, it's always good to reach out to the stakeholder and close it by providing facts. The first step in solving the issue is to understand and hear what the client says. It could be a matter of perception, and sending the status report may not help. The best thing to do is an interactive meeting (call meetings)
2. D	A resistive stakeholder is aware of the project and potential impact and is resistant to change.
3. C	Clients, sellers, and any entity outside the project team are considered to be outside of the team. People having an influence on either of them are said to have outward influence.
4. B	Stakeholders with high power and high interest should be managed closely. Hence, B is the correct answer.
5. A	Stakeholders' analysis is done early in the project and then re-assessed on a continuing basis in the controlling processes. The question here is the FIRST time, so Harry is executing the process Identify Stakeholders of Initiating Process Group. Choice A is the best answer.
6. B	Will is not a valid assessment of stakeholder dimension and hence is a wrong answer.
7. D	Stakeholders' analysis is a continuous process that is performed throughout the project life cycle.
8. C	The stakeholder falls under High authority and Low interest. Don't copy him on emails. Work towards finding his information needs and provide to efficiently.
9. B	The Project Manager needs to communicate effectively on issues, status, and reporting. When and how to raise issues and escalation path and criteria as part

of the communication management plan and should be adhered to for effective communication

10. C Using elimination technique:

> A. Invite the stakeholders to attend project status meetings: Will not work for stakeholders who are not interested: Not the best choice
>
> B. Send status reports to the stakeholders: May not increase involvement to a higher degree. Not the best choice.
>
> C. Have the stakeholders touch base periodically, leading to stakeholder analysis and planning ahead: Engaging with stakeholders and adapting to their expectations is a good way to increase stakeholders' engagement. Best choice.
>
> D. Constantly update the stakeholders on the status of all project changes: This choice may not work for senior executives (high authority and low interest)

Out of all the given choices, Option C is the best.

Stakeholder Engagement needs to be assessed initially, re-assessed periodically and adjustments made as appropriate.

11. A Roman voting: Individuals vote with either a thumbs up (agreement) or thumbs down (dis- agreement).

12. B To represent three aspects for stakeholders, a cube would be the best choice. A Salience model is a predefined combination of 3 aspects which are power, urgency, and legitimacy, and is not the correct option. Choice B is most correct.

13. B The salience model describes classes of stakeholders based on their power (ability to impose their will), urgency (need for immediate attention), and legitimacy (their involvement is appropriate).

14. B Ray is participating in project activities and showing initiative to engage with other stakeholders. Ray is a supportive stakeholder. His active support of the project puts Ray in the leading stakeholder bracket.

15. D Planning for the stakeholder engagement is done at the time of planning. The stakeholder management planning process is Plan Stakeholder Engagement.

16. A This question can take you by surprise. The question is, essentially, what is the output of Manage Stakeholder Engagement? One of the main outputs of

	Manage Stakeholder Engagement is issue logs. You meet with stakeholders to understand if there are any issues and take them from there.
17. B	The ability to understand and relate to others' emotions is empathy, a core skill of emotional intelligence. Fill in the blank.
18. B	Let's use the elimination technique: A. Confront Steve: Not the best option. B. Manage Steve's expectations: This can be a good choice – let's see if there is a better alternative. C. Send project reports more often to Steve and the customer: Yes, it can be a choice to look at but still not the best answer so far. D. Analyze stakeholders and their information need again: This is, so far, the best answer in case you get data/report requests again, as well as from a few stakeholders, which may point to a weak communication planning. You need to understand the communication needs again and change the communication as per the feedback. Choice D is the best answer.
19. B	Brainwriting is achieved by asking the participants to write their ideas before the meeting.
20. C	Identify Stakeholders should focus on identifying all people or organizations impacted by the project and documenting relevant information regarding their interest, involvement, and impact on project success

12. COMMUNICATIONS

IMPORTANT TOPICS FOR THE PMP EXAM

Communication Planning	Communication Channels
Type Of Communication	Communication Model
Communications Dimensions	Non-verbal communications

12.1 COMMUNICATION MANAGEMENT OVERVIEW

Objective: Communication management focuses on developing and communicating artifacts that meet the information needs of stakeholders.

Process Name	Process Group	Why
Plan Communications Management	Planning	Who, how, what, and when to communicate
Manage Communications	Executing	Doing communications
Monitor Communications	Monitoring & Controlling	Checking and taking action if not effective

In any major project, a gap in communication, no matter how small, impacts the project in an adverse way. That's the reason that a Project Manager who is good at communication management is much more successful in managing the stakeholders. Communication involves access to the right information and distributing project information to achieve successful project results.

12.2 PROJECT COMMUNICATION DIMENSIONS

Communication takes place all the time, even while you are not communicating actively (voluntary versus involuntary)

There are various forms of communication, ranging from gestures, also called nonverbal communication or tone of voice, known as para-lingual communication.

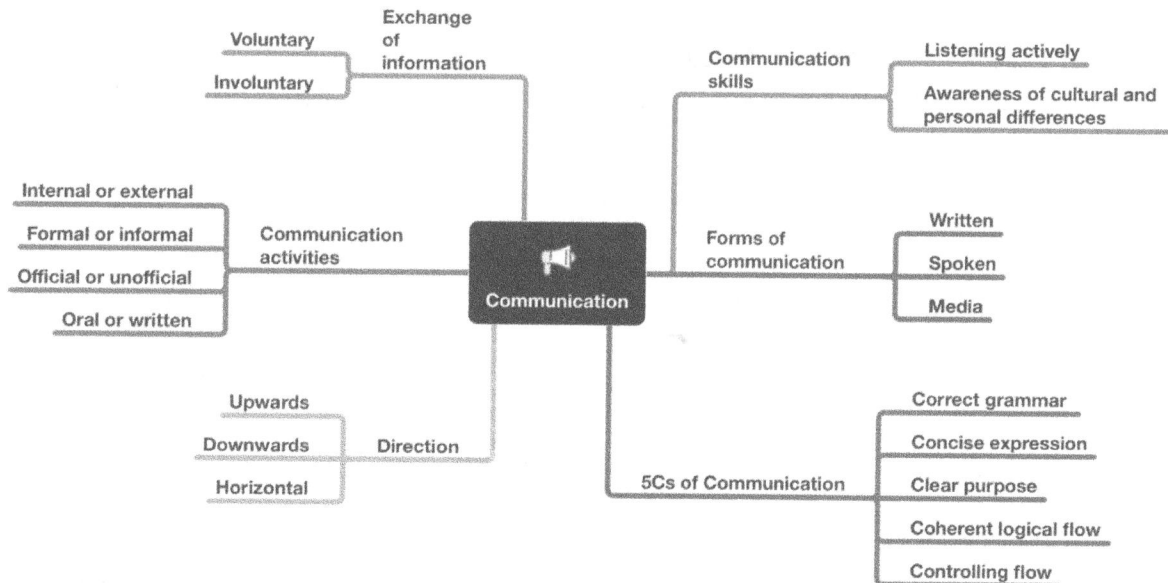

A risk of miscommunication is always present in project scenarios, and hence it is imperative that the Project Manager be aware of that risk and ensure that all communications are planned thoughtfully, keeping the 5Cs of communication in mind.

A Project Manager also needs to listen actively and manage stakeholders' expectations while understanding any personal or cultural differences.

Efficient communication is the need of the hour to work with virtual teams comprising of various cultures and beliefs.

12.2.1 LET'S PLAY: COMMUNICATION DIMENSIONS

Match the following

S.no.	Communication Characteristics	Category
1	Correct grammar, concise expression, clear purpose, coherent, logical flow, controlling the flow	With peers
2	Gestures	Internal, upwards
3	Horizontal communication	Communication skills
4	Sending an internal note to the supervisor	5Cs of communication
5	Listening actively	Nonverbal communication

12.3 PLAN COMMUNICATIONS

Developing an appropriate communication approach is usually based on stakeholders' information needs and requirements.

Stakeholder register

Environment

Planning communications

Communication requirements analysis

Communication models

Communication methods

Think of daily meetings, steering team meetings, Change Control Board (CCB) meetings, client calls, and the escalation matrix. All of this should be planned in the communication plan.

If I had to plan whom to communicate information to and when to communicate that information, how would I begin? I would check stakeholder requirements and the project environment to start planning for any communication in my project. Plan Communications Management is part of the planning process group and results in documenting who, when, and how any communication between parties will take place. Most of the Project Management Planning activities are carried out simultaneously and will constitute the integrated Project Management Plan.

COMMUNICATIONS REQUIREMENT ANALYSIS

Do you need to set up a complex system to communicate, or do you just need to wave your hands and talk? All of this depends on many things. One very important aspect is finding and managing the number of communication channels.

COMMUNICATION CHANNELS

If there are only 2 members on a team, how many ways can information reach each of them - only one. If there are 5 team members, then how many communication channels could there be?

It quickly becomes a web of communications, as shown.

So how would you calculate the total no of communication channels?

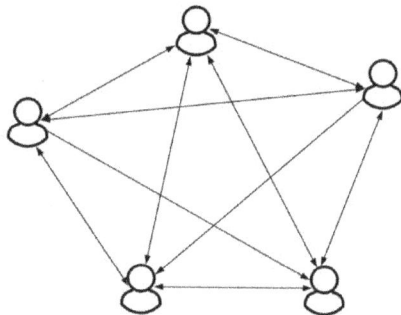

Communication channels = n(n – 1)/2,

Where n represents the number of stakeholders.

For example, a project with 10 stakeholders has 10(10 – 1)/2 = 45 potential communication channels.

Why do we calculate the total number of communication channels? One reason would be because there will be questions in the PMP exam on this topic. :)

The customer and you as Project Manager are also involved in communication and should be considered as an entity while calculating the communication channels.

How does knowing the number of communication channels helps?

You may want to restrict the communication channels if there are too many. The way to achieve that is by ensuring that there is an official mapping of people for communication. It can be top-down communication or horizontal communication. What's that about?

HOW DO WE COMMUNICATE? (COMMUNICATION MODEL)

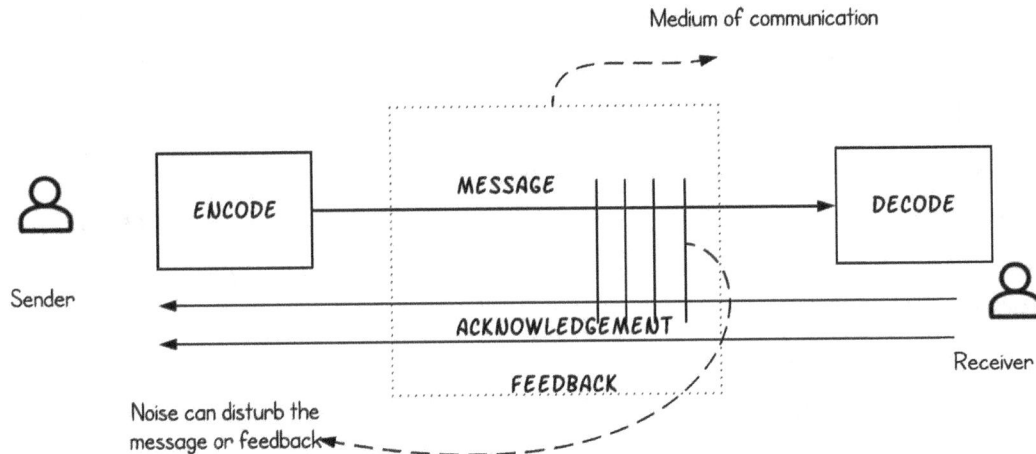

In any communication, there is a sender and a receiver. The sender has the responsibility to encode the message in such a way that the receiver understands the message. The receiver, on the other hand, has the responsibility to decode the message and provide feedback to the sender, explaining if he has understood the message or not.

Noise can be internal (things like views or perceptions about a person) or external (a car horn) and can alter the message.

Term	Meaning
Sender	The entity which initiates the message
Receiver	The entity the message is intended for
Medium	The mechanism by which a message is transmitted
Feedback	A response to the message
Noise	Can interfere with message
Encode	Encryption/modification so that the message can be sent and is clear to all recipients
Decode	Decryption/modification ensures that the message is understood by all receivers

COMMUNICATION METHODS

When you plan for project communication, you may want to consider the environment, the urgency of the information, and what type of communication will work the best.

There are basically three types of communication methods, Interactive (two-way), Push (one way from sender), and pull (receiver pulls communication in). Various situations demand different methods. A good project communication plan consists of all three methods.

INTERACTIVE COMMUNICATION.
A Multi-directional exchange of information. It is the most efficient way to ensure a common understanding
Used when quick decisions are required, or a complex discussion is needed. Examples are meetings, phone calls, video conferencing, etc.

PUSH COMMUNICATION
Push communication is initiated by the sender, and the receiver does not have any control over when they receive the information. Think SMS, emails, and notice boards. Using the push method does not certify that the message reached the recipient or was understood. Examples are letters, memos, reports, emails, faxes, voice mails, press releases, etc.

PULL COMMUNICATION.
Pull communication is a very good way to handle a large volume of data or information archives. Things like minutes, plans, and reports can be stored in a shared repository where the project team can look for information without disturbing others. Yes, you need to implement configuration management (who can access what), but that will make your life as a PM easier. In pull communications, recipients can access information when they need to. Examples are Intranet sites, e-learning, knowledge repositories, etc.

FEW MORE THINGS TO REMEMBER
NONVERBAL COMMUNICATION
These are gestures, facial expressions, and physical appearance when you are communicating your message

PARA LINGUAL COMMUNICATION
Is the tone and pitch of your voice when you are telling people what is going on with your project

12.3.1 LET'S PLAY: COMMUNICATION MODEL

Match the following

Element	Description
1. Sender	Used for transmitting the message
2. Receiver	The entity for which the message is intended
3. Medium	This can change the message
4. Feedback	Done at receiving end
5. Noise	Confirming the receipt of the message
6. Encoding	Done at the sender's end
7. Decoding	The entity that initiates the communication
8. Acknowledgment	Response to message

12.3.2 LET'S PLAY: COMMUNICATION TYPES

Mia and Jay were selecting the candidates for replacing Alex. Choose the kind of communication used in the scenarios given:

1. One applicant came in 30 minutes late and was dressed unprofessionally. Mia and Jay knew that he would not be a good fit for the position.

   A. Paralingual

   B. Nonverbal

   C. Feedback

   D. Communication competence

2. Jay asked an applicant, Rachel, about her background. Her tone of voice was sarcastic, and Jay got the impression that she didn't take the job seriously. Jay and Mia decided to pass on her, too.

   A. Paralingual

   B. Nonverbal

   C. Feedback

   D. Communication competence

3. Jay asked the next applicant, Ron, if he knew what the process requirements were? Ron inquired, "Can you please repeat the question?"

   A. Paralingual

   B. Nonverbal

   C. Feedback

   D. Communication competence

4. Ron told Jay and Mia about his background. As he spoke, he made eye contact with them and made sure to confirm agreement with them.

   A. Paralingual

   B. Nonverbal

   C. Feedback

   D. Communication competence

12.4 MODULE END QUESTIONS - PMP STYLE

1. Project success is measured by the perception of the project, which includes the team and the Project Manager, their actions, and their communication styles. Effective managers spend most of their time in:

   A. Creating Work Performance Reports

   B. Communicating

   C. Working on scheduled activities

   D. Managing risks

2. Catherine is working towards introducing a new product in the firm. The stakeholders have asked her for certain information about the project. She is in the process of identifying the right communication method for information distribution to project stakeholders who are working at different locations. She decided to have the performance reports uploaded on the intranet where only specific stakeholders can access them. This information is available 100% of the time. Which sort of communication method has she opted for?

   A. Push

   B. Interactive

   C. Pull

   D. Mass Communication

3. Jessica is a Project Manager launching a new product of in-flight food service. One of her stakeholders has asked for an immediate status report of the project. She decided to send a FAX with the information. Which sort of communication BEST describes this?

   A. Push

   B. Interactive

   C. Pull

   D. Written

4. You set up a call with the client. However, the client says in an angry tone, "We are not satisfied with the project status." Which sort of communication BEST describes the way the client resorted to showing their displeasure?

   A. Nonverbal

   B. Paralingual

   C. Feedback

   D. Formal

5. Gina is assigned a new project, RUGBY, as the Project Manager. She has 6 team members, 2 sponsors, and 1 client. She wants to inform all of them about the progress of her project. How many lines of communication are present in the project?

   A.   45
   B.   36
   C.   3
   D.   50

6. Jane is working as the Project Manager to develop ERP software for her client JENGA. Three members have been added to her team. Now she has seven team members, one sponsor, and one client. How many communication lines (channels) have been added?

   A.   24
   B.   21
   C.   45
   D.   40

7. In a team meeting, Jane asked her team members if anyone knew how to write a particular type of code requiring C language expertise. James responded, "C language? Yes, Ma'am, I have learned the language." What sort of communication has James used?

   A.   Paralingual
   B.   Nonverbal
   C.   Feedback
   D.   Noise

8. Today is the annual event in your company where everyone is asked to be in formal dress. One of your team members turns up in a casual dress. Your other team members raised their eyebrows and hands in a questioning way. What kind of communication is being used?

   A.   Paralingual
   B.   Nonverbal
   C.   Feedback
   D.   Active listening

9. You are the Project Manager working with KFCD. You are creating a communication plan for your project. A communication plan allows a Project Manager to document the approach for communicating most efficiently and effectively with stakeholders. You sent an information note to all the managers about the project's best practices. This communication would be classified as:

   A.   Horizontal communication

B.   Informal communication

C.   Upward communication

D.   Downward communication

10. Jaimie sent minutes of the meeting to all the stakeholders and customers who attended the meeting. The communication between Jaimie and the customer will be classified as follows:

A.   External formal communication

B.   Internal formal communication

C.   Internal official communication

D.   External official communication

11. You called the client, John, as per the project plan. He showed some comfort in the way the teamwork is progressing and also mentioned a few issues which you noted down. John discussed some assignments along the way and mentioned that it was his birthday today. Which process are you in?

A.   Plan communication

B.   Manage communication

C.   Control communication

D.   Manage stakeholders

12. Active listening is, EXCEPT:

A.   Nodding while another person is talking

B.   Repeating to confirm the message

C.   Listening while replying to an urgent email

D.   Looking in the eye

13. There are a lot of emails floating around. One of the emails which you got was marked as very urgent. So, you responded to all. One of the recipients wrote back to keep him out of these emails as he is not interested. What action would you take?

A.   Send him an email and apologize

B.   Meet/call him to understand his information needs and update the communication plan accordingly

C.   Do nothing - this is normal.

D.   Acknowledge his email by responding to all.

14. In a communication model, the sender is responsible for, EXCEPT:

A.   Information is clear and complete

B.   Encoding the information

C.   Confirming the understanding

D.   Confirming the agreement on the shared information

15. Mia sends a status report to all the stakeholders every week. This time, she needed some opinions on the new format of the dashboard, so she sent out a survey to all. Which communication method is used when Mia uses the survey as the tool for getting a response?

    A.   Push

    B.   Interactive

    C.   Pull

    D.   Email

16. You are a Project Manager with a telecom service provider and are working on the project ROLTA. The project is to enable on-demand pricing for prepaid customers along with offers and discounts with channel partners. Most of your time is spent responding to channel partners with the information they seek. What is left is taken up by requests which are asking for information you are not the owner of. Connecting the right people to each other is your response. What should you do?

    A.   Nothing. This is how big projects work

    B.   Delegate, that's where you may be lacking

    C.   Have team and seller meetings so that the people know each other and reach out to the right person for information

    D.   Implement a pull communication system and ensure that everyone is aware of it.

17. An audit was performed a few days ago, and now you need to close a few of the observations that were part of the audit. Many stakeholders need to be updated every day about how many observations are still open. You have a lot of other work planned and are already short of resources. Which communication model would be most helpful?

    A.   Interactive communication.

    B.   Push communication

    C.   Pull communication.

    D.   Oral communication

18. In a long-running project, the information on the old data is crucial for experts to make any project decisions and further planning. What kind of communication method would be the best for working with this information?

    A.   Push

    B.   Pull

    C.   Interactive

    D.   Focus groups

19. **Select the incorrect statement**

    A.   Encode is to translate the idea

    B.   Decode is to translate the idea

    C.   Decoding is performed by the receiver

    D.   Encoding is performed by the receiver

20. **You have been sending a regular status report as per the communication plan, the organization structure changed last month, and as a result, new people have replaced older ones. What would you do next?**

    A.   Update the stakeholder register

    B.   Meet with new tagholders to understand their interest in the project

    C.   Wait for a few weeks to let people settle in new roles

    D.   Let the new supervisor reach out to you

12.5 ALL ANSWERS

ANSWERS: 12.2.1 LET'S PLAY: COMMUNICATION DIMENSIONS

S.no.	Communication Characteristics	Category
1	Correct grammar, concise expression, clear purpose, coherent, logical flow, controlling the flow	5Cs of communication
2	Gestures	Nonverbal communication
3	Horizontal communication	With peers
4	Sending an internal note to the supervisor	Internal, upwards
5	Listening actively	Communication skills

ANSWERS: 12.3.1 LET'S PLAY: COMMUNICATION MODEL

Communication Element	Description
1. Sender	The entity that initiates the communication
2. Receiver	The entity for which the message is intended
3. Medium	Used for transmitting the message
4. Feedback	Response to message
5. Noise	This can change the message
6. Encoding	Done at the sender's end
7. Decoding	Done at receiving end
8. Acknowledgment	Confirming the receipt of the message

ANSWERS: 12.3.2 LET'S PLAY: COMMUNICATION TYPES

Question	Answer	WHY
1	Nonverbal	Dressed unprofessionally
2	Paralingual	Her tone of voice was sarcastic
3.	Feedback	Ron inquired, "Can you please repeat the question?"
4.	Communication competence	As he spoke, he made eye contact with them and made sure to confirm agreement with them.

ANSWERS: 12.4 MODULE END QUESTIONS - PMP STYLE

1 . B	Effective Project Managers need to network and be good communicators to manage people and stakeholders effectively.
2. C	The pull communication method is the technique of posting information so that stakeholders can get it when they need it.
3. A	Push communication is initiated by the sender and is unidirectional. FAX is one-way communication (in a non-technical sense)
4. B	Paralingual communication is in the tone and pitch of the person's voice when they are talking. Nonverbal communication means gestures, facial expressions, etc. Feedback is when you respond to communication. Formal communication is written, and hence B is the correct choice.
5. A	The formula to calculate the lines of communication is {n*(n-1)} / 2. Here you have 9 people plus Project Manager. N is 10 hence Communication channel is {10*(10-1)}/2 = 45.
6. A	Here you have 7 team members, 1 sponsor, 1 client and 1 as Project Manager, so: {10*(10-1) }/2 = 45; Previously Project Manager had 1 as herself, 4 team members, 1 sponsor and 1 client, so: {7 * (7-1)}/2 =21. So, additional communication lines: 45 - 21 = 24.
7. C	James repeated the question, and this is an example of feedback.
8. B	Nonverbal communication means your gestures, facial expressions, and physical appearance.
9. A	Information sharing among peers is horizontal communication.
10. A	Minutes distribution is formal communication. Sending the minutes to the customer is formal external communication. Sending the minutes to the team is formal internal communication.
11. B	This is tricky, and it could be both managing communication and managing stakeholder. Notice that you called as per the plan. This is the communication when to meet with whom and how - ALL part of the communication plan.
12. C	This is an EXCEPT question. Doing another task is not active listening.
13. B	Understanding the information needed and changing the communication plan is a continuous process.
14. D	The receiver may not agree with the sender. The sender is responsible for transmitting the message in such a way that the receiver understands it.
15. A	Surveys are push communication.

16. D	Spending time as a gatekeeper for information is not a valuable addition to the Project Manager's time. Implementing a shared server will help all stakeholders to find the right information, leaving the Project Manager to do effective management.
17. B	Push communication would be most helpful in sending the information to many stakeholders.
18. B	Pull communications are a good way to store significant data, and it can be accessed by stakeholders when they need it.
19. D	Doing TRUE/FALSE technique: A. Encode is to translate the idea: TRUE B. Decode is to translate the idea: TRUE C. Decoding is performed by the receiver: TRUE D. Encoding is performed by the receiver: FALSE Encoding is performed by the sender, so option D is the correct option.
20. B	A project manager should be proactive. Whenever the organization structure changes, the project stakeholder register will undergo changes. You should meet the new people/team to understand their interest levels and information needs in order to engage with them better for project success.

13. TEAM

IMPORTANT TOPICS FOR THE PMP EXAM

Organizational Theories	Resource Plan
Organizational Charts	Conflict Management
Team Stages	Organizational Theories
Team Charter	Virtual Team
Team Stages	Emotional Quotient
Influencing	Co- Location
Leadership styles	People motivation
Emotional Intelligence	Mentoring

13.1 INTRODUCTION: A GOOD TEAM

THE CALL

I received an email from the COO asking me to drop everything and join a call because I was taking the handover as Program Manager.

I joined the call in the evening.

Several senior people on the call:

- The Vice President acting as the Customer Delivery Head,
- Two group heads,
- Current program manager,
- On-site and Offshore Project Managers and
- Few SMEs

The agenda of the meeting was to develop the Project Roadmap URGENTLY.

The next day when I arrived at the office, I noticed the offshore Project Manager wearing the same clothes as the day before. He told me that the team worked overnight on the Roadmap.

Hmm – Great Team...

Within a few days, I was in front of the customer.

The customer gave me a long list of issues. This was a surprise.

WITH TEAM

I asked for the project plan from the on-site Project Manager. She had none.

Offshore PM again had no plan.

The team was working without a plan...

THE ROOT CAUSE

The role and responsibilities were not defined.

13.2 RESOURCE MANAGEMENT OVERVIEW

Aim: Resource management is planning, acquiring, and managing resources to successfully complete the project.

Process Name	Process Group	Why
Plan Team	Planning	Defining Team, Reporting structure, when to acquire and release, training requirements
Acquire Team	Executing	Getting resources onboard / getting approvals as per the plan
Develop and Manage Team	Executing	Building trust and providing training, understanding team dynamics, using EQ, and managing conflicts

13.3 PLAN TEAM

Resource planning includes identifying and documenting project roles & responsibilities, required skills set, reporting relationships, and creating a staffing and resource management plan.

TEAM GOVERNANCE

→ You can use hierarchical charts to show who reports to whom.

→ A text format can be used to describe roles and responsibilities.

→ RAM stands for Responsibility Assignment Matrix. A RAM chart can be used to clearly assign responsibilities of the work to your team.

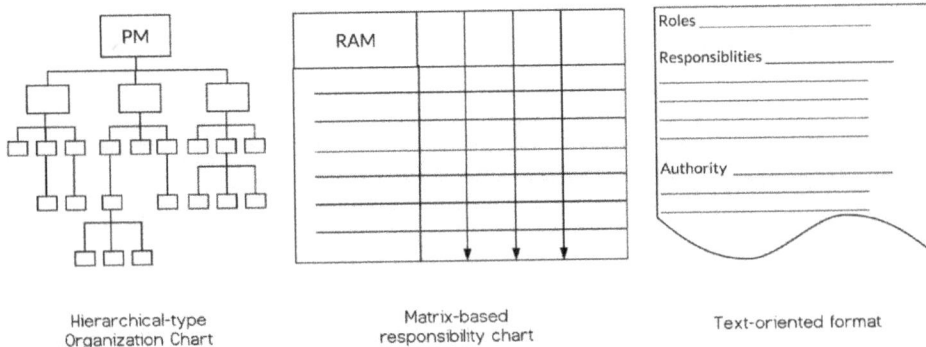

Hierarchical-type Organization Chart

Matrix-based responsibility chart

Text-oriented format

A good example of RAM is a RACI (Responsible, Accountable, Consult, Informed) chart.

A RACI chart can be helpful in a matrix organization where the resources report to many supervisors. In such cases, a clear direction and accountability will help the team to function effectively.

Activity	Team Member				
	Emma	Ana	Mia	Ben	Ethan
Testing	A	R	I	I	C
Module 2 Plan	C	A	I	I	I
Module 4	I	C	A	R	I
Module 2	R	I	I	A	C

R = Responsible   A = Accountable   C = Consult   I = Inform

Follow the rule of clear accountability, so have only one A. You can have many R's.

A good example is creating the Project Plan. Project Manager(A) is accountable for making the project plan, but the module leads (R) can work and collaborate to fill in the module details.

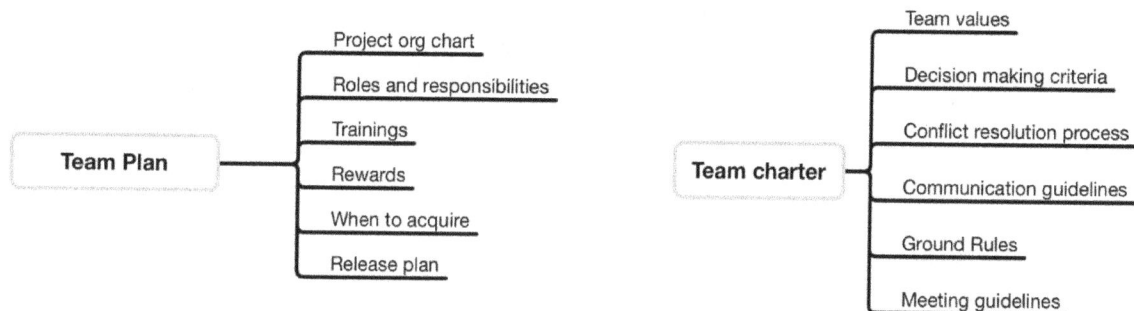

Team Plan
- Project org chart
- Roles and responsibilities
- Trainings
- Rewards
- When to acquire
- Release plan

Team charter
- Team values
- Decision making criteria
- Conflict resolution process
- Communication guidelines
- Ground Rules
- Meeting guidelines

TEAM CHARTER

The team charter defines the group norms. This helps align the thought process, a vision of the group, and expected ways to behave.

Team Values like openness and respect will help the team come together and discuss the conflicts when they arise.

Team culture can be built on the ways to communicate, e.g., open-door policy or WhatsApp any time culture. You decide how formal your team could be.

GROUND RULES

Ground rules detail the code of conduct for a group, explaining the behavior that's expected of all members. Ideally, ground rules are created and agreed to by all in the team. A few ground rules as an example are:

→ Meetings on time

→ No interruptions while one speaks

→ Put your name as owner of a task only if you can make the target date

If you miss the target date or a ground rule, a fine can be imposed. This will help the team come together and help to understand the acceptable behavior and non-acceptable behavior in the group.

A good idea is to publish the ground rules in a visible place for the team to view.

13.4 ACQUIRE AND DEVELOP TEAM

Get the team on board as per the project plan. Selection of the team members plays a tremendous role in getting the right people on board.

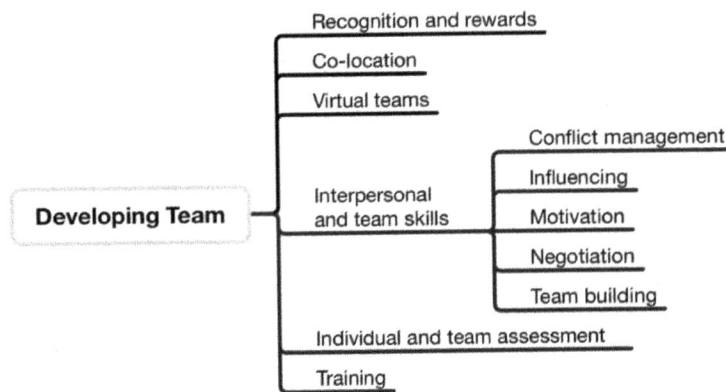

If you do not get people with the right skills in one place, you may opt for a virtual team and build the team.

A few of the methods to manage and develop teams are:

CO-LOCATION

Co-location, also referred to as Tight Matrix, involves placing many or all of the most active project team members in the same physical location to enhance their ability to perform as a team.

Tacit information is information in the air. That is the reason why a person located in headquarters knows the undercurrents. However, a person based in Canada and working from home might have little knowledge about the urgency in the air at the head office.

If you want your team to be aggressively working on a few critical milestones, the best thing to do is to co-locate your team. This way, you avoid all the miscommunication, or worse, lack of communication.

Co-location strategies can include a team meeting room (sometimes called a "war room"), places to post schedules, and other conveniences that enhance communication and a sense of alliance.

VIRTUAL TEAMS

Virtual teams are groups of people with a shared objective who fulfill their roles with little or zero time spent meeting face to face. There can be disadvantages related to virtual teams. For example, the possibility of misinterpretations, feeling of loneliness, and one head to catch. Communication planning becomes increasingly important in a virtual team environment. Tools that can be used by virtual teams to work effectively:

COMMUNICATING EFFECTIVELY

→ Schedule some time for teams to get together using the group conferencing tools. A daily meeting with all group members will help. Find a common time.

→ Chat windows – let your team have a way to leave messages using WhatsApp group or any official tool like zoom chat

→ Shared storage space like Dropbox or SharePoint site can help the team to refer to the right documents without wasting time

→ Use pair programming with the virtual conferencing tool. You don't have to talk. It is just on so that it feels like you are working together, also referred to as sliding windows.

→ Use collaboration tools to share the tasks and progress.

TASK ALLOCATION AND TRACKING

A clear understanding of tasks and tracking the progress using tools like ZIRA or common workspace tools can help the team understand the tasks and update the progress without dependencies.

BUILD TRUST

Using a virtual game hub or chit-chat space will help the team to feel together. There are games like guess the movie or let's make a dish. Find out some time for your team to spend some chill time together.

SCHEDULING MENTORSHIP CALLS

A great leader should know the team, and the best way is to spend some time in a one-on-one meeting. This is a time to understand any challenges faced by your team members at an individual level and coach/mentor them.

Here we focus on improving competencies and team member interactions to improve overall team productivity.

INTERPERSONAL SKILLS

You build your team by spending time with them, bonding with them, and using your interpersonal skills.

I know a manager who remembers most of the things about his team, like location preference, the way of working, and even personal issues if someone is facing distracting challenges. The result? Teams love him and are willing to do whatever he asks for.

RECOGNITION AND REWARDS

Part of the team development process involves recognizing and rewarding desirable behavior. People are motivated if they feel they are valued in the organization, and this value is demonstrated by the rewards given to them.

Money is viewed as a tangible aspect of any reward system, but intangible rewards can be equally more effective.

Most project team members are motivated by an opportunity to grow, accomplish, and apply their professional skills to meet new challenges. A good strategy for Project Managers is to reward the team and recognize them throughout the life cycle of the project rather than waiting until the project is concluded.

INDIVIDUAL AND TEAM ASSESSMENT

A key task to improve the performance of the team is to understand the skill gaps. A plan to identify and improve skill gaps will help the team. The skill gaps can be addressed in various ways:

- → External training
- → Internal Training
- → On The Job learning
- → Mentorship
- → Shadow and reverse shadow

You can use a combination of the training to build your team competency.

13.5 TUCKMAN LADDER – MODEL OF TEAM DEVELOPMENT

Each team goes through these stages. Some pass through them fast. Some take a little more time. It depends on the complexity, size, and culture of the team. The first stage of the team formation is:

FORMING

This phase is where the team meets and learns about the project and what their formal roles and responsibilities are. Team members tend to be independent and not as open in this phase.

STORMING

During this phase, the team begins to address the project work, technical decisions, and the project management approach. If team members are not collaborative and open to differing ideas and perspectives, the environment can become destructive.

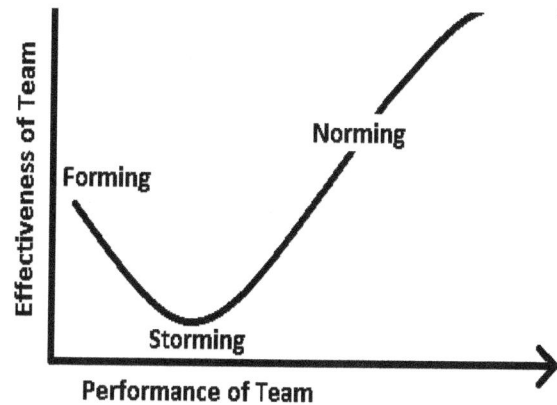

NORMING

In the norming phase, team members begin to work together and adjust work habits and behaviors that support the team. The team begins to trust each other during this phase.

PERFORMING

Teams that reach the performing stage function as a well-organized unit. They are interdependent and work through issues smoothly and effectively.

ADJOURNING

In the adjourning phase, the team completes the work and moves on from the project. It's common for these stages to occur in order. However, a team may get stuck in a particular stage or slip back to an earlier stage, based on the leadership and climate of the organization/team.

13.5.1 LET'S PLAY: TEAM STAGES

Identify and match the team stage in the given scenarios:

Scenario.	Team Stage
1. Kyle and Joanna are working together on the project POSH. They disagree on everything most of the time. They are at a point now where they are barely talking to each other.	Forming
2. Norman manages project APOLLO. Norman understands the team aspirations, ensures that the team enthusiasm is high, and allocates the right tasks to the right people. The team trusts Norman and contributes with high enthusiasm. It seems like a great, happy group.	Storming
3. A new member, Amy, joined the task force; everyone seemed polite and offered assistance if she needed it. She is trying to understand her duties.	Norming
4. Now that the project is over, the team is analyzing the failures and is looking forward to meeting each other while packing their bags.	Performing
5. Sarah is torn by the behavior of her fellow colleague, Amy. She had differences of opinion, but now she has made up her mind to focus on her task, realizing that the points Amy made were not so bad after all and helped her arrive at a few good decisions.	Adjourning

13.6 CONFLICT MANAGEMENT

Now that your team is trained, working with each other, and producing project deliverables. They might run into some conflicts, as per usual inherent human nature. If the conflicts are small, you, as a Project Manager, do not need to get into them; they get solved on their own. But if conflicts are affecting project performance, or if they escalate, then as a PM, you need to take appropriate actions.

Conflict Happens

Some conflict is beneficial for the team, as it gets the team to think differently.

Sources of conflict include

- Scarce resources,
- Scheduling priorities, and
- Personal work styles.

Team ground rules, group norms, and solid project management practices, like communication planning and role definition, reduce the amount of conflict.

Good things to note about conflict

Successful conflict management results in greater productivity and positive working relationships.

- Differences of opinion can lead to increased creativity and better decision-making.
- If the differences become a negative factor, project team members are initially responsible for their resolution.
- If the conflict escalates, the Project Manager should help facilitate a satisfactory resolution.
- Conflict should be addressed early and usually in private, using a direct, collaborative approach.
- If the disruptive conflict continues, formal procedures may be used, including disciplinary actions.

CONFLICT RESOLUTION TECHNIQUES

FORCING

- Get your way.
- "I know what's right. Don't question my judgment or authority."
- It is better to take a risk causing a few hard feelings than to abandon a position you are committed to.
- You feel you have proved your point, but the other party feels defeated and possibly humiliated.

AVOIDING

- Avoid having to deal with conflict.
- "I'm neutral on that issue. Let me think about it."
- Disagreements are inherently bad because they create tension.
- Interpersonal problems don't get resolved, causing long-term frustration manifested in a variety of ways.

ACCOMMODATING

- Don't upset the other person.
- "How can I help you feel good about this encounter? My position isn't so important that it is worth risking bad feelings between us."
- Maintaining harmonious relationships should be our top priority.
- The other person is likely to take advantage of you.

COMPROMISING

- Reach an agreement quickly.
- "Let's search for a mutually agreeable solution."
- Prolonged conflicts distract people from their work and engender bitter feelings.
- Participants become conditioned to seek a convenient rather than an effective solution.

COLLABORATING

- Solve the problem together.
- "This is my position. What is yours? I'm committed to finding the best possible solution."
- The positions of both parties are equally important (though not necessarily equally valid). Equal emphasis should be placed on the quality of the outcome and the fairness of the decision-making.
- Participants find an effective solution.

As per PMBOK, Collaboration/Problem Solving is the BEST STRATEGY.

13.6.1 LET'S PLAY: CONFLICT MANAGEMENT

Appraisal discussions were taking place. Mark, the Project Manager, has a team of 35 people and had a lengthy task to discuss the results and the expectations to keep his team motivated. Here are a few scenarios of 1-1 discussions Mark had with his team members.

Find the conflict resolution technique selected by Mark:

1.	Rita started crying when Mark handed over the appraisal results and told her that she was rated as an underperformer. Since it was difficult to converse, Mark said, "why don't you go home today, sleep on it, and we will discuss your appraisal again tomorrow?"	A. Forcing B. Avoiding C. Accommodating D. Compromising E. Collaborating
2.	Mark to Rob: "Rob, I don't want to hear the same excuses again. The rest of the team is working harder and producing better results. I'm convinced that you should be rated as an average 5/10 as your final rating. If you have any complaints, speak to the Human Resource Department."	A. Forcing B. Avoiding C. Accommodating D. Compromising E. Collaborating
3.	Mark to Jason: "Jason, you can select either a promotion or a role change but not both. Let me know so that I can proceed."	A. Forcing B. Avoiding C. Accommodating D. Compromising E. Collaborating
4.	Mark, while addressing the team in the daily team meeting: Team, let's move beyond appraisal ratings. You are a dynamic group, and I'm sure this year we will rock."	A. Forcing B. Avoiding C. Accommodating D. Compromising E. Collaborating
5.	Noah, a member of the team, resigned. When Mark and Noah discussed the reasons, Noah mentioned that he needs to spend more time at home since his wife Carol is working. Mark knows that Noah is an asset to the team. He called a meeting with Noah and the human resource manager, Susan, to see if there could be a better option, such as allowing Noah to work from home.	A. Forcing B. Avoiding C. Accommodating D. Compromising E. Collaborating

13.7 GETTING THINGS DONE:

Video Available You Tube

SEARCH THIS TOPIC AT THE CHANNEL

A key task for the manager is to get things done, and hence it is important for a PM to understand different ways to get things done.

A quick comparison of powers you can use as a Project Manager. You can combine a few types of powers to be more effective based on the project and organization dynamics.

Power type	Description	Keyword
Position/authority	Formal power by being in a position	Formal/designation
Referent	Being associated with someone of credibility	Using someone's name
Personality	Using own personality	Charm
Relational/ networking	Using network	People in the network
Expert	How much you know	SME power (most lasting power)
Reward	Ability to give monitory rewards	Rewards
Coercive	Ability to withhold rewards	Negative power (least lasting power)
Persuasive	Ability to provide counters	
Ingratiating/flattery	Using common ground	Flattery
Pressure- based	Limiting choices	Time pressure, work choices
Avoiding	Refusing to participate	
Guilt based	Using a sense of duty	Duty/guilt
Situational	Using part of the situation	
Information	Control of gathering or distributing information	

13.8 LEADERSHIP STYLES

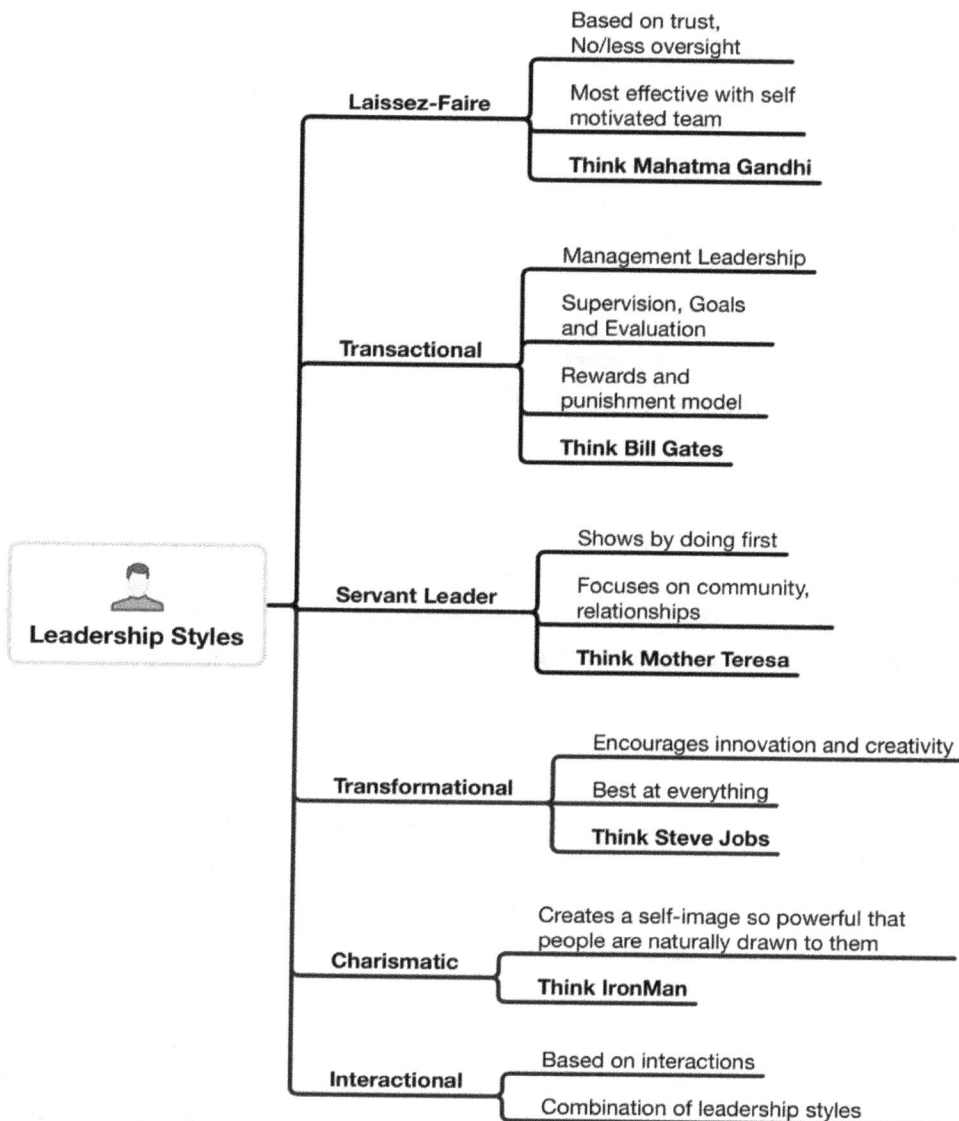

Leadership Styles

- **Laissez-Faire**
  - Based on trust, No/less oversight
  - Most effective with self motivated team
  - **Think Mahatma Gandhi**

- **Transactional**
  - Management Leadership
  - Supervision, Goals and Evaluation
  - Rewards and punishment model
  - **Think Bill Gates**

- **Servant Leader**
  - Shows by doing first
  - Focuses on community, relationships
  - **Think Mother Teresa**

- **Transformational**
  - Encourages innovation and creativity
  - Best at everything
  - **Think Steve Jobs**

- **Charismatic**
  - Creates a self-image so powerful that people are naturally drawn to them
  - **Think IronMan**

- **Interactional**
  - Based on interactions
  - Combination of leadership styles

SERVANT LEADER?

→ Educate stakeholders

→ Support the team through mentoring and encouragement. Advocate for team members' training and career development. The quote "We lead teams by standing behind them."

→ Help the team with technical project management activities like quantitative risk analysis

→ Celebrate team successes

→ Support and bridge-building activities with external groups

13.8.1 LET'S PLAY: LEADERSHIP STYLES

Describe the leadership style displayed by the manager in the scenario:

A.	Laissez-faire		B.	Transactional
C.	Servant leader		D.	Transformational
E.	Charismatic		F.	Interactional

1. Chris works in the organization BLUE. The team reports to him as he is the Functional Manager. However, the team members are often busy with the project and usually are traveling. Chris does not bother anyone until and unless any escalation from fellow managers reaches him.

Answer: _____

2. Roy is an athlete and ensures that he gets his work done. Sometimes the logic works, and in some cases, the charm. He knows the audience, and he knows what will work with them.

Answer: _____

3. Aron works with the team and ensures that he is always available for any need. If the team is working on weekends, Aron will make sure that he is present in the office just to talk to and motivate the team. He often laughs and says that my job is to ensure you guys are fed and hydrated so that you can focus on work.

Answer: _____

4. Joy is busy setting the team goals for the coming year. The goal-setting exercise will help the team and her stay focused on the job at hand. It's a big task, and she wants to do justice to it.

Answer: _____

5. When Liam speaks to the team, everyone listens. He is so clear in his thought processes and very good at painting the big picture. The new product which Liam is launching will take the market by storm. Everyone is excited to be part of this next big phenomenon.

Answer: _____

13.9 PEOPLE MANAGEMENT THEORIES

MASLOW'S HIERARCHY OF NEEDS BY ABRAHAM MASLOW

Once a lower-level need has been met, it no longer serves as a motivator, and the next higher level becomes the driving motivator.

The most fundamental and basic four layers of the pyramid contain what Maslow called "deficiency needs" or "d-needs":

- Esteem
- Friendship and love
- Security
- Physical needs

If these "deficiency needs" are not met – with the exception of the most fundamental (physiological) need – there may not be a physical indication, but the individual will feel anxious and tense.

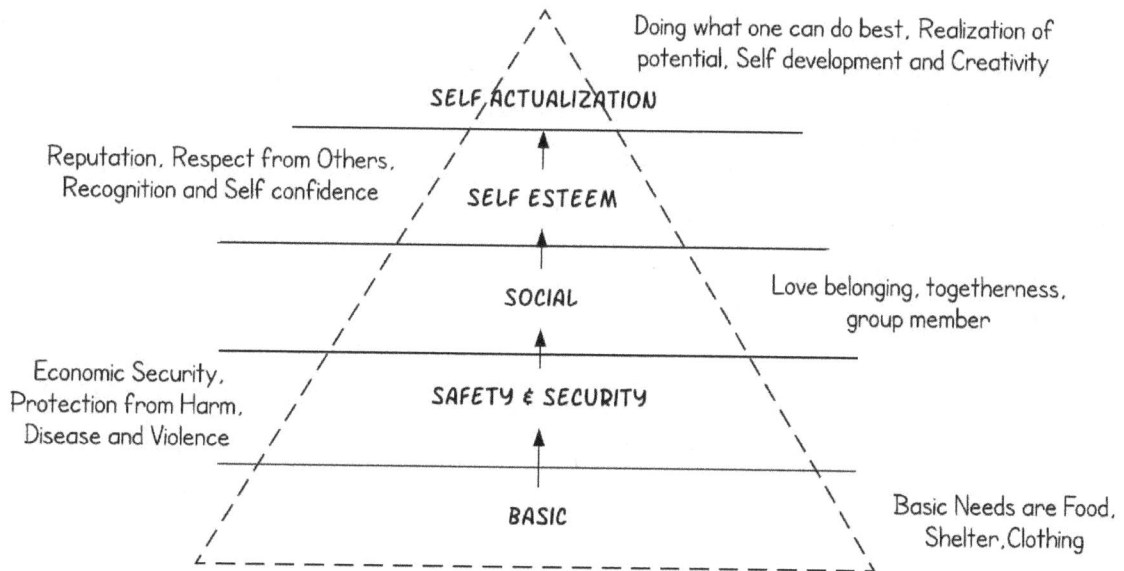

Doing what one can do best, Realization of potential, Self development and Creativity

SELF ACTUALIZATION

Reputation, Respect from Others, Recognition and Self confidence

SELF ESTEEM

SOCIAL

Love belonging, togetherness, group member

Economic Security, Protection from Harm, Disease and Violence

SAFETY & SECURITY

BASIC

Basic Needs are Food, Shelter, Clothing

Maslow's Hierarchy of Need

HERZBERG'S MOTIVATION THEORY

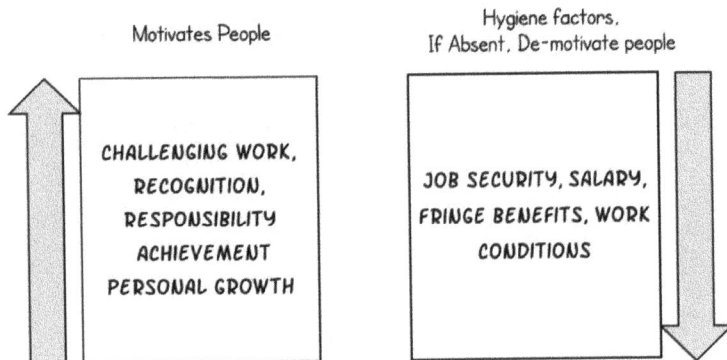

Motivates People

CHALLENGING WORK,
RECOGNITION,
RESPONSIBILITY
ACHIEVEMENT
PERSONAL GROWTH

Hygiene factors,
If Absent, De-motivate people

JOB SECURITY, SALARY,
FRINGE BENEFITS, WORK
CONDITIONS

- A "hygiene factor" is something like a paycheck or status – things that people need to do the job.
- Having their hygiene factors met does not motivate people, but the absence of hygiene factors de-motivates and reduces performance.
- What motivates people is the work itself and not hygiene conditions (ex: working conditions, Salary, personal life, security, and status)

MCGREGOR'S THEORY X AND THEORY Y:

Theory X and Theory Y are theories of human motivation that were created and developed by Douglas McGregor at the MIT Sloan School of Management in the 1960s. These theories describe two contrasting models of workforce motivation that have been used in human resource management, organizational behavior, organizational communication, and organizational development.

Theory X and Theory Y have to do with the perceptions that managers hold of their employees, which in turn, influence their management style.

THEORY X

According to this theory, type X individuals are considered to be inherently lazy and not happy with their jobs. As a result, an authoritarian management style is required to ensure that individuals fulfill their objectives. Workers managed this way need to be closely supervised under comprehensive systems of control.

THEORY Y

In this theory, management assumes employees can be ambitious, self-motivated, and exercise self-control. It is believed that employees enjoy their mental and physical work duties. According to them, work is as natural as play. They possess the ability for creative problem solving, but their talents are underused in most organizations. Theory Y managers believe that, given the proper conditions, employees will learn to seek out and accept responsibility and exercise self-control and self-direction in accomplishing objectives to which they are committed. A Theory Y manager believes that, given the right conditions, most people will want to do well at work. They believe that the satisfaction of doing a good job is a strong motivation. Many people interpret Theory Y as a positive set of beliefs about workers.

THEORY Z BY WILLIAM OUCHI:

- Formulated from Quality movement and Quality circles
- Both Management and Workers need to be involved, and they should trust each other
- Based on the book "How American Business Can Meet the Japanese Challenge."

EXPECTANCY THEORY BY VICTOR VROOM

You need to give people an expectation of a reward to motivate them.

The rewards or awards should be achievable. If they are impossible to achieve, they will de-motivate people.

MCCLELLAND'S ACHIEVEMENT THEORY

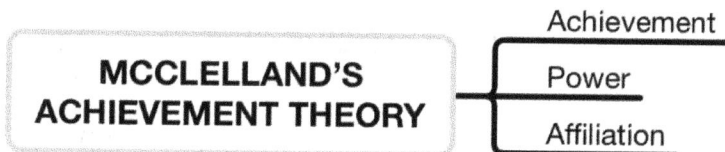

Need theory, also known as the Three Needs Theory proposed by psychologist David McClelland, is a motivational model that attempts to explain how the needs for achievement, power, and affiliation affect the actions of people from a managerial context.

People need achievement, power, and affiliation to be motivated.

- Achievement is when someone performs well and is recognized for it
- Power means he or she has a lot of control or influence in the company

- Affiliation, a strong sense of being a part of a working team and having good relationships with co-workers

HALO EFFECT 😇

Extending the impression of a particular outstanding trait to influence the total judgment of a person.

Ex: Technical Architect to Management

13.10 MENTORING - A MUTUALLY BENEFICIAL PARTNERSHIP

Nowadays, the organization has a special focus on mentorship. Even if yours does not, It's a good idea to start thinking in terms of developing a mentorship program for your team.

A Mentor:

A person who has been there and done that can develop leadership skills by helping others learn, grow, and improve.

A mentee:

You are new in the field and want someone who can help you do these things.

More professionals these days are actively pursuing mentoring to advance their careers. And whether you're on the giving or receiving end, these types of partnerships can benefit your career.

A mentoring partnership can be rewarding to both people, personally and professionally. It's an opportunity to develop communication skills, expand your viewpoints, and consider new ways of approaching situations. And both partners can advance their careers in the process.

As a leader of the group, you can initiate the program, foster an environment and give time for relationships to develop. Let new people be mentored by experienced individuals.

A policy of pairing the people can be adopted to enable mentorship.

13.11 EMOTIONAL INTELLIGENCE AND MBTI

Video Available [YouTube]

SEARCH THIS TOPIC AT THE CHANNEL

Emotional intelligence/ quotient (EQ) is the ability to understand, use, and manage your own emotions. Mastering EQ will work positively to relieve stress, communicate effectively, empathize with others, overcome challenges and defuse conflict.

EQ can help you build stronger relationships, succeed at school and work, and achieve your career and personal goals.

Self-awareness	Self-management
Social awareness	Relationship management

Emotional Intelligence

EQ helps you understand your feelings, turn intention into action, and make informed decisions about what matters most to you.

4 attributes commonly define emotional intelligence:

SELF-AWARENESS

Recognizing your own feelings and emotions and knowing how they change your thoughts and behavior. You are aware of your strengths and weaknesses and have self-confidence.

SELF-MANAGEMENT

Controlling impulsive feelings and behaviors, managing emotions in positive ways. Taking the initiative and adapting to changing circumstances.

SOCIAL AWARENESS

Having empathy. Understanding others' emotions, needs, and concerns. Observant to pick up on emotional cues and comfort others. You feel comfortable socially and recognize the power dynamics in a group or organization.

RELATIONSHIP MANAGEMENT

Developing and maintaining good relationships, communicating clearly. You inspire and influence others, work well in a team, and manage conflict.

You can start with knowing yourself and the reasons why you react the way you react. A few tools which can help with that are:

- DISK Analysis
- MBTI - Myer Brigg Type Indicator

Search for the assessment using the above tools, and you can get many links. One of the links which I liked is   https://www.16personalities.com

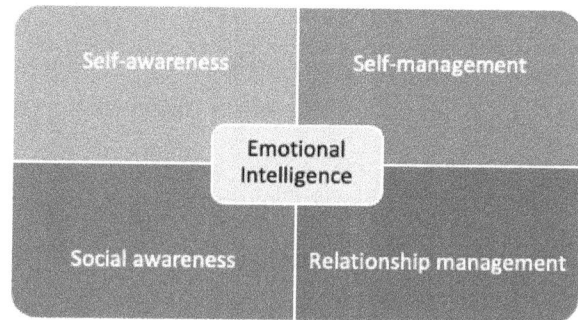

13.12 MODULE END QUESTIONS - PMP STYLE

1. Select the correct order of team development stages:

    A.   Adjourning, Forming, Storming

    B.   Storming, Norming, Adjourning

    C.   Performing, Norming, Forming

    D.   Forming, Adjourning, Storming

2. Which of the following team development stages characterize the team stage where the team meets and learns about the project and their formal roles and responsibilities?

    A.   Forming

    B.   Storming

    C.   Norming

    D.   Performing

3. People need hygiene factors to work efficiently. The absence of those factors will demotivate people. This is taken from:

    A.   Maslow's Need theory

    B.   Herzberg's motivation theory

    C.   Theory X by Victor Vroom

    D.   Theory Z by William Ouchi

4. The BMB restaurant chain started from a single truck in 1946 by Bob. The chain has grown to nearly 600 locations in 19 states. All locations are corporately owned, not franchised. Truck drivers and other patrons began telling Bob that his food was excellent. He did not have the capacity to fill large orders. He contracted with Tim to package BMB products. Tim agreed to do that because of the BMB's reputation in the market. Which power did Bob use on Tim?

    A.   Expert power

    B.   Legitimate power

    C.   Reward power

    D.   Referent power

5. You work as part of a development team in an agile project. There are times when you are so angry that you do not want to talk to anyone on your team. This is leading to bad relationships and negative reviews. It has started affecting your mental well-being noways. Which EQ aspect should you start with to understand your emotions?

    A.   Self-awareness

    B.   Self-management

C.   Social awareness

D.   Relationship management

6. **Which of the following is NOT a valid Conflict Management Technique?**

A.   Force

B.   Withdraw

C.   Focus Groups

D.   Avoid

7. Donald and Doris are currently in a conflict over the location of an upcoming store. Donald is emotional about the site, whereas Doris is more of a logical thinker. Both, after a lengthy discussion that involved storming out and tears, decided to go with their next store location as Boston. Both liked this option. Which conflict management strategy was used in the scenario?

A.   Withdrawal

B.   Problem Solve

C.   Reconcile

D.   Forcing

8. **A key barrier in developing a team is:**

A.   Members working in a virtual environment

B.   Members in the forming team stage

C.   Members trusting each other

D.   Members not trusting each other

9. **Which of the following is not correct regarding the Manage Team process?**

A.   Manage Team focuses on improving competencies and team interactions.

B.   Manage Team process results in change requests

C.   Manage Team process results in providing feedback on work

D.   Manage Team process results in resolving issues

10. Ana is the Project Manager for project AXA. She has few team members on board. Each team member came from a different background, and few of them lacked the necessary skills. People are still at a distance. They started working on some of the allocated work. Which team development stage is the team AXA?

A.   Forming

B.   Storming

C.   Norming

D.   Performing

11   You and your senior manager have differences over which observation to be closed first. You set up a meeting with the senior management. He declined the meeting request. You called to confirm the availability, but he did not pick up the phone. Which conflict management technique did the senior manager use?

    A.   Withdraw/Avoid.

    B.   Smooth/Accommodate

    C.   Compromise/Reconcile

    D.   Collaborate/Problem Solve.

12.   A Project Manager needs to be forward-reaching in addressing the conflicts early and obtaining a consensus. However, it would be not a great action to resolve an issue if the Project Manager said:

    A.   Let's work on it and try to find the root problem.

    B.   Let's gather more information and then analyze it properly.

    C.   I have another point for discussion if this is too difficult to solve now.

    D.   I feel we can now come to an agreement on this issue.

13.   Project NEO is going as per the plan. Everyone was tuned to work with each other. People laugh at each other's jokes, and there is harmony amongst the team. A new person, Koel, joined the team last week. Out of nowhere, the team suddenly seems to be always at war. What is happening?

    A.   The team has moved to the forming stage

    B.   The team has moved to the storming stage

    C.   The team is not happy with Koel

    D.   Koel may have some serious personality issues

14.   A new team member, Jack, joined the team last month. For no reason, the team suddenly seems to be always at war with Jack. Jack sought a meeting with you. What would you do?

    A.   Accept the meeting to hear him out and do nothing. He just needs to be heard.

    B.   Accept the meeting and hear him. Also, talk to other members to understand the issue and then get to the cause to solve the current problem

    C.   Talk to the team minus the person and tell them to behave

    D.   Talk to the new team member and ask him to do better

15. There have been many disputes within the team. You approached your manager to ask for his advice. He looked at you, smiled, and said, "Really? You are such a charismatic person. I know you don't need me to solve this for you." And walked away. Which conflict resolution technique did he use?

   A.   Avoid

   B.   Smooth

   C.   Compromise

   D.   Force

16. How does the Team Charter help the project?

   A.   It is an information radiator

   B.   It helps in meeting management

   C.   Team charter helps in planning better holidays

   D.   It helps to understand the expected behavior within the team and set clear guidelines, which in turn help teamwork better

17. You started the project, and team members are getting on board. A few people joined the team last week, and a few more are joining now. Which stage is the team at?

   A.   Forming

   B.   Storming

   C.   Norming

   D.   Performing

18. A new project is kicked off, and you are the project manager of this new team. The expectation of senior management is on-time deliveries. You start checking the team on required skills and find that the team lacks in certain aspects. What kind of training can you use to impart skills to your team: (Select 3 that apply):

   ☐ A.   External training vendor

   ☐ B.   At home, brainwriting

   ☐ C.   In-office peer programming

   ☐ D.   Using sliding windows

   ☐ E.   On the job training

   ☐ F.   Online self-study

19. The motivational theory that people are most motivated by one of the three primary needs - achievement, affiliation, and power is coined by:

    A.   Herzberg

    B.   Maslow

    C.   McClelland

    D.   McGregor

20. Which of the following is the best type of Project Manager authority that a Project Manager should possess to earn the team's respect and to get them on his side?

    A.   Referent power

    B.   Legitimate power

    C.   Penalty power

    D.   Expert power

12.13 ALL ANSWERS

ANSWERS: 13.5.1 LET'S PLAY: TEAM STAGE

Scenario	Team Stage	Keywords
1. Kyle and Joanna are working together on the project POSH. They disagree on everything most of the time. They are at a point now where they are barely talking to each other.	Storming	"Barely talking to each other3
2. Norman manages project APOLLO. Norman understands the team aspirations, ensures that the team enthusiasm is high, and allocates the right tasks to the right people. The team trusts Norman and contributes with high enthusiasm. It seems like a great, happy group.	Performing	"Enthusiasm is high and allocates the right tasks to the right people. The team trusts Norman and contributes with high enthusiasm. It seems like a great, happy group."
3. A new member, Amy, joined the task force; everyone seemed polite and offered assistance if she needed it. She is trying to understand her duties.	Forming	"She is trying to understand her duties as of now."
4. Now that the project is over, the team is analyzing the failures and is looking forward to meeting each other while packing their bags.	Adjourning	"Looking forward to meeting each other while packing their bags."
5. Sarah is torn by the behavior of her fellow colleague, Amy. She had differences of opinion, but now she has made up her mind to focus on her task, realizing that the points Amy made were not so bad after all and helped her arrive at a few good decisions.	Norming	"Focus on her task, realizing that the points Amy made were not so bad."

ANSWERS: 13.6.1 LET'S PLAY: CONFLICT MANAGEMENT

Scenario	Conflict resolution technique
1. Rita started crying when Mark handed over the appraisal results and told her that she was rated as an underperformer. Since it was difficult to converse, Mark said, "why don't you go home today, sleep on it, and we will discuss your appraisal again tomorrow?"	Avoid – The conflict stays at 100 percent.
2. Mark to Rob: "Rob, I don't want to hear the same excuses again. The rest of the team is working harder and producing better results. I'm convinced that you should rate it as the average for the final rating. If you have a complaint, speak to HR."	Forcing – One Point of View and decision is taken.
3. Mark to Jason: "Jason, you can select either a promotion or a role change but not both. Let me know so that I can proceed."	Compromising – Full resolution not implemented. One is not fully satisfied.
4. Mark, while addressing the team in the daily team meeting: Team, let's move beyond appraisal ratings. You are a dynamic group, and I'm sure this year we will rock."	Smoothing – Conflict is reduced by some percentage.
5. Noah, a member of the team, resigned. When Mark and Noah discussed the reasons, Noah mentioned that he needs to spend more time at home since his wife Carol is working. Mark knows that Noah is an asset to the team. He called a meeting with Noah and the human resource manager, Susan, to see if there could be a better outcome, such as allowing Noah to work from home.	Problem Solve – Group thinking to eliminate the problem to zero percent.

ANSWERS: 13.8.1 LET'S PLAY: LEADERSHIP STYLES

Question	Answer	Why
1.	Laissez-faire	Minimum oversight
2.	Interactional	Combination of management styles
3.	Servant leader	Serving the team
4.	Transactional	Supervision, Goal setting, feedback
5.	Transformational	Vision, Inspiration

ANSWERS: 13.12 MODULE END QUESTIONS - PMP STYLE

1. B	The right Answer is Storming, Norming, and then Adjourning.
2. A	Forming is where the team meets and learns about the project and its formal roles and responsibilities. The team members tend to be independent and not as open in this phase.
3. B	Herzberg's motivation theory - A "hygiene factor" is something like a paycheck or status – things that people need to do the job. - Having their hygiene factors met does not motivate people, but the absence of hygiene factors de-motivates and reduces performance. - What motivates people is the work itself and not hygiene conditions (ex: working conditions, Salary, personal life, security, and status
4. A	Since Bob was the expert in making excellent food, Tim was influenced to work with him due to the expert power exhibited in the scenario.
5. A	*SELF-AWARENESS* Recognizing your own feelings and emotions and knowing how they change your thoughts and behavior. You are aware of your strengths and weaknesses and have self-confidence.
6. C	Focus-Groups is not a valid Conflict Management Technique.
7. B	Both the parties liked the decision. Problem solved. Incorporating multiple viewpoints and insights from differing perspectives requires a cooperative attitude and open dialogue that typically leads to consensus and commitment.
8. D	A key aspect of developing a Team is to develop the trust level of the team so that they can take on the challenges together and can solve them. Building trust is one key thing to ensure that your team performs at an optimal level.
9. A	Improving competencies, team interactions, and the team environment are characteristics of the Develop Team Process and not the Manage Team Process.
10. A	Forming is where the team meets and learns about the project and their formal roles and responsibilities. Team members tend to be independent and not as open in this phase.

11. A	The manager used avoidance as the technique.
12. C	The Project Manager should try to resolve a conflict early and not delay it because of other reasons. Hence, Option C is the correct answer as the Project Manager is trying to avoid the conflict.
13. B	The storming phase of the team sees personality clashes and lesser productivity.
14. B	If an issue is escalated, then the Project Manager should solve it. Collaboration/problem solving is the best thing to do.
15. B	Smoothing – The manager uses praise to help you feel better about yourself so that you can take on the challenge and solve it.
16. D	The team charter sets clear expectations, and an early commitment to clear guidelines decreases misunderstandings and increases productivity.
17. A	Forming. This phase is where the team meets and learns about the project and their formal roles and responsibilities.
18. A, E, F	Training or skill development can be achieved by providing external training, Online training, or on-the-job training by self-learning or mentorship. Brainwriting is information gathering technique. Peer programming is the way to work in teams to reduce resource attrition or dependency. The sliding window is an efficient way to work in virtual environments.
19. C	Need theory, also known as Three Needs Theory, proposed by psychologist David McClelland, is a motivational model that attempts to explain how the needs for achievement, power, and affiliation affect the actions of people from a managerial context.
20. D	Expert power is the most lasting power and works beyond the direct subordinates.

14. ECO MAPPING

ECO REF.	DOMAIN 1: PEOPLE (42%)	CHAPTER/TOPIC REFERENCE
TASK 1	MANAGE CONFLICT	
1.1	Interpret the source and stage of the conflict	
1.2	Analyze the context for the conflict	Team - Conflict Management
1.3	Evaluate/recommend/reconcile the appropriate conflict resolution solution	
TASK 2	LEAD A TEAM	
2.1	Set a clear vision and mission	
2.2	Support diversity and inclusion (e.g., behavior types, thought process)	
2.3	Value servant leadership (e.g., relate the tenets of servant leadership to the team)	Team Management
2.4	Determine an appropriate leadership style (e.g., directive, collaborative)	
2.5	Inspire, motivate, and influence team members/stakeholders (e.g., team contract, social contract, reward system)	
2.6	Analyze team members and stakeholders' influence	Stakeholder Management
2.7	Distinguish various options to lead various team members and stakeholders	Team – Team Management Theories
TASK 3	SUPPORT TEAM PERFORMANCE	
3.1	Appraise team member performance against key performance indicators	
3.2	Support and recognize team member growth and development	Team – Develop Team
3.3	Determine appropriate feedback approach	
3.4	Verify performance improvements	

TASK 4	EMPOWER TEAM MEMBERS AND STAKEHOLDERS	
4.1	Organize around team strengths	Team – Team Management Plan RACI
4.2	Support team task accountability	
4.3	Evaluate demonstration of task accountability	
4.4	Determine and bestow level(s) of decision-making authority	
TASK 5	ENSURE TEAM MEMBERS/STAKEHOLDERS ARE ADEQUATELY TRAINED	
5.1	Determine required competencies and elements of training	Team – Trainings
5.2	Determine training options based on training needs	
5.3	Allocate resources for training	
	Measure training outcomes	
TASK 6	BUILD A TEAM	
6.1	Appraise stakeholder skills	Team – Estimations And Trainings
6.2	Deduce project resource requirements	
6.3	Continuously assess and refresh team skills to meet project needs	
6.4	Maintain team and knowledge transfer	Integration – Knowledge Management
TASK 7	ADDRESS AND REMOVE IMPEDIMENTS, OBSTACLES, AND BLOCKERS FOR THE TEAM	
7.1	Determine critical impediments, obstacles, and blockers for the team	Team – Servant Leadership Integration – Direct and Mange Project
7.2	Prioritize critical impediments, obstacles, and blockers for the team	
7.3	Use network to implement solutions to remove impediments, obstacles, and blockers for the team	
7.4	Re-assess continually to ensure impediments, obstacles, and blockers for the team are being addressed	
Task 8	NEGOTIATE PROJECT AGREEMENTS	
8.1	Analyze the bounds of the negotiations for agreement	Agile – Product Backlog Grooming Integration – Project MBR
8.2	Assess priorities and determine ultimate objective(s)	
8.3	Verify objective(s) of the project agreement is met	

TASK 9	**COLLABORATE WITH STAKEHOLDERS**	
9.1	Evaluate engagement needs for stakeholders	
9.2	Optimize alignment between stakeholder needs, expectations, and project objectives	Stakeholder Management
9.3	Build trust and influence stakeholders to accomplish project objectives	
TASK 10	**BUILD SHARED UNDERSTANDING**	
10.1	Break down situation to identify the root cause of a misunderstanding	Agile – Consensus Management
10.2	Survey all necessary parties to reach consensus	Quality – RCA, Problem Resolution
10.3	Support outcome of parties' agreement	
10.4	Investigate potential misunderstandings	
TASK 11	**ENGAGE AND SUPPORT VIRTUAL TEAMS**	
11.1	Examine virtual team member needs (e.g., environment, geography, culture, global, etc.)	
11.2	Investigate alternatives (e.g., communication tools, colocation) for virtual team member engagement	Team Management – Virtual Teams
11.3	Implement options for virtual team member engagement	
11.4	Continually evaluate effectiveness of virtual team member engagement	
TASK 12	**DEFINE TEAM GROUND RULES**	
12.1	Communicate organizational principles with team and external stakeholders	
12.2	Establish an environment that fosters adherence to the ground rules	
12.3	Manage and rectify ground rule violations	
TASK 13	**MENTOR RELEVANT STAKEHOLDERS**	
13.1	Allocate the time to mentoring	Team – Charter, Mentoring And EQ, MBTI
13.2	Recognize and act on mentoring opportunities	
TASK 14	**PROMOTE TEAM PERFORMANCE THROUGH THE APPLICATION OF EMOTIONAL INTELLIGENCE**	
14.1	Assess behavior through the use of personality indicators	
14.2	Analyze personality indicators and adjust to the emotional needs of key project stakeholders	

ECO REF.	DOMAIN 2: PROCESS (50%)	CHAPTER/TOPIC REFERENCE
TASK 1	EXECUTE PROJECT WITH THE URGENCY REQUIRED TO DELIVER BUSINESS VALUE	
1.1	Assess opportunities to deliver value incrementally	INTEGRATION MANAGEMENT
1.2	Examine the business value throughout the project	
1.3	Support the team to subdivide project tasks as necessary to find the minimum viable product	
TASK 2	MANAGE COMMUNICATIONS	
2.1	Analyze communication needs of all stakeholders	
2.2	Determine communication methods, channels, frequency, and level of detail for all stakeholders	Communication Management
2.3	Communicate project information and updates effectively	
2.4	Confirm communication is understood and feedback is received	
TASK 3	ASSESS AND MANAGE RISKS	
3.1	Determine risk management options	Risk Management
3.2	Iteratively assess and prioritize risks	
TASK 4	ENGAGE STAKEHOLDERS	
4.1	Analyze stakeholders (e.g., power interest grid, influence, impact)	
4.2	Categorize stakeholders	Stakeholder Management
4.3	Engage stakeholders by category	
4.4	Develop, execute, and validate a strategy for stakeholder engagement	
TASK 5	PLAN AND MANAGE BUDGET AND RESOURCES	
5.1	Estimate budgetary needs based on the scope of the project and lessons learned from past projects	
5.2	Anticipate future budget challenges	Cost Management
5.3	Monitor budget variations and work with governance process to adjust as necessary	
5.4	Plan and manage resources	
TASK 6	PLAN AND MANAGE SCHEDULE	
6.1	Estimate project tasks (milestones, dependencies, story points)	Schedule Management

6.2	Utilize benchmarks and historical data	
6.3	Prepare schedule based on methodology	
6.4	Measure ongoing progress based on methodology	
6.5	Modify schedule, as needed, based on methodology	
6.6	Coordinate with other projects and other operations	
TASK 7	**PLAN AND MANAGE QUALITY OF PRODUCTS/DELIVERABLES**	
7.1	Determine quality standard required for project deliverables	
7.2	Recommend options for improvement based on quality gaps	Quality Management
7.3	Continually survey project deliverable quality	
TASK 8	**PLAN AND MANAGE SCOPE**	
8.1	Determine and prioritize requirements	
8.2	Break down scope (e.g., WBS, backlog)	Scope Management
8.3	Monitor and validate scope	
TASK 9	**INTEGRATE PROJECT PLANNING ACTIVITIES**	
9.1	Consolidate the project/phase plans	
9.2	Assess consolidated project plans for dependencies, gaps, and continued business value	
9.3	Analyze the data collected	
9.4	Collect and analyze data to make informed project decisions	
9.5	Determine critical information requirements	
TASK 10	**MANAGE PROJECT CHANGES**	Integration Management
10.1	Anticipate and embrace the need for change (e.g., follow change management practices)	
10.2	Determine strategy to handle change	
10.3	Execute change management strategy according to the methodology	
10.4	Determine a change response to move the project forward	

TASK 11	PLAN AND MANAGE PROCUREMENT	
11.1	Define resource requirements and needs	
11.2	Communicate resource requirements	
11.3	Manage suppliers/contracts	Procurement Management
11.4	Plan and manage procurement strategy	
11.5	Develop a delivery solution	
TASK 12	MANAGE PROJECT ARTIFACTS	
12.1	Determine the requirements (what, when, where, who, etc.) for managing the project artifacts	
12.2	Validate that the project information is kept up to date (i.e., version control) and accessible to all stakeholders	Integration Management
12.3	Continually assess the effectiveness of the management of the project artifacts	
TASK 13	DETERMINE APPROPRIATE PROJECT METHODOLOGY/METHODS AND PRACTICES	
13.1	Assess project needs, complexity, and magnitude	
13.2	Recommend project execution strategy (e.g., contracting, finance)	The Basics
13.3	Recommend a project methodology/approach (i.e., predictive, agile, hybrid)	Project Life Cycle
13.4	Use iterative, incremental practices throughout the project life cycle (e.g., lessons learned, stakeholder engagement, risk)	
TASK 14	ESTABLISH PROJECT GOVERNANCE STRUCTURE	
14.1	Determine appropriate governance for a project (e.g., replicate organizational governance)	Team
14.2	Define escalation paths and thresholds	Roles And Responsibility
TASK 15	MANAGE PROJECT ISSUES	
15.1	Recognize when a risk becomes an issue	
15.2	Attack the issue with the optimal action to achieve project success	Risk Management
15.3	Collaborate with relevant stakeholders on the approach to resolve the issues	Issue And Risks
TASK 16	ENSURE KNOWLEDGE TRANSFER FOR PROJECT CONTINUITY	INTEGRATION MANAGEMENT
16.1	Discuss project responsibilities within team	Knowledge Management

16.2	Outline expectations for working environment	
16.3	Confirm approach for knowledge transfers	
TASK 17	**PLAN AND MANAGE PROJECT/PHASE CLOSURE OR TRANSITIONS**	
17.1	Determine criteria to successfully close the project or phase	
17.2	Validate readiness for transition (e.g., to operations team or next phase)	Integration Management Close Project/Phase
17.3	Conclude activities to close out project or phase (e.g., final lessons learned, retrospective, procurement, financials, resources)	

ECO REF.	DOMAIN 3: BUSINESS ENVIRONMENT (8%)	CHAPTER/TOPIC REFERENCE
TASK 1	**PLAN AND MANAGE PROJECT COMPLIANCE**	
1.1	Confirm project compliance requirements (e.g., security, health and safety, regulatory compliance)	
1.2	Classify compliance categories	
1.3	Determine potential threats to compliance	**BUSINESS ENVIRONMENT**
1.4	Use methods to support compliance	Risk Management
1.5	Analyze the consequences of noncompliance	Risk Categories
1.6	Determine necessary approach and action to address compliance needs (e.g., risk, legal)	
1.7	Measure the extent to which the project is in compliance	
TASK 2	**EVALUATE AND DELIVER PROJECT BENEFITS AND VALUE**	
2.1	Investigate that benefits are identified	
2.2	Document agreement on ownership for ongoing benefit realization	
2.3	Verify measurement system is in place to track benefits	The Basics – Project Selection Methods
2.4	Evaluate delivery options to demonstrate value	
2.5	Appraise stakeholders of value gain progress	
TASK 3	**EVALUATE AND ADDRESS EXTERNAL BUSINESS ENVIRONMENT CHANGES FOR IMPACT ON SCOPE**	

3.1	Survey changes to external business environment (e.g., regulations, technology, geopolitical, market)	The Basics - EEF
3.2	Assess and prioritize impact on project scope/backlog based on changes in external business environment	Agile – Product Backlog Grooming
3.3	Recommend options for scope/backlog changes (e.g., schedule, cost changes)	Risk – Identify Risks
3.4	Continually review external business environment for impacts on project scope/backlog	
TASK 4	SUPPORT ORGANIZATIONAL CHANGE	
4.1	Assess organizational culture	
4.2	Evaluate impact of organizational change to project and determine required actions	The Basics – Organization Structures
4.3	Evaluate impact of the project to the organization and determine required actions	

15. ABOUT KAVITA SHARMA

Kavita Sharma
Significant Contributor
PMBOK- Sixth Edition

Kavita Sharma has two decades of project management experience in IT, Project Management, Program Management, Account Management, and Project and Leadership Coaching.

She worked with Microsoft, Tech Mahindra, Sapient, and Satyam in her career. While working as an end-to-end program manager, she managed multi-skilled virtual teams ranging from 30 - 90 members having widespread skill sets.

In the last few years (approx. 10), she has evolved as a great mentor to the PMP aspirants and conducts project management workshops.

She authored many books, including the best seller:

Pass PMP in 21 Days - Study Guide.

You can see her name in the PMBOK as a significant contributor and CAPM (eLearning by PMI) reviewer.

Her focus is now shifting to mindfulness. We hope to see something new from her pretty soon.

YouTube: https://www.youtube.com/channel/UCLjfEAI-EmgzsDQnXiTth9g

Linkedin: https://www.linkedin.com/in/kavitasharmapmp

Official Website: https://KavitaSharma.net

THANK YOU

Hi, this is Kavita Sharma. Thanks for buying the book and staying with it till the end. I assume that you have gone through the book and stayed with it. And that is the reason you are reading this page.

A lot of effort has gone into producing this book.

I keep receiving feedback from people like you and ensure that the feedback is acted upon.

That's the reason you see book updates.

The credit goes to all of you.

I hope that you found the book helpful. If there is any feedback do write to me. I will look forward to hearing from you.

You can reach me at kavita.sh@gmail.com.

Thanks, and wishing you success.

Kavita Sharma

Author, Coach, and Thinker

DISCLAIMER

With this book, I have put in my best effort to bring you the right tools to pass the PMP examination. However, this should not be interpreted as a promise or guarantee of your success. Any positive or negative outcome is ultimately dependent on your competency, commitment, and the overall effort put into the PMP exam preparation.

You have the right tools with you. Use them and pass the PMP exam.

www.ingramcontent.com/pod-product-compliance
Lightning Source LLC
Chambersburg PA
CBHW080617030426
42336CB00018B/2999